Peculiar Rhetoric

RACE, RHETORIC, AND MEDIA SERIES
Davis W. Houck, General Editor

Peculiar Rhetoric

Slavery, Freedom, and the African Colonization Movement

Bjørn F. Stillion Southard

University Press of Mississippi / Jackson

The University Press of Mississippi is the scholarly publishing agency of
the Mississippi Institutions of Higher Learning: Alcorn State University,
Delta State University, Jackson State University, Mississippi State University,
Mississippi University for Women, Mississippi Valley State University,
University of Mississippi, and University of Southern Mississippi.

www.upress.state.ms.us

The University Press of Mississippi is a member of
the Association of University Presses.

Copyright © 2019 by University Press of Mississippi
All rights reserved

First printing 2019

∞

Library of Congress Cataloging-in-Publication Data

Names: Stillion Southard, Bjørn F., author.
Title: Peculiar rhetoric : slavery, freedom, and the African colonization
movement / Bjørn F. Stillion Southard.
Description: Jackson : University Press of Mississippi, [2019] | Series:
Race, rhetoric, and media series | "First printing 2019." | Includes
bibliographical references and index. |
Identifiers: LCCN 2019002912 (print) | LCCN 2019005747 (ebook) | ISBN
9781496823717 (epub single) | ISBN 9781496823700 (epub institutional) |
ISBN 9781496823731 (pdf single) | ISBN 9781496823724 (pdf institutional)
| ISBN 9781496823694 (hardcover : alk. paper) | ISBN 9781496823830 (pbk. :
alk. paper)
Subjects: LCSH: American Colonization Society—History—19th century. |
African Americans—Colonization—Liberia—19th century. | Free
blacks—America—History—19th century. | Slavery—United
States—History—19th century. | Rhetoric—Political aspects—United
States—History—19th century. | Lincoln, Abraham, 1809–1865—Political
and social views. | Clay, Henry, 1777–1852—Political and social views. |
Caldwell, Elias Boudinot, 1776–1825—Political and social views. |
Sheridan, Louis—Political and social views. | Teage, Hilary—Political
and social views.
Classification: LCC E448 (ebook) | LCC E448 .S84 2019 (print) | DDC
973/.0496073009034—dc23
LC record available at https://lccn.loc.gov/2019002912

British Library Cataloging-in-Publication Data available

For Ella and Finna

Contents

ACKNOWLEDGMENTS ix

INTRODUCTION 3

CHAPTER 1—Peculiar Argumentation: Henry Clay, Elias B. Caldwell, and the Establishment of Colonization's Deliberative Discourse 18

CHAPTER 2—Peculiar Voice: The Counter Memorial of the Free People of Colour of the District of Columbia and the Unsettling of Colonization's Deliberative Discourse 40

CHAPTER 3—Peculiar Planning: Louis Sheridan and the Negotiation of Diasporic and Deliberative Discourse 65

CHAPTER 4—"Peculiar Obligations": Hilary Teage and the Constitution of Civic Identity in Liberia 86

CHAPTER 5—Peculiar Proposal: Abraham Lincoln and the Public Policy Advocacy for Colonization 113

CONCLUSION—Middle Passages, Emigration, and Peculiar Legacies 132

NOTES 143

INDEX 173

Acknowledgments

This book and its author benefited in many ways from the support of many people. James F. Klumpp, Shawn J. Parry-Giles, Trevor Parry-Giles, Robert N. Gaines, Andrew D. Wolvin, Mari Boor Tonn, and Kathleen E. Kendall supported the germ of this project. That early idea has grown in unexpected and wonderful ways and is now the book before you. I thank Davis Houck, Vijay Shah, Lisa McMurtray, Lisa Williams, the two reviewers, and the entire team at University Press of Mississippi for helping me to bring this book to fruition.

The librarians at the Library of Congress Manuscript Reading Room were swift and helpful during my multiple visits to work through the American Colonization Society Papers. Tiffany Lewis connected me with Aimee Roberge, who procured some vital letters related to Louis Sheridan from the New York Historical Society.

Angela G. Ray and Paul Stob convened a conference at the Alexandria Lyceum in the Fall of 2015. My engagement with Hilary Teage and the Liberia Lyceum began there. Parts of chapter 4 appeared as "A Lyceum Diaspora: Hilary Teage and a Liberian Civic Identity," in a volume titled *Thinking Together: Lecturing, Learning, and Difference in the Long Nineteenth Century*, edited by Ray and Stob (Penn State University Press, 2018). I appreciate their editing and support of my contribution to the book.

Earlier versions of chapter 2 and chapter 5 have appeared, respectively, as "Polyvocality and the Personae of Blackness in Early Nineteenth-Century Slavery Discourse: The Counter Memorial against Colonization, 1816," *Rhetoric & Public Affairs* 15, no. 2 (2012): 235–66; and "Abraham Lincoln's 'Second Annual Message to Congress' and Public Policy Advocacy for African Colonization," *Rhetoric & Public Affairs* 21, no. 3 (2018), both copyright Michigan State University Press. I thank G. Mitchell Reyes and Charles E. Morris III for their comments on the former essay and the reviewers for both essays for providing feedback that helped in the development of those projects. Special thanks to Martin J. Medhurst, the editor of *Rhetoric & Public Affairs*, for his guidance on both projects.

My colleagues at the University of Georgia foster a culture of rigor that has pushed me to be a better scholar. In their respective terms as department head, Barbara Biesecker and Edward Panetta have each been supportive of my research in every way possible. Dave Tell has been a constant source of intellectual engagement. Maegan Parker Brooks, Cindy Koenig Richards, Lisa M. Corrigan, Michael Phillips-Anderson, M. Kelly Carr, and Richard Benjamin Crosby have been great interlocutors along the way.

Sally J. Spalding read every word of this manuscript, providing edits, insights, and good humor.

My parents, Barb and Fred Southard, have supported me in countless ways for my entire life. My brothers, Gerrit and Tor, are the best. My extended family—in-laws, aunts, uncles, and cousins—were always kind to listen to me when they would ask the seemingly innocuous question, What is your book about? Nieces and nephews were smart not to ask.

I've spent two decades admiring the intellect and drive of Belinda Stillion Southard. Our partnership has seen many states, schools, degrees, jobs, and phases. There is no one whose opinion I sought or trusted more than hers. I could not have gotten through it without her. We carry each other.

This book is dedicated to Ella Rose and Finna Helene. They are fierce and funny and better than me. I love them so very much.

Peculiar Rhetoric

Introduction

In 1816 a group of "gentlemen who are friendly to the promotion of a plan for colonizing the free blacks of the United States" convened at Davis's Hotel in the Georgetown neighborhood of Washington City.[1] According to the chair of the meeting, Henry Clay, their purpose was to consider the "propriety and practicability" of a colonization scheme.[2] The influential attendees of the meeting included Clay, Daniel Webster, Ferdinando Fairfax, John Randolph, Francis Scott Key, Rev. William Meade, and at least a dozen more political, religious, and social leaders.[3] Free blacks—the objects of their scheme—were not truly free; as Clay observed: "That class, of the mixt population of our country, was *peculiarly situated*. They neither enjoyed the immunities of freemen, nor were they subject to the incapacities of slaves."[4] Because of the "unconquerable prejudices resulting from their color," Clay surmised, "they never could amalgamate with free whites of the country."[5] The remarks delivered at this germinal gathering foreshadowed the decades-long effort to remove free blacks from the United States and resettle them in another country, most notably in what became the country of Liberia on the western coast of Africa. From this meeting the American Society for Colonizing the Free People of Colour of the United States (later shortened to the American Colonization Society) was formed.

As Clay attested, free blacks were indeed peculiarly situated in early nineteenth-century American society. In fact, "free" blacks lived a life that was not entirely free or enslaved. This peculiarity influenced not only the social position of free blacks within these early communities but also the formation of a black identity.[6] As Paul Gilroy argues, attempting to be both black and a member of white-dominated society

> requires some specific forms of double consciousness. By saying this I do not mean to suggest that taking on either or both of these

unfinished identities necessarily exhausts the subjective resources of any particular individual. However, where racist, nationalist, or ethnically absolutist discourses orchestrate political relationships so that these identities appear to be mutually exclusive, occupying the space between them or trying to demonstrate their continuity has been viewed as a provocative and even oppositional act of political insubordination.[7]

In the early-to-mid-nineteenth century, free blacks in the United States occupied the "space between" that Gilroy describes. Due to the perceived threat that free blacks allegedly posed to white slaveholding society, colonization was a solution worthy of pursuit. Colonization could also be framed in ways that appealed to antislavery whites, as removal to Liberia provided free blacks with an opportunity for freedom and self-rule. If colonization could "drain off" the free black population, as Clay put it, then clear racial categories could be better maintained within America's borders *and* the freedom of already free blacks could be respected. This logic manifested in state laws that simultaneously urged support for colonization and created restrictions on citizenship and economic interactions for free blacks.[8] Promoted out of respect for racial hierarchy and the liberty of free blacks, colonization aimed to remove the segment of the population that could not be easily defined in American society.

Much like the population they sought to expel from the United States, the American Colonization Society (ACS) was also peculiarly situated. In the second quarter of the nineteenth century, public discourse regarding slavery became more polarized and hostile. While radical abolitionists battled with firebrand proslavery advocates, the ACS attempted to negotiate the extreme positions of the two sides. Clay was well aware that these negotiations would not be easy and thus believed it was necessary to focus the ACS's efforts on free blacks only. "It was proper and necessary distinctly to state," Clay reassured his audience, that "no part of the object of this meeting to touch or agitate, in the slightest degree, a delicate question connected with another portion of the colored population of our country."[9] The other "portion of the colored population," the enslaved population, was not under consideration. To an extent, colonizationists' efforts to negotiate between pro- and anti-slavery discourses succeeded. Over fifteen thousand free blacks were transported from the United States to Liberia.[10] In fact, the arguments for colonization, espoused by the "gentlemen" in that Georgetown hotel and hundreds of advocates that followed (including

Abraham Lincoln), animated colonization discourse for decades, only to be abandoned in favor of emancipation.

The ACS formed at a time of rising colonization sentiment throughout the United States. Early supporters of colonization were few but powerful. For example, in 1790 wealthy white planter Ferdinando Fairfax, an attendee of the first ACS meeting, argued for the "propriety" of gradual emancipation and colonization in light of sectional tensions.[11] As one of the most outspoken and prominent free black men to support colonization, Captain Paul Cuffe stated his belief in the scheme in the early 1810s after visiting the British free black colony in Sierra Leone.[12] It was around this time that colonization groups formed in the North, West, and South. In the North, religious leaders like Samuel J. Mills and Robert Finley preached that colonization aligned with the principles of Christianity.[13] In the West, groups formed in Ohio and Kentucky that focused on the relocation of free blacks to locales removed from white society.[14] In the South, Virginians secretly contemplated colonization in the General Assembly in 1800 and renewed their interest when the journals from that session were later discovered by Assemblyman Charles Fenton Mercer.[15] Many of these local and state efforts aimed for national support, such as a small group in New Jersey that asked their state legislature "to use their influence with the National Legislature to adopt some plan of colonizing the *Free Blacks*."[16] The ACS represented a unification of purpose, as well as a recognition that the efficacy of colonization required the considerable resources of the national government.

Despite the support from many corners of the country and the creation of the ACS to amplify the message, the quantitative insignificance and qualitative denouncement of colonization seems to make clear that the African colonization movement failed. The ACS relocated over fifteen thousand free blacks during its *entire* history (1816 to 1899). By comparison, there were more than one hundred thousand free blacks living in northern states and more than 1,500,000 enslaved blacks in the United States in 1820 alone.[17] Moreover, colonization was incredibly unpopular among prominent abolitionists. For example, "Article Four" of David Walker's well-known antislavery tract, *Walker's Appeal, in Four Articles*, was devoted entirely to criticizing the ACS. Even though he was once a member of the ACS, William Lloyd Garrison denounced colonization in his pamphlet *Thoughts on African Colonization*, and in his newspaper, *The Liberator*.[18] Maria W. Miller Stewart poetically ridiculed colonizationists' willingness to fund removal rather than pay for free blacks to remain in the country. She stated, "Methinks their [colonizationists'] hearts are so frozen towards us, they had rather their money should be sunk in the ocean than to administer it to our relief."[19] In 1849 Frederick Douglass proclaimed that "the Colonization Society is one of the most impudent Societies in the world."[20] The ACS could not claim significant success in the number of free blacks colonized, nor could it count on the support of some of the country's most vocal opponents of slavery.

Defenders of slavery similarly decried the scheme. Thomas R. Dew's *Review of the Debate in Virginia Legislature of 1831 and 1832* was influential in the development of the political economic argument for slavery and launched a rebuke of colonization similar to Walker's. Dew attacked colonization, stating, "The whole history of colonization, indeed, presents one of the most gloomy and horrific pictures to the imagination of the genuine philanthropist which can possibly be conceived."[21] In another widely circulated proslavery text, George Fitzhugh attacked the colonization movement for its moderation, arguing, "The negroes despise the Clay clique of Colonizationists, because, believing slavery morally wrong, they have not the courage to say so, nor the justice to give the slave up."[22] For a movement supposedly keen to unite abolitionists and slaveholders across regions of the country, colonizationists seemed only to unite both sides in opposition to colonization.

Rhetorical scholarship has adopted this narrative of failure, though for different reasons. In addition to colonization's statistical failure to "repatriate" blacks to Africa, Philip C. Wander renders judgment on what he called the "abortive scheme" of colonization and its retrenchment of racism: "The great leaders of the nineteenth century, including Madison, Monroe, Clay, Webster, Lincoln, and Douglas, created and sustained what in our view must be called racist institutions."[23] Despite colonization's questionable beginnings, other scholars offer more favorable commentary on the movement by focusing on the rhetoric of colonization opponents. For example, Jacqueline Bacon argues that the anticolonization discourse that fomented in the black newspaper *Freedom's Journal* "creates an identity for African Americans that allows them to speak for themselves and assert agency."[24] Stephen H. Browne examines the "radical critique" of Garrison as expressed in *Thoughts on African Colonization*, arguing that the pamphlet "took on a formidable opponent and sought, literally, to speak it out of existence."[25] Alisse Portnoy illuminates the role that women played in the kind of radical critique with which Garrison and other male anticolonizationists have been credited.[26] Ousmane K. Power-Greene takes a similar approach by focusing on the history of the black struggle to challenge colonization.[27] Altogether, then, rhetorical studies of how racism and rights have been contested in American history position colonization as an antagonist or foil to abolitionist and antiracist discourses.

Colonization discourse was more rhetorically complex than the narrative of failure suggests. Such a narrative emphasizes the quantitative and ideological effect of colonization advocacy. These effects are worthy of critique, but the force of those criticisms has tacitly deemed the case closed on colonization rhetoric. However, as David Zarefsky reminds us, "a more complex view of the rhetorical transaction" is one that "emphasizes contingency and choice rather than predictability and control."[28] There is far more contingency and choice in colonization discourse worthy of examination when the movement is not seen as a fait accompli. Specifically, the narrative of failure sublimates the complex rhetorical processes that constituted colonization and blackness in the middle of the public debate about slavery and antislavery for a half century. The middle of colonization discourse was, in part, a matter of its compromise position on the issue of slavery. However, the middle demands attention for the novel rhetorical maneuvers of rhetors navigating between more clearly identified end points. Erik Doxtader argues that public life is a critical domain in which the "weight" of the middle is often lost. Political agents choose *between* things: self and collective, stability and change, principles and practice. "To resolve these tensions," Doxtader continues, "we frequently turn from this middle" to consider beginnings and endings. Indeed, "middles are hard to define."[29] When the middle is discussed, the focus tends to be on the concept of moderation and the pejorative connotations of the middle with mediocrity.[30] Like Doxtader, Bradford Vivian resists the diminution of the middle, instead turning toward it and developing what he calls a "rhetoric in the middle voice." Vivian offers a rethinking of rhetoric in the middle that "emphasizes processes and relations instead of subjects and objects" that "cannot be suppressed or domesticated by appeals to essential truth, knowledge, virtue, or being."[31] Viewing colonization as a failure discourages a focus on the middle, away from the processes and relations and complexities of public life that constituted a sustained, strange, and serious conversation about African colonization for a half century.

Peculiar Rhetoric engages in an examination of colonization in the middle of public life, exploring the variety, complexity, contradictions, virtuosity, and, yes, failure of a significant and often polarized discourse about race in America. The case of colonization offers compelling insights into a specific kind of middle rhetoric, what I refer to as *peculiar rhetoric of colonization*. "Peculiarity" refers to something that is different from normal (often in a strange way), something particular or special.[32] When applied to slavery, "peculiar" is the euphemistic word that many whites used in public discourse to denature the horrors of slavery, that "peculiar institution."[33] The phrase "peculiarly situated" functioned differently; it conveyed a vision of social hierarchy that recognized the existence of free blacks and their inability to fit into the scheme created by those in power. In both cases, the litotic designation of "peculiar" understated the savagery and anxieties of slavery in America. The concept of "peculiar rhetoric" captures the odd, strange, uneasy, and at times transgressive discourses that whites and blacks generated in relation to the subject of colonization.

The approach taken in this book could be called a peculiar rhetorical history. The peculiar rhetorics examined herein affirm Zarefsky's claim that "rhetorical history is a vibrant, multidimensional field."[34] Zarefsky discusses the dynamism of rhetorical history in terms of two kinds of studies: synchronic (emphasizing rhetors' response in a particular moment) and diachronic (emphasizing the development of rhetorical practice over time). *Peculiar Rhetoric* examines individual rhetors in particular moments but situates those rhetors within the nearly fifty-year span during which colonizationists advocated for widespread, federal support. This approach contributes to the corpus of rhetors and discourses in American public address while also illuminating what Zarefsky refers to as "the rhetorical climate of an age."[35] Daniel Walker Howe explains that focusing on individuals rather than organizational action "offers advantages of accuracy and subtlety that too often are lost in collective portraits of an age or movement."[36] By "pausing to dart sideways and slantways, in order to examine the interplay of particular texts and contexts in sometimes microscopic detail," as Janell Johnson puts it, those close readings can illuminate the particulars of a moment that provides texture to the broader histories.[37] In a Venn diagram of diachronic and synchronic approaches to rhetorical history, this study vibrates in the overlapping middle section, oscillating between particular texts and broader contexts to capture the peculiarity that colonization engendered.

The linkage between diachronic and synchronic approaches to rhetorical history is enriched by the study of the constitutive potential of language. A constitutive approach to rhetoric allows for a more complicated understanding of effect, shifting emphasis away from how rhetoric represents reality to how rhetoric shapes reality through identification.[38] As James Jasinski argues, "discursive constitution specifies the way textual practices structure or establish conditions of possibility, enabling *and* constraining subsequent thought and action in ways similar to the operation of rules in a game." Indeed, as Jasinski goes on to state, language can function to "organize and structure ... the norms of political culture and the experience of communal existence," providing "the linguistic resources of the culture."[39] The discourse of white colonizationists, who were operating from a position of political and social power relative to free blacks, shaped those "linguistic resources of the culture." Another facet of a constitutive approach highlights how rhetoric contributes to "self-constitution and formation of subjectivity."[40] This perspective is particularly important when attempting to understand the rhetorical history of disempowered and oppressed peoples. When social, rhetorical, and political norms create barriers to full participation in the deliberative public sphere, the typical methods and forms of discourse will provide little insight into the perspectives of those who are excluded. The constitutive framework realizes that the traditional relationship between rhetor and audience can be refigured in order to comprehend alternative perspectives and understand the impact of language that is not tied to persuasive success.

Part of the critical space opened by the constitutive approach is to allow for theoretical play in the examination of historical discourse. There was a moment in rhetorical studies in which the recovery of unheard voices seemed at odds with contemporary theorizing about power. Writing about Karlyn Kohrs Campbell's anthologies of women's rhetoric, Barbara Biesecker argues that collecting individual speakers and speeches amounts to "female tokenism."[41] Biesecker's concern, expressed in her quotation of Adrienne Rich, was that "there's a false power which masculine society offers to a few women who 'think like men' on condition that they use it to maintain things as they are."[42] Biesecker argues for "working against the ideology of individualism" in favor of a "plurality of practices" that builds upon contemporary scholarship on power and subjectivity.[43] This debate seemed to pit the study of speakers and speeches against contemporary theory.

In the decades since Campbell and Biesecker's exchange, however, a robust scholarship has emerged that sees value in recovery *and* critique. As Bonnie J. Dow notes, "feminist scholars expanded on Biesecker's call for the integration of post-structuralists' insights into public address in a variety of ways."[44] Dow shows how the turn toward the constitutive functions of rhetoric allows for the critical interrogation of subjectivity while also attending to "women's public rhetorical activities," which includes, but is certainly not limited to, individual speakers and speeches.[45] Similar statements apply to the study of race. For example, Eric King Watts critiques a tendency in studies of "black speech," arguing that "the complex and radically contingent operations that make (and unmake) 'race' were backgrounded."[46] Watts analyzes a song by W. E. B. Du Bois in order to show "how the concept of voice may help public address scholars contend with the instabilities constitutive of the trope of 'race.'"[47] What Dow and Watts separately demonstrate is that the study of public address can appreciate rhetorical performance by diverse rhetors and engage in critique without forgetting history or canonizing it. Such methodological flexibility helps to more fully investigate the peculiar rhetorics of colonization because of the differences in the kinds of discourse that contribute to this concept.

Peculiar Rhetoric, Deliberation, and Diaspora

The texts examined in each chapter constitute peculiar rhetorics through the negotiation of deliberative and diasporic discourses. I use the concept of deliberation to describe a discourse in which rhetorical power is invested in "carefully weighing" costs and benefits in "the performance of a set of communicative behaviors that promote thorough group discussion."[48] This performance occurred within a context that included rules and power relations (implicit and explicit), which "reproduce themselves" through the process of deliberation. Deliberative discourses focused on the costs and benefits of colonization through the language of policy making. Colonizationists addressed their deliberative discourses to other whites, specifically the white men who held the power of the national purse. Although popular discourse in the early nineteenth century was becoming more crude and vulgar than it had been the century prior, colonizationists maintained the gentlemanly decorum in their deliberative discourse.[49] Clay made this principle clear in his speech at the founding of the ACS, stating that he "hoped, in their deliberations, they would be guided by that moderation, politeness and deference for the opinion of each other, which were essential to any useful result."[50] The polite deliberative discourse of white colonizationists was a cipher for their ideological commitments. Robert Asen reminds us, "Public policy deliberations constitute polysemous texts."[51] Indeed, the attention to deliberation by white colonizationists exemplifies the definition of policy offered by Fred Moten and Stefano Harney: "a resistance to the commons from above." [52] The emphasis on policy in deliberative discourse asserted the power of whites over the free black "commons" that troubled the racial dynamics of antebellum America.

The deliberative discourse of colonizationists failed to address blacks in a meaningful way, but that did not mean that blacks did not grapple with the feelings of inclusion and exclusion wrought by the scheming of white political agents. The notion of diasporic discourse describes how free blacks confronted belonging and alienation engendered in deliberative discourse. As noted above, some free blacks rejected colonization outright. Other free blacks participated in colonization, with varying degrees of willingness. Diasporic discourses of free blacks expressed the complex relationship between acceptance and rejection of colonization. The complexity of their position highlights the "cultural indeterminacy and spaces in between" that undergird postcolonial approaches to discourse.[53] The literal meaning of diaspora denotes the diffusion of people with a shared identity beyond their homeland.[54] Similar to Stuart Hall, I use the term metaphorically, as "diaspora does not refer us to those scattered tribes whose identity can only be secured in relation to some sacred homeland." Instead, I see diaspora, and diasporic discourse more specifically, as not marked by some fixed sense of purity or essence, "but by the recognition of a necessary heterogeneity and diversity . . . ; by *hybridity*."[55] A key element of the hybridity of the black diaspora was, as Nadia Ellis describes, "a distinctive desire to belong 'elsewhere,' which desire produces a productive tension between attachment and a drive toward intense and idiosyncratic individuation."[56] Although a term like "diaspora" can run the risk of "becoming a promiscuously capacious category," as Khachig Tölölyan warns, the peculiar rhetorics of free blacks discussed in this book offer distinct expressions of the tensions in the black diaspora between what Ellis calls "the desire to belong" and "the desire to flee."[57] It seems fitting that the concept of diaspora lacks boundaries and fixed meaning, for this is precisely what the free blacks grappled with. Diasporic discourses show how free blacks, or texts marked with blackness, worked through these competing desires in different ways.

Analyzing the peculiarity that emerged within and between deliberative and diasporic discourses contributes to the larger conversation about the rhetorical strategies about race and racism. By focusing on the tensions of white colonizationists' peculiar rhetorics, notions of unity and transcendence are rendered in more complicated terms. When public address scholars examine the struggle within discourse between white and black, free and slave, Africa and America, the impulse has been to examine rhetors, texts, and strategies that emphasize the resolution of racial tensions. Some strategies, like compromise, seem unable to bear the weight of issues as contentious as race. Zarefsky observes, "Compromise rhetoric is more likely to work with issues that are central but not so volatile, where diametrically opposed principles are not deemed to be at stake, where the hairsplitting and 'logic chopping' nature of compromise does not have to contend with the stark simplicity of a position."[58] Other strategies, like consilience, offer "an approach in which disparate members of a composite audience are invited to 'jump together' out of their separate experiences in favor of a common set of values or aspirations."[59] David A. Frank and Mark Lawrence McPhail argue that consilience "has the potential of moving Americans *beyond* the complicity of racial division and toward coherent *reconciliation*."[60] John B. Hatch further emphasizes the resolution of tension in rhetorics of race, linking reconciliation with Kenneth Burke's comic frame to show how both concepts "[transcend] the serious commitments of each distinct perspective of human motives and can appreciate their differences as complementary, not conflictual."[61] The underlying assumption of this line of research is that unity and resolution are the desired outcomes. This is often, but not always, the case in the complicated matters of race.

Attending to the peculiar rhetorics of colonization also contributes to the enrichment of the scholarship on African American rhetoric. Many of the eminent black rhetors of the mid-nineteenth century addressed their troubled feelings of belonging in the United States. However, those luminaries, men and women like Douglass, Walker, Stewart, and Henry Highland Garnet, remained in the United States and actively resisted colonization. The rhetorical scholarship on these figures reveals a particular attention to the radicalism displayed in their rhetoric.[62] Black radicalism remains a vital area of inquiry, but part of the ongoing effort to expand the study of African American rhetoric ought to include complicated texts, texts authored by lesser-known figures, and texts that are part of the diffuse black diaspora.[63] This project turns to the archive and brings lesser-known rhetors and texts into the corpus of African American rhetoric, thus making that corpus diasporic.

While this project participates in the ongoing project of amplifying lesser-known voices of the past, it is also a response to what Britt Rusert refers to as the "disappointment in the archives of Black freedom."[64] Rusert notes that "scholars of the black Atlantic have thoroughly plumbed the depths of nihilism, negativity, and 'bad feelings' in the history of slavery" but also that "studies of black freedom continue to be structured by an optimism that does not always align with the content."[65] Are the peculiar rhetorics of free blacks part of the archive of slavery or of black freedom? The answer to this question is yes. This means that although the peculiar rhetorics of free blacks rhetorically and geographically expand the corpus of black discourse, their diasporic disposition also leaves their status within that corpus less settled than past efforts at recovering black voices.

Peculiar Rhetorics of the Colonization Movement

The structure of this book reflects the tension between deliberative and diasporic discourses that constituted peculiar rhetorics of colonization. The book is framed by the analysis of deliberative discourses of white colonizationists, in the first and last chapters. The deliberative discourse of colonizationists aimed for certainty, for definition, in the racial hierarchy by appealing to the familiar processes of public policy. Speeches at the founding of the ACS by Clay and Elias B. Caldwell (chapter 1) and the second Annual Message of Lincoln (chapter 5) attempted in different ways to persuade Congress to provide federal support for the transportation of free blacks to colonies beyond the United States. These speeches evaluated the costs and benefits of taking action for the public good, the province of deliberative discourse dating back to the beginnings of rhetoric in the Western tradition.[66] Clay presided over the first meeting of the ACS, at which both he and Caldwell argued for the advantages of colonization to address the problem of free blacks living in the United States. Clay was a particularly important figure for colonization due to his early, frequent, and influential advocacy that defined the early colonization years. Lincoln, who idealized Clay's political prowess, pursued colonization efforts from the elevated political position of president before issuing the Emancipation Proclamation and functionally ending colonization's viability in the United States. That Clay, Caldwell, and Lincoln had access to the deliberative sphere of public life illustrates a power dynamic that is important to understanding deliberative and diasporic discourses in this book. The diasporic discourses of free blacks chronologically and rhetorically operate between the deliberative discourses of Clay, Caldwell, and Lincoln. In varying ways, the diasporic discourses of these middle chapters expressed a lack of belonging to the social world occupied by the deliberative discourses. A Counter Memorial by the "free people of colour" of the District of Columbia (chapter 2), letters written by Louis Sheridan (chapter 3), and speeches by settler colonist Hilary Teage (chapter 4) highlight the variety of peculiar rhetorics by disempowered free blacks. Using the deliberative discourses of white colonizationists as a frame illuminates how the diasporic discourses of free blacks asserted their understanding of belonging as a part of, and apart from, American society.

In chapter 1, I examine the deliberative discourses of Clay and Caldwell and the manner in which those texts represent the vision of the national colonization effort. The speeches at the founding meeting not only function as a chronological starting point for the national movement for African colonization, they also serve as representational discourses of the political, and overwhelmingly white, strand of colonization advocacy. Peculiar rhetoric in Clay's introductory remarks and Caldwell's featured address constructed the case for federally supported colonization through *peculiar argumentation*. Peculiar argumentation highlights how Clay and Caldwell attempted to appeal to two opposing audiences without reconciling the key differences that caused tension between them. Such argumentation functioned as one manifestation of peculiar rhetoric in the larger discourse of colonization. What makes the peculiar argumentation at the ACS's founding particularly important is that it was a key reference point for much of the subsequent discourse on colonization. This chapter functions both as a context chapter and as a critique of the argumentative strategies of the ACS. The peculiarity of Clay's and Caldwell's argumentation emerged in the unresolved tensions that colonizationists constructed in their effort to attain federal support for colonization.

In chapter 2, I begin an account of the diasporic voices of disenfranchised black people through an examination of an immediate response to the creation of the ACS in 1816 and the articulated motivations of that group. In the pages of the *National Intelligencer*, the very newspaper that published the account of the ACS meeting in Georgetown, a "Counter Memorial against African Colonization by free people of colour" was published. The uncertainty of whether the "free people of colour" included one or many authors, of one or varied races, sets this chapter apart from the others in this book that focus on the voices of individuals instead of groups. However, this ambiguity over authorship is part of the peculiarity examined in this chapter. Specifically, the uncertainty of the authorship and the purpose of the Counter Memorial creates a *peculiar voice* defined by the suspension of the text's meaning between more stable and knowable authors and discourses. This chapter examines how the Counter Memorial challenges the deliberative efforts of the ACS through direct refutation, but also, more importantly, through rhetorical strategies that create interpretive slippages based on the uncertain authorship and intent of the text. The instability of the Counter Memorial's meaning invites three readings of the text, each activated by examining a different strand of black rhetorical discourse from that time. The peculiarity arises from the polyvocal performance of the Counter Memorial, which resists a single interpretation.

Chapter 3 traces the unusual process of a free black man negotiating with the ACS for the emigration of himself and his party to Liberia. A former slave who purchased his freedom, Louis Sheridan became a successful merchant and slaveholder in North Carolina. Despite his success, Sheridan felt that he was not being treated equally by his white peers and sought through his contact with the ACS the opportunity to achieve true liberty and equality. Sheridan's negotiation with the ACS calls attention to his *peculiar planning*. Drawing on theories of Afro-Pessimism and black optimism, this chapter explores how Sheridan's attempts to constitute his identity through the planning of his voyage to Liberia were met with "resistance from above" in the form of the ACS's policy orientation.[67] Sheridan's unusual position as free black, successful merchant, and slaveholder brings the tension between Afro-Pessimism and black optimism into stark relief. Sheridan's desire to be treated the same as any man with his means, and the failure of white society in North Carolina or the ACS to do so, provided a fraught context in which he struggled to understand his position. Sheridan's felicity with words allows readers to begin to comprehend his struggle between two orientations toward black subjectivity. Sheridan's correspondence was rendered peculiar by his vacillation between the critical dispositions of Afro-Pessimism and black optimism.

Chapter 4 analyzes a more traditional rhetorical relationship, that of speaker and speech. But the identity of the speaker and the location of the speech—a settler colonist speaking in Liberia—provide important insights into how diasporic and deliberative discourses were coordinated within the constitution of civic identity for settler colonists in Liberia. Teage—editor, author, political activist, and speaker—was an active participant in the attempt to create a civic identity for a people that were not American or African or African American. Teage articulates the *peculiar obligations* of settler colonists in Liberia, obligations that bear the mark of American civic life with the experience of being excluded from the very civic life they seek to create. Illumination of these peculiar obligations builds from the deliberative and epideictic speeches Teage delivered, illuminating his adherence to the conventions of those genres while also extending how scholars understand the public speaking and public memory in the black diaspora. The obligations that Teage encouraged illuminated the peculiar position of settler-colonist civic identity, as neither free nor slave, neither American nor African, neither citizen nor chattel.

In chapter 5, I return to an investigation of colonizationist rhetoric through an exploration into Lincoln's support for colonization in his second Annual Message from 1862 as a *peculiar proposal*. Lincoln's "message" serves as the final chapter in this project for two reasons. First, as the chapter argues, Lincoln's second Annual Message was the last, best policy argument for colonization before the president's Emancipation Proclamation took effect. Once the Proclamation was signed, the president no longer made public statements in favor of colonization. Even more, it was difficult for colonizationists to advocate for their compromise when the president made emancipation the law of the land. Analysis of Lincoln also recalls his political idol, Clay. It is ironic that, despite his best efforts, Lincoln ended the national importance of colonization that Clay began. Like chapter 1, this chapter examines Lincoln's deliberative argumentation, particularly in its engagement with policy advocacy of colonizationists. The peculiarity of Lincoln's proposal emerged from the timing of the second Annual Message (communicated between the preliminary and final Emancipation Proclamation), as well as from colonization's seemingly minor role in the larger scheme of the proposal.

In the conclusion, I map the traces of peculiar rhetorics of colonization in the various iterations of "Back-to-Africa" emigrationist movements that took shape in the post-Reconstruction era and persisted into the early twentieth century. During this period, the ACS continued to exist and provided modest support to blacks seeking immigration to Liberia. More significant was the endurance of the ideological struggle between many blacks as to the meaning of immigration to Africa. This conclusion, which highlights the tensions that remain within a discourse of the middle, offers a final accounting of the book's primary purpose: beholding the tensions between and resisting the easy resolution to notions of beginnings and endings, or success and failure. The conclusion ends the book, but it also begins a conversation about peculiar rhetoric in the postbellum context of black life in America. In doing so, I discuss perhaps the best-known figure associated with colonization, Marcus Garvey, who was more accurately defined as an emigrationist and not as a colonizationist. The conclusion opens to peculiar rhetorics of *emigration* in the speeches and writings of Douglass, Henry McNeal Turner, Garvey, and W. E. B. Du Bois.

Peculiar Rhetoric turns toward the middle and examines the interplay of deliberative and diasporic discourses of colonization. This rhetorical inquiry focuses on particular rhetors and moments, while also assembling a new narrative of colonization that resists the binary of success and failure. In the process, some black rhetors previously unexamined by rhetorical scholars—the free people of colour of the District of Columbia, Sheridan, and Teage—are appreciated for their complex negotiation of colonization's promise of liberty and assumptions of inequality. Even the well-known white rhetors like Clay and Lincoln are cast in a new light when situated within the tension between deliberation and diaspora that undergirds a peculiar rhetoric of colonization. Ultimately, *Peculiar Rhetoric* beholds the rhetorical processes through which Americans, black and white, struggled to understand race and identity within the context of African colonization.

CHAPTER 1

Peculiar Argumentation

Henry Clay, Elias B. Caldwell, and the Establishment of Colonization's Deliberative Discourse

On January 2, 1817, the *Maryland Gazette* reported that a meeting of "numerous and respectable" participants had assembled in Georgetown to consider the creation of a colony of free blacks. The *Gazette* noted that the meeting's "proceedings [were] fraught with interest." In this preliminary introduction to the colonization movement, the newspaper saw fit to convey that "the hon. Henry Clay" served as chair and that "Elias B. Caldwell, Esq., in a speech of considerable length, developed the views of the friends of the project" and promised that complete proceedings of the meeting would be published at a later date.[1] Indeed, the *Gazette*'s observation of Caldwell's speech being "of considerable length" was not surprising, as it was Caldwell who was assigned the task of articulating the weighty purpose of this new national organization. The timing of these speeches, delivered at the meeting that created the first and most significant national colonization society, makes them important elements of the movement's history, but also important sources for theorizing the discourses of the middle and the peculiar rhetorics that emerged.

Peculiar rhetoric was part of colonization's origin story. Colonizationists believed that their solution to the "problems" associated with free blacks was morally and politically optimal for slaveholders, abolitionists, and, to a lesser extent, free blacks. Their discourse fits neatly into the deliberative genre of the early nineteenth century because of colonizationists' direct appeals to the genre's *topoi*, specifically, the good and the unworthy, the advantageous and the disadvantageous.[2] The presence of Clay at the founding meeting was apt. The Kentuckian came to be known as "the Great Compromiser" for his efforts to unite North and South on many issues. However, a close examination of the ACS's germinal discourses reveals that no such rhetorical unity was achieved. Instead, the foundational arguments constructed a case for colonization through what I call *peculiar argumentation*. What made the argumentation peculiar were the ways in which colonizationists offered incompatible claims in tenuous suspension between competing white audiences. Such incompatibility manifested, at times, in Clay's and Caldwell's inconsistent internal reasoning. At other times, the colonizationists' peculiar argumentation failed to address the well-circulated counterarguments of the movement's detractors.

Clay's and Caldwell's peculiar argumentation was rhetorically significant for whites and blacks in nineteenth-century America. For the white audiences to which Clay and Caldwell appealed, the speeches attempted to articulate a middle ground between slaveholders and abolitionists. Colonization sentiment fomented in the North, South, and West of the United States, leading to the creation of a national organization that united these smaller groups into a larger effort to effect change at a national level.[3] The speeches of Clay and Caldwell functioned as significant indices of colonization sentiment in their moment and became a foundation upon which the movement's discourse was built in the ensuing decades. Mentions, excerpts, and reprints of the speeches circulated throughout the country immediately after the 1816 meeting and for years beyond.[4] The rhetorical significance of Clay's and Caldwell's speeches was further amplified by the spread of colonization discourse throughout the United States. At its height, the ACS had around 150 auxiliary societies in nearly every state.[5] Those auxiliaries fundraised for the ACS, advocated for support from state legislatures, subscribed to the ACS monthly periodical, the *African Repository*, and often created their own newspapers. ACS materials percolated through the states, referencing Clay's and Caldwell's speeches and putting the two men on a very short list of the movement's founding fathers.[6] Even when Clay and Caldwell were not mentioned by name, the arguments they made about the expediency and practicability of colonization remained a part of the public discourse of colonization in antebellum American society.[7] Although there were other colonization discourses before and after, the speeches at the founding of the ACS allow for critical insights into the context in which the national colonization movement emerged, the reasoning offered for federal colonization support, and the rhetorical appeals that defined a central deliberative discourse of white colonizationists in the nineteenth century.

The analysis of Clay's and Caldwell's speeches is also vital to understanding the diasporic discourse of black rhetors explored in later chapters. How

Clay and Caldwell spoke about the character of free blacks and of Africa became a reference point for later discourses that negotiated what it meant to engage in colonization as a black person. Dickson D. Bruce Jr. argues that the creation of the ACS "redefined the character" of colonization and emigration programs in the eyes of the black population.[8] Prior to the formation of the ACS, blacks pondered the relationship between emigration, empowerment, and a distinctive African "nationality" within the context of post–American Revolution appeals to freedom and liberty.[9] However, the peculiar argumentation of Clay, Caldwell, and their ilk constrained the transformative power of such appeals in the context of colonization. As Bruce observes, "the Colonization Society presented more of a threat than a promise for African Americans concerned about the future."[10] Black opponents referenced the founding speeches of the ACS, albeit in critical terms. For example, David Walker quoted at length from the 1816 speeches in "Article Four" of his *Appeal*.[11] More important than the absolute denunciation of the peculiar argumentation of the ACS was the manner in which some black rhetors grappled with the thorny and complex issues of colonization: the hope of freedom and belonging in another country, but also the sense of difference and exclusion that undergirded the reasoning of Clay, Caldwell, and the ACS.

Examining the peculiar argumentation that framed the ACS proceeds in three parts. First, I establish the context for colonization advocacy in terms of the competing audiences the movement attempted to unite in support of its supposedly moderate solution. Second, I turn to the speeches of Clay and Caldwell at the creation of the ACS, analyzing the peculiar argumentation that constructed their justifications for colonization. Finally, I trace the legacy of their peculiar argumentation in order to establish the tensions that would be the generative force of other peculiar rhetorics discussed in this book.

Colonization's Audiences

In April of 1816 two old schoolmates from the College of New Jersey met in Washington to discuss colonization. These men, Elias B. Caldwell and Charles Fenton Mercer, enlisted the support of another friend, Francis Scott Key, and Caldwell's brother-in-law, Robert Finley.[12] The connections between Caldwell, Mercer, Key, and Finley underscore some of the diversity of regions and motivations that supported colonization. Within particular regions the appeals could be more narrowly tailored to the audience. For example, Finley, living in New Jersey, spoke and wrote about colonization because of his "sympathy for the colored race" and his "dislike to slavery ... and antipathy to all the phases of it he had ever seen."[13] Finley helped establish the ACS, yet his point of view would likely offend a Virginia planter whose primary concern was keeping a docile slave population. If colonization was going to gain widespread, national support, its supporters needed to find appeals that could create compromise between regional and ideological extremes. Understanding colonization's audiences, specifically southern slaveholders and northern antislavery advocates, provides the context for the peculiar argumentation of Clay and Caldwell at the founding of the ACS.

In the South, colonization support was informed by the fear of slave insurrections. The successful slave revolt in Saint-Domingue (present-day Haiti) and the attempted slave uprisings in the United States, such as Gabriel Prosser's rebellion (1800) seemed to justify the South's fears. After all, the Saint-Domingue slave rebellion brought about the first wholesale emancipation of a major slave society (1793), the granting of full racial equality in a US colony (1792), and the first independent nation in Latin America (1804).[14] In the United States the increased anxiety led to a redoubled emphasis on maintaining a pacified slave population. Officials attempted to censor any word of the uprising and passed legislation to prohibit the importation (or immigration) of nonwhites from Saint-Domingue.[15]

Similar fears pervaded local efforts in the South. For example, in 1792 South Carolina banned the importation of African and West Indian (which included Saint-Domingue) slaves. Maryland, North Carolina, and Kentucky passed similar laws.[16] In 1803 South Carolina reopened the African slave trade yet maintained a ban on West Indian slaves.[17] The same year, North Carolina sent a memorial to Congress regarding the recent arrival of free blacks from Guadeloupe (another West Indian island). The memorial reported a feeling of "much danger to the peace and safety of the people of the Southern States of the Union," to which the House committee considering the petition agreed. In their response, the committee declared that "the system of policy stated in the said memorial to exist, and to be now pursued in the French colonial governments, of the West Indies, is fraught with danger to the peace and safety of the United States."[18]

"Gabriel's Rebellion," organized by a slave, Gabriel, against his owner, Thomas Prosser, actualized the fears of Saint-Domingue within US borders. As in Saint-Domingue, Gabriel's plot escalated slaveholding society's fears because of the expansive potential of the event. Unlike most previous slave-revolt plots, particularly those before the American Revolution, John R. McKivigan and Stanley Harrold note, Gabriel's insurrection clearly contemplated "*political* violence."[19] Like the revolt in Saint-Domingue, Gabriel was not seeking to flee from the area but sought to overthrow the slave system and create a new government. In the trial that followed the uprising, another one of Prosser's slaves, Ben, provided testimony that illuminated this dimension of the plot. Gabriel's plan was to begin with the murder of Prosser and the "White Neighbors." The group was then "to repair to Richmond and Seize upon the Arms and Ammunition."[20] Unlike runaway slaves—whose escape simply inconvenienced their white owners—slave insurrections were perceived as an attack on the entire social and economic system on which most southern whites depended.

Insurrections struck at the core of the southern slave society, leading whites to intensely respond to real or rumored insurrections. David Brion Davis argues that Gabriel Prosser's "well-organized slave conspiracy" proved to be the "critical event that helped to paralyze antislavery zeal in the South." Davis goes on to state, "By 1806, few ties remained between the southern antislavery societies and the larger 'parent' groups in Philadelphia and New York."[21] The problem was larger than one failed uprising. With the promises of the Revolution unfulfilled, rebellious activities among slaves rose from 1810 to 1816.[22] Fear of insurrection spread to new corners of a still-expanding United States. The population of slaves was again on the upswing after a decade where the free population had grown faster than the enslaved.[23] By 1816 the potential for insurrection grew with the population of slaves and the proliferation of natural rights rhetoric in the United States. Colonization developed as a solution that responded to this tension, providing relief to slaveholders by removing the population they most feared would incite rebellion and granting rights to free blacks in their new Liberian home.

One of the most common reactions by southern whites to slave uprisings was to contain the public discourse about such unrest. This was the case in 1800 with Gabriel's Rebellion when the Virginia General Assembly met in secret to consider what could be done to stop such acts of violence and freedom. After Mercer, a member of the House of Delegates, discovered in February of 1816 the journals documenting this secret meeting, the assemblyman became captivated with the concept of colonization.[24] The discovered journals included official communications from Virginia governor James Monroe to President Thomas Jefferson asking that land in western territories, or elsewhere, be set aside as a colony for blacks.[25] While Jefferson did not oblige, during Monroe's time as president significant funds were allocated to explore African colonization.[26] Such support was years away. For Mercer, the legislative session ended in February, and he was unable to act on the subject.

Mercer's advocacy for colonization went beyond the Virginia General Assembly, as he began to spread word of the benefits of such a plan. On a trip to Washington, Mercer encountered Caldwell and Francis Scott Key. During this April 1816 meeting, Mercer relayed his intent to introduce a colonization measure in the next session of the Virginia Assembly. Curiously, in March of 1816, a group of men had called a meeting to discuss the merits of colonization.[27] Though no formal actions came from this March colonization gathering, that such a meeting was called demonstrates colonization's growing appeal.

The social and political relevance also interested Mercer's interlocutors. Key intimated that he might pursue a seat in the Maryland legislature with colonization as a policy objective. Caldwell took interest in Mercer's ideas but could not return to New Jersey to garner support, due to the financial needs of his family. Instead, he wrote letters to his acquaintances extolling the virtues of colonization. One such correspondent was his brother-in-law, Finley, a Presbyterian minister who directed the Andover Theological Seminary in New Jersey. The communication campaign undertaken by Mercer, Key, and Caldwell enhanced the exigency of colonization, arguing that the scheme provided a politically viable solution to the problems of slave revolts.[28]

Caldwell's correspondence with Finley may or may not have been the first time that the latter had heard of colonization.[29] Regardless, Finley identified with the aims of colonization. For Finley, though, colonization was less a political solution to slave rebelliousness and more of a moral cause. The increasing numbers of moral improvement societies during the early nineteenth century created an environment encouraging outreach, evangelism, and missionary zeal. Prior to the colonization meeting, Finley pondered his own actions toward moral improvement: "When I consider what many others have effected for the benefit of their suffering fellow-creatures at an earlier age than mine, I am humbled and mortified to think how little I have done."[30] In November of 1816 Finley shared his thoughts on colonization with the New York and New Jersey Synod of the Presbyterian Church. In this setting Finley revealed a colonization scheme that differed from that of Mercer, whose colonization plan aimed at having numerous states send requests to the president to remove free blacks to Africa. Finley sought to create a national organization to lobby Congress for the funding needed to make colonization a reality.[31]

Religious sentiment against slavery fomented in the North for over century prior to the establishment of the ACS. The earliest advocacy against slavery was plainly styled and seemed tame compared to later abolitionist screeds. Yet, for its time, it was a powerful statement against chattel bondage.[32] Pockets of confrontational discourses throughout British North America argued for the universal humanity of all peoples, slaves included.[33] But these few bold challenges to slavery were not the norm, even in the North. The American Revolution and its clarion call for the protection of natural rights authorized firmer stances on slavery. In 1764 James Otis penned one of the initial salvos against the government in London and stated, "In order to form an idea of the natural rights of the colonists, I presume it will be granted that they are men, the common children of the same Creator with their brethren of Great Britain."[34] This appeal to natural rights, almost by definition, could not be limited only to the political situation with Britain.

After the war, the natural rights appeal spread in northern religious groups and their stance on the slavery. Numerous religious sects that were previously silent or ambivalent about slavery began opposing the practice. In 1780 American Methodists drafted and passed statements that supported emancipation because slavery was "contrary to the laws of God, man, and nature."[35] In 1784 Methodist circuit riders voted to expel members of the church who sold or bought slaves, on the grounds that the action was "nonhumanitarian."[36] In 1787 Charles Carroll, a member of the Catholic Church, supported emancipation in Maryland. Baptist opposition to slavery came after the Revolution as well, with a 1785 acknowledgment from the Baptist General Committee that slavery was against the word of God.[37] Even among Friends, the Revolutionary era fostered greater determination against slavery, with the Philadelphia Yearly Meeting being nearly slaveholder free by 1779.[38] Antislavery and other benevolent organizations were formed based on many of the same transcendent appeals to the humanity and rights of all.[39] Natural rights rhetoric and the revolutionary zeal of the 1770s and 1780s provided an opportunity and a language by which reluctant Christians were empowered to oppose slavery.

The activities of colonization supporters during 1816 advanced the cause of a national colonization movement. Key and Caldwell engaged the political and legal dimensions of slavery in Washington since their meeting with Mercer. In the summer of 1816, Key offered free legal services to a man who came to Washington to sue for his freedom and that of other free blacks who were kidnapped and sold into slavery. Caldwell helped to advertise the case and raised money for the cause of the kidnapped free blacks.[40] Planning for the colonization meeting began in earnest in December of 1816. Finley traveled from New Jersey to Washington in early December, where he continued to discuss the benefits of colonization in the familiar settings of religious institutions. Finley garnered an audience at the F Street Presbyterian Church (often called Dr. Laurie's Presbyterian Church, as Rev. Dr. James Laurie was the sole pastor there) with Caldwell, Samuel J. Mills (who would become the Colonization Society's first agent to Liberia), and Dr. Laurie, among others.[41] The moral virtues of colonization drove Finley's interest in colonization. But to spread the word about the moral virtues of colonization, preaching in religious circles would not be enough. Finley began to engage the political process as well. Upon arriving to Washington, Finley distributed his pamphlet *Thoughts on the Colonization of Freed Blacks*, among members of Congress.[42] Finley also became a presence in Washington social circles. Escorted by Caldwell's wife, Finley visited the home of Samuel Harrison Smith and Margaret Bayard Smith on December 4. The social event that evening included President James Madison and President-elect James Monroe. In a letter, Mrs. Smith reported that Finley was introduced to Monroe and "several other gentlemen" and that Finley "went home, to use his own expression, perfectly satisfied and gratified."[43] Although colonization advocates continued to appeal to specific audiences, supporters also took actions that attempted to spread colonization sentiment beyond their core audience.

The audience that colonizationists addressed least directly was free blacks. They were treated as objects of the scheme, not subjects to be addressed. Such an occlusion seemed consistent with the antiblack ideology that undergirded many whites' support for colonization. Or it might have represented the ignorance of northern white reformers about free blacks' views. In either case, it was clear that colonizationists were not focused on rallying black support; rather, the audience they thought needed convincing was whites and, more specifically, white legislators. Curiously, the most prominent free black colonization advocate in the 1810s, the sea captain Paul Cuffe, was similarly focused on garnering the support of the US government rather than appealing to free blacks. In 1810 Cuffe sailed to Sierra Leone with the support of the African Institution, a British organization that was supporting the emigration of blacks. The experience proved positive for Cuffe, who wrote in 1814, "The most advantageous means of encouragement to be rendered towards civilization of Africa is that the popularity of the colony be encouraged . . . families of good character should be encouraged to remove from the United States and settle at Sierra Leone in order to become farmers; and to lend them aid in such useful utilities as they are capable of; and in order for this accommodation it appears to me there should be an intercourse kept between America and Sierra Leone."[44] Cuffe made many of the same arguments advanced by white colonizationists and, like white supporters, seemed more concerned with government support than with free black interest. Cuffe became a spokesperson for African colonization, and during the blockade of trade with Britain during the War of 1812, Cuffe asked Congress for permission to continue sailing to Sierra Leone.[45] Cuffe's frustration was indicative of the significance of the federal government for the success of colonization: "Nothing: Nothing of much amount can be affected by an individual or private bodies until the government removes the obstruction in the way."[46] The obstruction for Cuffe was the blockade during the war. However, Cuffe's statement could apply to the subjects of slavery and colonization more generally. The philanthropy of individuals and groups could not ameliorate the problems of slavery through colonization. The strength of the federal government was needed. This served as a core principle for colonizationists. It also meant that the audience of free blacks was far less important to them than whites who controlled the government purse.

In sum, early colonization discourse aimed to address two primary audiences: northern reformers and southern slaveholders. If colonizationists could unite these groups, and their congressional representatives, the removal of free blacks to Africa could address the growing racial and sectional tensions (as perceived by the colonizationists). Left out of colonizationists' concern was the free black population that would be the object of the plan. Because of the difficulty in addressing the needs of two fundamentally different white audiences and the lack of concern for free blacks, colonizationists like Clay and Caldwell struggled to find a message that could resonate across audiences.

The Peculiar Argumentation of the ACS: Clay, Caldwell, and the Deliberative Appeals for a National Colonization Movement

The speeches of Clay and Caldwell at the formation of the ACS attempted to clarify the deliberative arguments for colonization. The peculiar argumentation in these speeches arises as a function of both the weakness in their policy claims and their failure to account for obvious contextual factors that compromised the strength of their plan. To demonstrate this peculiar argumentation, this section begins by laying out Clay's and Caldwell's advocacy in detail in order to better understand how they viewed colonization on their own terms. Next, I illustrate the dialectical order exposed when comparing Clay's and Caldwell's claims. These claims show how the speakers' peculiar argumentation generated ideological conflicts that would shape and constrain colonizationist discourse in the decades that followed. Lastly, the lack of argumentation on important matters created weaknesses in their advocacy that would compromise the resonance of their arguments with their audiences.

The speeches delivered at the inception of the ACS were direct in their approach. Clay and Caldwell each declared the subjects to be addressed in their speeches; Clay considered "the propriety and practicability of colonizing the free blacks of color of the United States," while Caldwell divided his address into "1st. The expediency; and 2dly. The practicability of the proposed plan."[47] This overt structure called attention to the act of justification in which the speakers were engaged. Both men tended to follow the road maps they provided for their listeners, except for a few telling exceptions, discussed in later sections.

Clay's opening remarks offered his own justifications for colonization and introduced the speaker and occasion. This was likely due to Clay's preparation to deliver the featured remarks at the meeting. The initial plan was for Bushrod Washington, nephew of George and a justice on the US Supreme Court, to lend his name and prestige to the meeting as its chair. Clay would have delivered the featured remarks. However, in Washington's absence, Clay took over the role as the presiding officer while also making the case for colonization's necessity.

Clay's reasoning in support of the propriety and practicability of colonization was more loosely structured than Caldwell's speech. First, on the subject of propriety, Clay made two main arguments. One argument was that the free black population, what he called "the mixt population of our country" was "peculiarly situated." According to Clay, free blacks "neither enjoyed the immunities of freemen, nor were they subject to the incapacities of slaves, but partook in some degree of the qualities of both." Due to this position and, he admits, the unconquerable prejudices that hinder any changes in the States, Clay concluded, "they never could amalgamate with the free whites of this country." The other propriety argument asserted that colonization had various moral benefits. First, it would benefit native populations in Africa with whom colonists would interact and introduce "the arts, civilization and Christianity." Additionally, colonization would return blacks "to the land of their fathers." Finally, white colonizationists, through their support of colonization could "extinguish a great portion of that moral debt which she [America] has contracted to that unfortunate continent [Africa]."

In addition to noting colonization's moral benefits, Clay made two other claims related to the propriety of colonization that appeared after he discussed the practicability of the scheme. Clay touched upon white society's fear of free blacks by asking, "Can there be a nobler cause than that which while it proposes to rid our own country of a useless and pernicious, if not dangerous portion of its population?" This was Clay's only mention of the slaveholder's fear of free blacks as the leaders of uprisings. The last element of propriety also functioned as Clay's peroration, as he "hoped, in their deliberations, they would be guided by that moderation, politeness and deference for the opinion of each other, which were essential to any useful result." Propriety took on a range of meanings for Clay and allowed him to address a variety of audiences in his brief speech (see table 1).

In comparison to its dialectic counterpart, Clay's discussion of practicability was much less diverse in its structure and appeal. Clay expressed two main ideas on colonization's practicality. The first claim on this subject concerned whether free blacks should be colonized domestically or to Africa. Clay said very little on this matter other than that he "had a decided preference for some part of the coast of Africa." This brief statement on the location of colonized free blacks occurred during the section on propriety. Clay's justification for Africa as the appropriate location espoused the moral virtues of sending

Table 1. The relational structure of Clay's claims of propriety and practicability in "Opening Remarks at the Creation of the American Colonization Society"
Free blacks should be colonized
○ Propriety
■ Free blacks cannot amalgamate
● Free blacks are peculiarly situated
♦ Neither slave nor free
♦ This might be prejudiced
■ Colonization has moral benefits
● Introduce arts, civilization, Christianity to Africa
● Better than the evil sufferings of free blacks remaining in US
● Extinguishes moral debt of the slave trade
■ Colonization will rid country of useless population
○ Practicability
■ Africa is optimal location
■ Sierra Leone is a promising example
● Supported for 20–25 years by private individuals
● Began with fugitive slaves from the American Revolution
● Struggled with ignorance, barbarity, prejudice, climate
● Made gradual progress

free blacks to that "benighted quarter of the globe." The second and far more substantive argument about practicability was his description of Sierra Leone and its promise as a location for free blacks. This British colony of supposedly repatriated blacks had existed for twenty-five years, had struggled in many ways, but, according to Clay, was making gradual progress. Clay also noted an American connection to the colony, stating, "The basis of the population of the colony consisted of the fugitive slaves from the Southern states during the Revolutionary War, who had been first carried to Nova Scotia, and who afterwards, about the year 1792, upon their own application, almost in mass, had been transported to the western coast of Africa." On practicability, Clay said relatively little beyond establishing an antecedent to what American colonizationists advocated (see table 1).

Caldwell's speech addressed many of the same issues as Clay's, but in much greater depth. Caldwell addressed similar topics, opting for "expediency" rather than "propriety" as his first area of argument, and practicability as his second. Caldwell's structure was more pronounced than Clay's, as each of these main areas was explicitly divided into subareas. Under the umbrella of expediency, Caldwell outlined colonization's "influence on our civil institutions, on the morals and habits of the people, and on the future happiness of the free people of colour" (see table 2). Caldwell's elaboration of these topics will be discussed in much greater detail in the next section, but one feature is particularly salient in a comparison between the two speakers' styles. Specifically, Caldwell used more direct refutation within his speech than Clay. For example, on the matter of civil institutions, Caldwell's discussion of civil institutions was similar to Clay's arguments about the peculiar situation of free blacks. Caldwell cites the Declaration of Independence "'that all men are created equal,' and have certain 'inalienable rights.'" Like Clay, he argued that free blacks will never be able to be truly equal and attain those rights. On this point, however, Caldwell continued his argument by addressing the potential arguments against his position: "Some persons may declaim, and call it prejudice. No matter—prejudice is as powerful a motive, and will as certainly exclude them, as the soundest reason." Caldwell's direct refutation differentiated his approach to expediency from Clay's propriety. Furthermore, Caldwell's refutation left little doubt that the purpose of his speech was to justify colonization, through argument or rebuttal.

Although both speeches at the ACS's founding meeting discussed the practicability of colonization, Caldwell devoted significantly more attention to the subject than Clay. Caldwell divided the subject into three parts: the territory, the expense, and the probability of obtaining free black consent (see table 3). The elaboration of the issue of territory included a lengthy digression about

Table 2. Caldwell's expediency arguments in his featured remarks
Free blacks should be colonized
○ Expediency
▪ Colonization improves "our" civil institutions
• Declaration of Independence says all men are created equal
• But free blacks do not have that equality
♦ For reasons of safety
♦ Some say this is prejudice
♦ But prejudice is a powerful motive
▪ Free blacks hurt the habits and industry of other blacks
• Acknowledged by all who are paying attention
▪ Being free hurts the happiness of the free blacks
• Free blacks want rights and privileges equal to those around them
• Current state of degradation is a state of unhappiness
♦ Debases the mind
♦ Cramps the energies of the soul
♦ Represses efforts toward greatness
• Increased improvement with equality makes free blacks miserable
♦ If free blacks stay, they must be kept in lowest state
♦ US cannot allow this debasement
♦ Keeping free blacks in US prevents their advancement

the moral benefit of bringing Christianity and civilization to Africans. Given the significant weight invested in the missionary aims of colonization, Caldwell suggested that it was self-evident that the endeavor would be financially supported. If colonization were not supported by the national purse, then Caldwell believed that private individuals would surely back the endeavor. He also argued that obtaining the consent of free blacks for their transportation was self-evident. Caldwell asked, "What sir, are they not men? Will they not be actuated by the same motives of interests and ambition, which influence other men? Or will they prefer remaining in a hopeless state of degradation for themselves and their children, to the prospect of the full enjoyment of civil rights, and state of equality?" Caldwell provided a more detailed discussion of the practicality of colonization, albeit without addressing the political economic details.

With the colonization speeches summarized and the justifications laid bare on their own merits, I will explore the peculiar argumentation that propelled Clay's and Caldwell's advocacy. Both speakers offered justifications

Table 3. Caldwell's practicability arguments in his featured remarks

Free blacks should be colonized
- ○ Practicability
  - ■ Territory?
    - Some argue free blacks should be colonized within US
    - Evils to domestic colonization
      - Free blacks will join the Indians
      - Free blacks will attract runaway slaves
      - Pacific NW of US is too cold for blacks
      - Difficult for US to acquire land within US
      - Costly to colonize within US
    - Africa is a better option
      - Territory is easier to acquire
      - Better climate for blacks
      - Cheaper for free blacks to live
    - Redeem the souls of the native African population
  - ■ Expense?
    - What affects part of the country affects all of it
      - Colonization should be supported by the national purse
      - If the nation does not support it, then individuals will
  - ■ Consent of free blacks?
    - Are they not men?
    - Free blacks would be like American colonists

for colonization that were meant to appeal to their fellow members of polite society and, more specifically, to those individuals who served as legislators in Congress. What made their deliberative discourses peculiar were the ways that both men attempted to strike a middle ground between opposing audiences and arguments. The presumptions they make about the free black population, the claims of argumentative self-evidence, and the avoidance of significant issues contributed to the ways in which this middle ground attempted and failed to build a strong rhetorical foundation for a national colonization policy.

Individual arguments in support of colonization frequently relied upon faulty presumptions, appeals to self-evidence, and argument avoidance. To begin, the rationale for colonization often presumed the perpetual inequality of free blacks. For example, Clay's argument about the peculiar situation of free blacks relied upon the presumption that this population could never be considered totally free. Their condition, he stated, was created by "unconquerable prejudices." Similarly, Caldwell argued that the guarantee of equality and rights in the Declaration of Independence could not apply to free blacks.

Such claims were also incongruous with some of colonization's northern audience. Almost immediately after the production of the Declaration of Independence, free blacks and reformers in the North were using the document to support the abolition of slavery. In 1777 Prince Hall and seven other black people petitioned the Massachusetts General Court for their freedom. The petition cited the war with Britain and the Declaration in support of black equality and rights.[48] In 1783 over five hundred members of the Society of Friends petitioned the Continental Congress to end the slave trade, based on the "solemn declarations often repeated in favor of universal liberty."[49] These are two examples of many in which blacks and whites publicly argued for the equality of the races. Certainly, many in the United States shared Clay's and Caldwell's belief that free blacks could never achieve true equality. However, presuming this to be a fact failed to account for or respond to a part of the public discourse on race and equality that had circulated for decades.

Appeals to self-evidence were another element of colonizationists' peculiar argumentation. This particular characteristic manifested multiple times in Caldwell's address. In his reasoning about the expediency of colonization and, more specifically, how free blacks hurt the morals and habits of the nation, Caldwell stated, "This state of society, unquestionably tends, in various ways to injure the morals and destroy the habits of industry among our people. This will be acknowledged by every person who has paid any attention to the subject." By this logic, such a claim both was obvious and supported "every person who has paid any attention," making the reasoning not only self-evident, but also *ad populum*. The appeal to self-evidence was also used in the discussion of the expense of colonization. Caldwell introduced the subject thusly: "On the subject of the expence [*sic*], I should hope there would not be much difference of opinion. All are interested, though some portions of the community are more immediately so than others." The *ad populum* appeal preceded the claim to self-evidence, in which Caldwell argued, "Besides, it is a great national object, & ought to be supported by the national purse." Caldwell assumed that colonization was important to the nation, meaning that it was self-evident that the government should fund it. In this instance, Caldwell's argument seemed to beg the question: Colonization should be funded by the nation because of its importance for the nation. If an audience held the same beliefs as the arguer, then appeals to self-evidence reinforced those beliefs. But when the audiences did not share the same beliefs, appeals to self-evidence offered weak support. Potential supporters from the North might not share the assertion that free blacks were "destroying" anything, while members of both audiences might have serious, specific questions about the costs associated with the government funding such a scheme.

Argument avoidance was a third characteristic of the colonization justifications. Caldwell avoided making practical arguments about territory with a digression about "redeeming fifty millions of people from the lowest state of ignorance and superstition, and restoring them to the knowledge and worship of the true god." The digression was amplified over the course of many lines and developed a strong case for missionary work in Africa. However, its relevance to practicability was dubious. It was the kind of argument he already made under the banner of expediency. The impact of such an argument might have been powerful, yet it failed to further establish the logistical bona fides of a plan that was seeking federal support.

Another form of avoidance occurred when Caldwell addressed the willingness of free blacks to be colonized. Through a series of rhetorical questions, Caldwell asserted that free blacks would participate. But the very fact that he used questions rather than providing examples avoided directly addressing the subject. Caldwell asked, "What sir, are they not men? Will they not be actuated by the same motives of interests and ambition, which influence other men? Or will they prefer remaining in a hopeless state of degradation for themselves and their children, to the prospect of the full enjoyment of civil rights, and state of equality? What brought our ancestors to these shores?" Perhaps most illuminating about this line of reasoning was its focus on the white audience's perceptions about what should motivate free blacks. Caldwell's allocation of motives made apparent the obvious omission of free black voices from the colonization movement, even as audiences to white orators.

Delving deeper into their advocacy illustrates how Clay's and Caldwell's arguments created an unstable dialectical order. Kenneth Burke describes the rhetorical creation of order, specifically as it relates to political deliberations, in terms of dialectical and ultimate order. Dialectical order is achieved when an arguer presents various reasons in favor of a proposition, where the relationship is loose, creating a "jangling relation with one another."[50] Ultimate order provides a line of reasoning that places these reasons into a "hierarchy, or sequence, or evaluative series." According to Burke, the difference between the dialectical and ultimate order is that in the ultimate order, a "guiding idea" or "unitary principle" brings together the different lines of argument.[51]

Another way in which ultimate order is achieved is through transcendence. To transcend, Burke notes, is to offer a single argument that appeals equally to both sides.[52] Transcendence moves beyond the original terms of the conflict, establishing a "new identity."[53] Burke explains the process of transcendence in the following terms: "When approached from a certain point of view, A and B are 'opposites.' We mean by 'transcendence' the adoption of another point of view from which they cease to be opposites."[54] The new point of view created through transcendence is not simply an additional point of view, but one that also eliminates the tension of the conflict. The compromise of dialectical order creates agreement by combining parts of "A" and "B," thereby reducing but not eliminating conflict. The transcendence of ultimate order creates a new position that moves beyond the tension of the conflict altogether.

Considering how arguments related to one another in the colonization movement's justifications brings the dialectical order of peculiar argumentation to light. The first problem with colonizationists' dialectical approach was that arguments made for one audience were later contradicted by arguments made for another audience. In the case of Clay and Caldwell, both speakers offered depictions of free blacks as both thoughtful Christians and violent agitators. For example, Clay argued that colonization will "rid our own country of a useless and pernicious, if not dangerous portion of its population," while in the same breath he goes on to suggest free blacks will aid in the "spreading of the arts of civilized life and possible redemption from ignorance and barbarism" in Africa.

Like Clay, Caldwell positioned free blacks as part of a missionary effort to redeem native Africans through Christianity. Yet, as noted above, Caldwell argued that it was self-evident that free blacks hurt the "habits and industry" of white Americans. Even more, he suggested that one of the reasons that equality and rights were "impossible" was due to the "safety of the state." The characterizations of free blacks as both dangerous and Christian addressed both audiences, but by including both undermined the strength of the appeal. Each audience could find their beliefs included in the justification for colonization, yet the presence of appeals directed to the other side of the issue raised concerns about the true intentions of the ACS.

The dialectical order of practicability arguments differed from those related to the perception of free blacks. The middling argumentation concerning practicability authorized the audience to wait, rather than act. Rather than appealing to both sides, the dialectical order created in some of the practicability arguments appealed to neither side. For example, Clay noted that he had some "preference" for Africa as the location for colonization. Then, he provided the audience with descriptions of the tremendous hardships suffered by settler colonists who founded Sierra Leone. Clay described, "This colony, after struggling with the most unheard of difficulties—difficulties resulting from the ignorance, barbarity and prejudices of the natives;

from the climate ... had made a gradual and steady progress." The tension in this case was more rhetorical than argumentative. His description of the hardship was overwhelming compared to the tepid notation of "gradual and steady progress." Given the financial and political costs to colonization, the description of Sierra Leone was not promising. Even more, it compromised the notion that civilization, arts, and Christianity could easily be introduced, because of the hardships settler colonists would face. The example of Sierra Leone weakened, rather than strengthened, either side's belief that colonization was a practical policy to address their individual concerns about free blacks in America.

Caldwell also left matters of practicability in jangling relation to one another. On the topic of expense, Caldwell argued that because colonization was a national issue, it deserved financial support from the national government. He went on to argue that if this money could not be secured from the government, he was certain that "the liberality and the humanity of our citizens will not suffer it to fail for want of pecuniary aid." Private citizens would pay if the government would not, Caldwell surmised, but he would "be sorry, however, to see our government dividing any part of the honor and glory which cannot fail of attending the accomplishment of a work so great, so interesting, and which will tend so much to diffuse the blessings of civil liberty and the happiness of man." Caldwell's demurring might be seen as part colonizationists' general position of moderation and balance. In terms of arguing for a policy, it provided any skeptic of the plan with an easy out by allowing the audience legislators to believe that they did not need to act in order to yield the potential benefits of colonization (aside from the possible forfeiture of honor and glory). Caldwell may have made the case that African colonization ought to be supported by someone; he did not make a compelling case that it should be supported by the federal government.

The Impact of Peculiar Argumentation: Advocacy, Benevolence, and Nostalgia

The peculiar argumentation of colonizationists constructed a case for colonization that offered weak but dialectically ordered appeals to the two audiences they sought to unite. The borrowing of appeals from competing traditions without ideologically uniting them reveals colonizationists' failure to create a rhetorical motivation for colonization that could move beyond the more hardline positions of abolitionists and slaveholders. This was evident in the logical tensions within Clay's and Caldwell's speeches and in their failure to effectively engage prevailing public arguments that would mitigate their position. Among the white audiences that colonizationists addressed, the cracks in their argumentation were almost immediately exploited.

First, the absence of political argument, most notably on the practicability of colonization, became clear in the relative lack of support that colonization received from the national government. In the immediate aftermath of the group's formation, the ACS began the process of petitioning the government for colonization support. The movement for federal support officially began with the delivery of a Memorial to Congress on January 14, 1817. The Memorial, signed by ACS president Bushrod Washington, continued to use the same appeals that Caldwell and Clay used in their speeches at the germinal meetings. The Memorial's description of the problem of slavery (i.e., the presence of free blacks within the United States) framed the issue in political terms, stating, "The intermediate species of population [free blacks] cannot be incorporated so as to render the Body Politic homogeneous and consistent in all its [members] which must be [the] essential consideration of every form of government."[55] The Memorial was received by the House of Representatives and assigned to the Committee on the African Slave Trade. The report, delivered by Timothy Pickering of Massachusetts, agreed with the ACS's assessment that free blacks were of "distinct character" and thus could not remain in the United States or be colonized on the continent. However, the report used Clay's analogy of Sierra Leone to argue for an alternative to establishing an American colony in Africa. The committee proposed that the president negotiate to send free blacks from the United States to Sierra Leone rather than create an American colony. Operating within the mode of public policy, this would maximize the benefit for white Americans. As Pickering stated, "Should an agreement with Great Britain be effected, no further negotiation, nor any extraordinary expenditure of money, will be required."[56] Not only did Clay's description of the Sierra Leone colony diminish the practicability of colonization, it also opened the door for an alternative that was a more economically and politically viable option. Although the report was ultimately supportive of colonization, it highlighted the seams in the argumentation of colonizationists.

The ACS was successful in receiving some federal funds, yet closer examination reveals that this had less to do with public advocacy than with a crafty interpretation of the Slave Trade Act of 1819. On March 4, 1819, the ACS convened a group of experienced lawyers, which included Washington, Francis Scott Key, and General Walter Jones, to communicate with President

James Monroe. They argued for an interpretation of the act that would allow the president to purchase land and create a colony in Africa. Monroe was supportive of colonization, but he was not sure the Slave Trade Act granted him such broad authority. Monroe took the issue to his cabinet, where John Quincy Adams was able to convince enough members that such an action by the president would fall beyond his legal authority. Secretary of the Treasury William H. Crawford, a colonization supporter, successfully altered the appeal. He argued that the president could appoint an agent and fund the transportation of that agent and free blacks to Africa. Monroe dedicated $100,000 to this endeavor, the largest sum of money allocated by the US government toward colonization until the Lincoln administration.[57] For his support, the eventual capital city of Liberia, Monrovia, bears Monroe's name. The federal support may have appeared, on its surface, to signal the success of colonization advocacy. However, the support did not come from Congress and was achieved only by the narrowest of margins in cabinet-level negotiations amongst colonization advocates. For colonization to work, it would require more support—financially, politically, and socially. To gain that support, the arguments would need to better address the ideological tensions among legislators.

Second, the emphasis on the moral arguments for colonization resulted in the framing of the group as a benevolent organization, a move that constrained the necessity for federal support and left the group open to criticism from the North and South. "Benevolence" connoted the well-meaning feeling of one person toward another. Benevolent societies proliferated during the 1810s, with Americans creating a variety of social outreach and moral improvement societies to help the public good.[58] The ACS certainly fit the description, even down to the inclusion of the word "American" in the association's name, which marked so many benevolent societies. Even more, Clay and Caldwell invested significant energies explaining the "propriety" (Clay's term) and "expediency" (Caldwell's) of colonization, both of which speak to the moral reasons to support the removal of free blacks. However, rather than strengthen the call for colonization, the framing of colonization as a benevolent organization revealed the lack of political efficacy in their arguments.

The reduction of colonization to benevolence began early on in the movement's history. In the Memorial to Congress of the Colonization Society from January 14, 1817, southern (slaveholding) supporters of colonization were described as "benevolent or conscientious proprietors."[59] The same characterization was conveyed twenty years later in Pennsylvania and Maryland.

In those instances, the ACS was described as "originated by benevolent and pious citizens of the south, and joined by citizens of the north."[60] Subsequent reports from the ACS continued to emphasize the benevolent motivation of colonizationists. In the Eleventh Annual Report of the Society, colonization to Africa was justified because "if ever the vast continent is to experience the blessings of civilization, it must be through the medium of foreign benevolence."[61] Another correspondent to the *African Repository* wrote of Liberia, "Let her have our help, and our great debt to Africa is paid by our benevolence."[62] Harking back to Clay's reference to the "great moral debt" owed to Africa, benevolence was given tremendous power as it was benevolence, not freedom, liberty, or justice that would settle the United States' debt to blacks.[63] By describing colonization and its supporters as benevolent, rhetors attempted to establish the motivations for colonization as beyond reproach.

The consolidation of colonization's motives to benevolence not only constrained the ability of the government to offer federal support; it also invited well-founded criticism of the ACS. In one criticism of colonizationists' benevolence, rhetors accepted benevolence as the guiding principle but noted that emancipation was a better means of enacting benevolence. A committee of free blacks in Wilmington, Delaware, drafted an address stating, "But we beg leave most respectfully to ask the friends of African colonization, whether their Christian benevolence cannot in the country be equally as advantageously applied, if they are actuated by that disinterested spirit of love and friendship for us, which they profess?"[64] Virginian Edmund Ruffin charged, "These counselors could act with similar facilities and success in inciting as a pious work the testamentary emancipation of the slaves." Emancipation was "unquestionably benevolent and pious," Ruffin stated, while many slaveholding supporters of colonization "had indicated anything but piety, benevolence, or a delicate sense of propriety."[65] Simply because colonizationists claimed their scheme to be benevolent did not make it so, nor was colonization the *most* benevolent option.

In *Thoughts on African Colonization*, prominent abolitionist William Lloyd Garrison tactfully and carefully unpacked the meaning of benevolence in relation to colonization, demonstrating that a claim of benevolence was not a justifiable motivation. Of colonizationists, Garrison "concede[d] to them benevolence of purpose and expansiveness of heart," but went on to state, "I blame them, nevertheless, for taking this mighty scheme upon trust; for not perceiving and rejecting the monstrous doctrines avowed by the master spirits in the crusade; and for feeling so indifferent to the moral, political and social advancement of the free people of color in this their only legitimate home."⁶⁶ Garrison's critique appreciated that colonizationists were attempting to do good, but he was also quite clear in asserting that colonizationists' perception of "good" was morally flawed. Three years after Garrison's *Thoughts* was published, William Jay similarly isolated the claims of colonization as a "benevolent system" and refuted the system as a self-interested scheme of slaveholders.⁶⁷ The peculiar argumentation of colonizationists was exploited for its weaknesses, providing opponents with clear inconsistencies to exploit in denouncing colonization.

Altogether the deliberative discourses of white colonizationists failed to acknowledge free blacks as humans deserving of freedom. They acknowledged free blacks as beings worthy of their benevolence and missionaries deployed to a continent deemed inhospitable to whites. These deliberative discourses indirectly impacted the diasporic discourse of free blacks, providing evidence to free blacks of their current tenuous position in the United States and the possibility of a tenuous position in Africa. The responses of white interlocutors to colonization's peculiar argumentation were decidedly not peculiar. They were direct claims that addressed the relative merits of the proposed action. However, as the next three chapters demonstrate, the issue and practice of colonization constituted peculiar rhetorics that do not fit neatly into either pro- or anticolonization. Turning toward the discourse of the black rhetors who were mostly ignored by colonizationists' peculiar argumentation, the nuances of peculiar rhetoric become more apparent.

CHAPTER 2

Peculiar Voice

The Counter Memorial of the Free People of Colour of the District of Columbia and the Unsettling of Colonization's Deliberative Discourse

On December 24, 1816, the *National Intelligencer* announced the formal creation of the ACS. The speeches of Henry Clay and Elias B. Caldwell, examined in the previous chapter, were printed, along with the resolutions establishing the organization, creating a committee to draft a memorial to Congress, and another committee to draft the society's constitution. A few questions posed by meeting attendees Francis Scott Key, John Randolph, and Robert Wright also appeared. Less than one week later, on December 30, the purported motivations of the ACS received a public rejoinder. The *National Intelligencer* published a response titled: "A Counter Memorial proposed, to be submitted to Congress in behalf of the free people of colour of the District of Columbia."[1] Labeling themselves as "free persons of colour, resident in the district of Columbia, born in the United States, and of parents born there also," the memorialists acted as spokespersons for the population that the ACS sought to remove to Africa. In response to the colonization scheme, the memorialists asserted their rights as human beings and suggested that white colonizationists—not free blacks—created violence and unrest.[2] Throughout most of the Counter Memorial, the memorialists denounced the peculiar argumentation of the ACS and offered reasons to oppose the removal of free blacks against their will.

Not only did the free people of colour marshal a compelling response to the colonizationists' peculiar argumentation, the conclusion of the Counter Memorial took an unexpected turn that called into question its meaning. Specifically, the free people of colour claimed that colonization was not the answer; instead, the prejudices of color would be remedied "at once natural, easy and efficacious" through "*amalgamation*," wherein the races would mix socially and, perhaps, sexually. Pushing the boundaries of social norms further, the free people of colour elaborated, "Among your memorialists are very many young men, of industrious and sober habits, of ordinary school education, and of mechanic trades, who would not feel themselves degraded by intermarriages with whites." As a consequence of interaction, intermarriage, and procreation, they averred, "the distinction of color would pass away."[3] Needless to say, this "easy" solution was far from easy. Indeed, this casual solution cloaked a very radical and, for the time, obscene thought—the merging of the races as opposed to separating them amidst the festering tensions caused by slavery in the United States.

The Counter Memorial's proposed solution provoked some editorializing. The editors of the *National Intelligencer*—Joseph Gales Jr. and William Seaton—affixed within brackets at the conclusion of the Counter Memorial the following subscription:

> The reader will not receive the arguments of the proceeding article as the serious opinion of the writer. His object, it is apparent, is to endeavor, by ridicule, to check the progress of the Colonization Plan, which has recently been started in Virginia and New Jersey, and taken up in this district—we have thought it proper to insert this note, lest any one might mistake for gravity the well-meant irony of our correspondent.[4]

The commentary by the editors was curious. If the Counter Memorial's irony was "apparent," then it would seem no comment was necessary. Further, because the force of irony relied on the assumption that some portion of the audience would not comprehend a duplicitous meaning, the power of the irony was lost if explained. Gales and Seaton told their readers how to interpret the Counter Memorial, a move that would be warranted only if there were multiple viable interpretations available to readers and if the effects of misinterpretation would produce significant anxieties.

This chapter focuses upon the uncertainty at the core of the editors' subscription and explores the potential range of meanings of the Counter Memorial within the context of the discourse on race in the 1810s. Rather than attempting to isolate the "real" author(s), this chapter argues that the Counter Memorial was speaking in a *peculiar voice*. "Voice" is an apt metaphor through which to examine the Counter Memorial and its contribution to our understanding of the peculiar rhetorics of colonization in the United States. As Eric King Watts argues, the concept of voice can be understood as an embodied and "authentic" expression of individual agency. But voice can also be examined as a relational and linguistic phenomenon that can be understood only within its context.[5] The question of the Counter Memorial's authorship is, initially, a question of the race and motives of the rhetor, questions that address the first sense of voice described by Watts. The potential to hear different voices in the Counter Memorial is actualized by enlarging the critical gaze to consider the linguistic context that authorizes each interpretation, a move that reflects the second meaning of voice. The tension between these two notions of voice, and among the various voices, or interpretations, of the Counter Memorial, demonstrates a different kind of peculiarity than the deliberative discourse of colonizationists.

The Counter Memorial serves as an example of the diasporic discourse of colonization rhetoric. The text struggles to "belong" to a particular author or audience, existing in the liminal space between its attachment to familiar discursive traditions and its "intense individuation" as something different from those traditions.[6] The struggle for this text to belong to a particular author or audience marks the Counter Memorial as hermeneutically diasporic; it both belongs to and flees from familiar interpretive frames.

The peculiar voice of the Counter Memorial emerges from the potential to hear three voices—serious, ironic, and signifying—which not only conveyed distinct motivations but came from *perceptions* about the bodies (specifically, the racialized bodies) of the implied authors. Interpreting the Counter Memorial as embodying a *serious* voice (to borrow the editors' term) assumes that the authors were the free people of colour in the District of Columbia, that their position was anticolonization, and that their motive was to educate the white readership of the *National Intelligencer*. Through this voice, the free people of colour were engaging colonizationists on the deliberative terms that Clay and Caldwell set forth in the ACS meeting. If taken from the perspective of the *ironic* voice—the voice promoted by the editors' subscription—the implied author was white, the author (likely a male, given the context) could be heard taking either an anti- or a procolonization position, and his motive was to subvert the efforts of the ACS and diminish support for colonization amongst the white readership of the paper. Finally, an assessment of the Counter Memorial as a *signifying* voice—a synthesis of the serious and ironic voices within the African American rhetorical tradition—assumes that the implied author(s) were free blacks, that their position was anticolonization, and that, ultimately, their motive was self-determination.[7] These voices connect with different rhetorical trajectories of the time; yet within the Counter Memorial they seep into one another, sometimes so powerfully as to make indiscernible the distinctions between deliberative and diasporic discourses.

As these three voices compete for the attention of the auditor, an important tension emerges that would likely pass unnoticed if one were to focus solely upon one interpretation. This tension concerns the depiction and performance of blackness in the Counter Memorial, which renders the text peculiar and diasporic in distinctly racial ways. As black feminist scholars have long theorized, blackness is not innate to the body, but a constantly contested performance. Michelle M. Wright contends, "Blackness cannot be located in the body because of the diversity of bodies that claim blackness." Instead, it is perceptions "of moments of performance" that define a particular body, and a particular voice, as black.[8] By extension, performing blackness facilitates the development of the diasporic discourse of colonization, at once illustrative of a particular blackness and always temporal and tenuous.

It is the performative nature of blackness that imbues it with rhetorical power. Toni Morrison refers to the development of the black persona in American literature as "American Africanism," which she describes as the "denotative and connotative blackness that African people have come to signify."[9] Morrison argues that the black persona has a paradoxical rhetorical power, "mak[ing] it possible to say and not say, to inscribe and erase, to escape and engage, to act out and act on, historicize and render timeless."[10] Although the free people of colour were given a voice in the Counter Memorial, the peculiar voice of the text invited much uncertainty. Colonizationists used the pages of the *National Intelligencer* in an attempt to quell the tensions of slavery with their supposedly moderate colonization plan, while the introduction of the Counter Memorial in the same publication introduces a level of rhetorical uncertainty into the existing discourse of the middle. As I argue, auditors' anxiety about the identity of the author and what they were arguing only reminded the reader of the social anxieties about race and slavery. Thus, the competing voices of blackness in the Counter Memorial expose the uneasy and unresolved tensions concerning the rhetorical performance of blackness in early nineteenth-century public discourse.

The approach to exploring the development of a peculiar voice requires some patience from the reader, who will be asked to consider three interpretations of the Counter Memorial. These three interpretations will require reading many passages more than once as the chapter develops. The layering of different voices over the same text highlights the "hermeneutic depth" of the text. As Leah Ceccarelli attests, through this method the critic "insists that an audience accept the multiplicity of meanings to fully appreciate the text's deeper significance."[11] Each voice discussed below is derived from the rhetorical practices of the era, yet as Watts states, "It is the critical act that generates textual 'voice.'"[12] Operating within the interpretive space between text and context, the aim is to appreciate the complexities of, and relationships amongst, the text (the Counter Memorial), the subject (colonization), and the historical moment (the early nineteenth century).

This examination of the Counter Memorial begins with a brief discussion of the historical and rhetorical context in which it was produced. Then, the analysis proceeds in terms of the three voices in which the Counter Memorial speaks: serious, ironic, and signifying. I conclude the chapter with a brief discussion of the relationship between the Counter Memorial's voices and the colonizationists' peculiar rhetorics.

The Context of Colonization and the Counter Memorial

The three voices that constituted the Counter Memorial's peculiar voice shared certain elements of rhetorical context: the slave trade practices in the 1810s, the force of *National Intelligencer*, and the rise of the public black rhetor. To begin, discourse in the 1810s represented the precariousness of the racialized social order. With the passage of the Slave Trade Act in 1808—which outlawed the United States' participation in the international slave trade—the end of all slavery seemed imminent to many.[13] Sensing that practicing slavery would simply decline on its own, those engaged in political debates about slavery focused on gradual reforms.[14] Studies of slavery concerning the time between the American Revolution and the rise of radical abolition in the late 1820s and early 1830s have labeled this epoch "the middle period," "the era of good feelings," "the neglected period of anti-slavery," and "the rain between the storms."[15] This was not a time in which Americans forgot about slavery; rather, as Edwin Black has argued, this period represented the suppression of emotion on the subject of slavery.[16] That suppression created the false ambition to ameliorate the tensions of slavery without abolishing the practice or allowing its unfettered existence.

To this point, colonization had lingered at the state and local levels since the late eighteenth century, but had not gone to the national level.[17] As I argue in chapter 1, with support from powerful political figures, colonizationists produced peculiar argumentation that attempted to "solve" the problems of slavery through deliberative discourse "guided by that moderation, politeness and deference for the opinion of each other, which were essential to any useful result."[18] Yet colonization was anything but a moderate action. The removal of thousands of free blacks against their will to a continent most had likely never visited, all with the funding of private donors (and the US government, the ACS hoped), was more radical (or absurd) than moderate. Not surprisingly, colonization's supporters did not see it that way, instead framing their efforts as a middle ground between the contentious status quo of slavery and the even more contentious possibility of abolition.

Next, the *National Intelligencer* played an important role as the medium of delivery for the free people of colour's peculiar voice. The *National Intelligencer* was a daily newspaper published in the District of Columbia, serving as one of the preeminent newspapers of record in the 1810s through the Civil War. Before the creation of a federal printing office, the *National Intelligencer* functioned as the communications organ of the government.[19] As such, editors Gales and Seaton were enveloped in the political milieu of the national government, including the timely issue of slavery. Reflecting their ambivalence toward the practice, the editors avoided the subject and, when necessary, spoke moderately about it. Typically, they advocated a moderate approach to slavery, seeing it as an evil practice but not one worth tearing the nation apart to end.[20] Gales supported the antislavery cause, but he found in colonization the gradualist approach that he believed would best serve the Union.[21] Thus, the circulation and reception of the editors' views on slavery magnified the peculiarity of the Counter Memorial. Additionally, the editors' moderate views reflected the immediate rhetorical context in which the Counter Memorial functioned (i.e., as an article published in the editors' paper).

Third, the rise of black rhetors in the early nineteenth century engendered particularly provocative meanings in the Counter Memorial. From 1808 to 1830 there was an "intense, interconnected social reevaluation" of slavery.[22] Celeste Michelle Condit and John Louis Lucaites note that free blacks at this time were symbolically transforming themselves from "free colored people to African-Americans," marking the creation of "a collectivity with its own identity and voice."[23] A significant factor in that reevaluation was the growing presence of black voices in public discourse.[24] When the Counter Memorial was penned in 1816, free blacks were, at best, newcomers to the white-elite-dominated public sphere and, at worst, wildly unwelcome participants.[25] Jacqueline Bacon characterizes the 1800s and 1810s as a time in black public life marked by community organizing, "an incipient militancy," and increasing oppression.[26]

Additionally, as Dickson D. Bruce observes, blacks were doing more than petitioning in the early nineteenth century. They were beginning to speak more in public, and those speeches were being turned into pamphlets.[27] These forces created a precarious situation for blacks in the period between the end of the international slave trade and the rise of radical abolition in the late 1820s. The motivation and in-group support for black discourse increased, but such support also led to increased anxiety and oppression in the white-dominated public sphere. Although free blacks in the North could occasionally seek an audience in the white-run newspapers (the first black newspaper would not be printed for another decade), their presence in periodicals was sparse and tightly controlled. The creation of the ACS and the response of the Counter Memorial interacted with a context in which the discourses of slavery shifted and attempted to make tenable a public space where black voices were heard and legitimized. A close textual examination of the Counter Memorial helps reveal this moment's political complexities.

The Serious Voice: Free Blacks Implied Author, Anticolonization Position, Education as Motive

The editors of the *National Intelligencer* claimed that the author of the Counter Memorial was simply engaging in an act of irony. The reader could take Gales and Seaton at their word. Yet there were many features that made the Counter Memorial seem to be the authentic work of free people of colour in the District of Columbia. Participation of blacks in petitioning in the late eighteenth and early nineteenth centuries justifies an interpretation of the Counter Memorial as a legitimate communiqué to Congress. The serious voice, then, constructed the author as a rational and engaged political agent engaging in deliberative discourse characteristic of white colonizationists like Clay and Caldwell. Such empowerment directly challenged the social norms as well as many of the assumptions upon which colonizationists built their arguments.

In the political context of the early nineteenth century, petitions allowed the public to communicate with Congress and seek redress of grievances. Blacks used the process of petitioning for their freedom and rights as early as the seventeenth century.[28] The Revolutionary War increased public discourse on slavery—most obviously through the metaphor of political slavery employed by American Patriots, which created a discursive opening for chattel slaves to appeal to the government for their freedom.[29] Within those petitions, Susan Zaeske argues, petitioners employed "flattering adjectives" and used language that reflected an awareness of petitioners' subordinate position.[30] Glen McClish observes that black rhetors adapted the conventions of the petition form, specifically in the construction of a "suppliant ethos," whereby blacks humbly but persuasively asserted their rights to a white audience.[31] Black petitioners faced the challenge of balancing accommodation of social norms with "forceful, even militant arguments to build community and challenge American society."[32] Bold pronouncements of equality by blacks, if perceived as hostile, could invite the overly restrictive responses used when whites felt a challenge to the racial hierarchy. Although petitioners employed the language of deference, the very act of petitioning was an act of citizenship—a bold step in their quest for equality.

The creation of a suppliant ethos was central to the critique of colonization in the Counter Memorial. The text stated that the "free persons of colour" have "good morals," were made "christian [sic] by the gospel," and "have at all times endeavored so to conduct themselves, as to merit the good will and friendship of their white brethren." The free people of colour also attempted to mitigate the negative depictions of free blacks. The Counter Memorial asserted, that "if, in particular instances, individuals have been found wanting in duty to God and to society, your memorialists trust that such instances have been regarded as exceptions to their general demeanor."[33] The admission that some small portion of the black population might behave poorly but most blacks were upstanding individuals allowed the free people of colour to retain the strength of argument against colonization while also gaining credibility by admitting reservations to their claim. A series of these descriptions characterizing free blacks helped reverse the negative portrayals on which colonization was based.

Having depicted free blacks as similar to whites—a feat achieved through a language noticeably void of confrontation—the free people of colour offered a clear statement about their rights. They stood resolved "against the assumed right of any individuals whatever . . . to pass judgment on their [blacks'] condition."[34] By building the argument inductively and providing opposing perspectives to those used by colonizationists to support their scheme, the free people of colour took the posture of educating their interlocutors—congressmen—on the disadvantages of removing blacks from the United States.

The nonthreatening posture of the free people of colour not only responded to and corrected characterizations of free black people; it also sounded a cautionary note to colonizationists. The prevailing notion (in racist white circles) was that whites must be secure from violent blacks; however, the memorialists warned that colonization "will easily pass from *persuasion to force*" causing "terror and anxiety."[35] Here, the free people of colour used one of the colonizationists' own assumptions to create an argument against colonization. Safety concerns had motivated many whites to consider colonization as a solution to the problems of slave insurrections.[36] In the Counter Memorial, the roles were reversed. Not only were the colonizationists' means contrary to their ends, but the free people of colour employed colonizationists' arguments to oppose the scheme. Situated after the carefully crafted discussion of the character of blacks in the District of Columbia, the potential for such a claim to be interpreted as confrontational was significantly reduced.

The free people of colour's scandalous claim that racial amalgamation would solve the problems of slavery called into question the reasonableness permeating most of the free people of colour's claims. The free people of colour responded to the notion that color was the source of racial tension by stating, "Philosophers and statesmen would see in those prejudices a remedy, at once natural, easy and efficacious . . . the remedy of *amalgamation*."[37] Despite the attempt to make amalgamation seem like the logical solution to the problems of color, the usage of the term "amalgamation" was jarring.

Encouraging amalgamation risked violence, not because interracial relationships were uncommon but because public discussion of such relationships challenged the hierarchy of race on which American slavery functioned.[38] Kenneth Stampp claims that "to measure the extent of miscegenation with precision is impossible"; however, the evidence suggests "that sexual contacts between the races were not rare aberrations of a small group of depraved whites but a frequent occurrence involving whites of all social and cultural levels."[39] The tension between the prevalence of interracial sex and the relative absence of public discussion about these relationships functioned as what Joshua D. Rothman calls "open secrets," which were "only dangerously scandalous if widely publicized."[40] White society "tolerated" interracial sex, viewing such interactions with "a measure of forbearance."[41] Still, to speak publicly about the blurring of racial lines would risk empowering slaves and compromising the racialized social order created by slavery.

Support for amalgamation offered a risky but not unwarranted solution to the problems created by color distinctions. Amalgamation was not a new concept; it simply had not been the stuff of polite public discussion. When faced with expulsion from the land that had become their home, the authors responded to one proposal with one of their own. Importantly, the free people of colour built toward this claim, such that its reception would be aided by ethos cultivated throughout the rest of the Counter Memorial. Still, there were few examples on which the authors could rely as models for discussing amalgamation publicly, only exacerbating the frankness of the argument. The free people of colour were on the forefront of holding up to public scrutiny the hypocrisy of "open secrets." Looking ahead, colonization and racial amalgamation would be intricately linked in slavery discourse during the 1830s.[42] In 1816, however, exposing amalgamation to public discussion proved uncomfortable, if not inflammatory. Either effect hued the colonization project with a shade of uncertainty that undermined colonizationists' efforts to unite competing factions.

Speaking in the serious voice, the free people of colour informed its interlocutors of an alternate perspective on colonization in a manner that was both rhetorically deft and historically legitimate. Arguments in the serious voice were to be taken as deliberative propositions, even if complicated by the bold claim that amalgamation would solve the problems of slavery better than colonization. Not all of the arguments were equally acceptable as straightforward claims against colonization. Still, in part or in whole, the serious voice of the Counter Memorial posed significant challenges to the rhetorical motivations of colonizationists and, more generally, to the authority of whites over blacks. If readers were to take the serious voice seriously, then free blacks would be entering a discourse of peculiarity that obfuscated many of the peculiarities to which Clay and Caldwell sought redress. However, the Counter Memorial can be read in at least two more voices, ensuring its rhetorical force as a peculiar voice.

The Ironic Voice: White Implied Author, Anticolonization or Procolonization Position, Subversion as Motive

The Counter Memorial could be read as a serious argument against colonization, but the editors of the *National Intelligencer* affixed a subscription suggesting subversive motives were at play. These motives, the editors surmised, were "to endeavor, by ridicule, to check the progress of the Colonization Plan."[43] In considering the deployment of the ironic voice, a white author is assumed (the use of irony by a black author comes with different assumptions and implications and will be discussed in the next section). Shifting the Counter Memorial from the realm of deliberation to the realm of irony, the editors invited complexity, not simplicity, into the interpretation of the text.

Irony works by imitating a referent text and altering key elements of that referent text to create meaning beneath the surface. The rhetorical impact of irony comes not from discerning the content-level meaning of the concept expressed; rather, irony demands that an auditor discern another meaning from that which is explicitly signified.[44] James P. McDaniel explains that irony "demands fuller recognition of surplus signification for effect."[45] By negotiating imitation and difference, an ironic text has the potential to be critical without making an explicitly critical argument. The fullness of irony offers a range of interpretation. Recognizing this broad range of interpretations, the editors of the *National Intelligencer* attempted to focus the meaning of the text by defining its intent.

The ability to mask criticism in some other discursive form made irony a particularly useful trope for the contentious subject of slavery. Benjamin Franklin cloaked one of his critiques of slavery under the pseudonym "Historicus." Franklin wrote of white Christians being enslaved by Africans. When an appeal was made for the Christians' freedom, Historicus reports, the leader of the African slaveholders replied, "The doctrine that plundering and enslaving the Christians is unjust, is at best *problematical*; but that it is the interest of this state to continue the practice, is clear; therefore let the petition be rejected."[46] Franklin's ironic voice in the allegory offered a thin veil over his bold critique of slavery as an institution, highlighting the absurdity of a Christian owning another without direct reference to the peculiar institution that does so.

Irony's ability to critique without overt critique could be more audacious in literature, as the potentially confrontational critique of real social problems could be explained away as mere fiction. In Hugh Henry Brackenridge's serially published book *Modern Chivalry*, the narrator, Captain John Farrago, reported on a lecture at the local philosophical society delivered by—to his surprise—a slave.[47] The slave, "Cuff," was sent by his master to argue "that men were all once black, and that by living in snowy countries, and being bleached by the weather, the skin had gradually become white."[48] Farrago offered a different account of the development of race and complexion: "I am of the opinion that Adam was a tall, straight-limbed, red-haired man, with a fair complexion, blue eyes, and an aquiline nose; and that Eve was a Negro woman."[49] Of their progeny Farrago concluded that some bore the likeness of Adam and some of Eve. Both explanations of race were absurd, suggesting that the claim was not a serious one. The irony—while viably offensive to particular audiences at the time—could be interpreted as an attempt at humor. But the humor comes through clenched teeth, as irony about slavery exposed the dramatic contradictions in the peculiar institution. The hypocrisy of slavery could be exposed with the protection of the critical distance afforded by irony.

Further aiding the impact of irony were the writings that traded in strange theories about the origins of races and extraordinary proposals to resolve the tensions that existed among the races. Writing two years after the Counter Memorial's publication, Hezekiah Niles, the editor of Baltimore's *Niles' Weekly Register*, believed that climate was the cause of the differences in color among the human race.[50] Even more extraordinary was Niles's plan to end racial tensions, or what he called his "final abolition of slavery and the extinction of the *slave species*."[51] That Niles viewed slaves as a distinct species shaped how he thought about the solution to slavery. Niles argued:

> If measures can be adopted simply to keep the colored population stationary, a great point will be gained—for the natural increase of the white people would soon swallow them up as it were: and by adventitious mixture, the effect of common association with the whites, and the operation of climate, the dark complexion might in time be nearly removed if not wholly eradicated.[52]

The "common association with the whites" that Niles mentioned involved the removal of all black women to the North to keep them from reproducing with black men in the South. Living in the cooler climates and not reproducing, the numbers of blacks would slow as the numbers of whites around them would increase. Despite being published two years after Counter Memorial, Niles's account mirrors a series of sexual and racial fictions that predated it. The possibility of the Counter Memorial to be read as serious argument was enabled by the existence of ideas that placed sexual reproduction and racial science at the center of the conversation about slavery, race, and colonization.

By demarcating the text as "well-meant irony," the editors suggested that the Counter Memorial was not "the serious opinions of the writer."[53] Many elements of the text supported the editors' observations about the use of irony. However, the assumption that the label of irony would protect the colonization movement from criticism greatly underestimated the potential rhetorical power wielded by those employing such a trope. To the contrary, when interpreted as irony, the Counter Memorial added more uncertainty and play to the reasons to support colonization. The ironic arguments of the Counter Memorial functioned by offering seemingly deliberative arguments with the inflection of latent ridicule and questionable authorship. With the peculiarity of the meaning and the author, however, it was questionable that an auditor would feel confident in their assessment of the text's irony.

The Counter Memorial ironically configured the concept of color to question the efforts of colonizationists. First, irony was generated through the Counter Memorial's likeness to a model discursive form. The form of the memorial—a statement of facts communicated to Congress—served as the model in this case. The Counter Memorial further established its likeness to institutional discourse by invoking many of the same arguments that the ACS discussed, such as appeals to the Declaration of Independence and the condition of free blacks in the United States. The Counter Memorial stated that free blacks in the District of Columbia "have been represented, by some, nuisances in the society in which they live, and that they will continue to be so, so long as the prejudices exist against the *color* of your memorialists."[54] Indeed, Clay stated, "From their condition, and the unconquerable prejudices resulting from their color, they never could amalgamate with the free whites of this country."[55] Meeting their burden of rejoinder, the memorialists offered a rebuttal to Clay and his ilk: "For their *color* your memorialists do not conceive themselves answerable to man, it being the gift of God—but they cannot dissemble their astonishment and indignation that those who profess to acknowledge them their *equals* in all things should make a difference of color the cause of their transportation and banishment."[56] The Counter Memorial still functioned within the code of serious public argument, identifying its interlocutors as "philosophers and statesmen" who would be amenable to a remedy that was "at once natural, easy and efficacious." The logical next step should have been a phrase of rights, equality, liberty, or freedom, as such appeals had been central to both the ACS claims and the memorialists' response.

The ironic voice of the Counter Memorial, however, offered the otherwise taboo solution of amalgamation. The justification for this "remedy" proceeded with tongue firmly planted in cheek. Ironic criticism of the colonizationists rings clear as the Counter Memorial addressed the plausibility of amalgamation (memorialists "would not feel themselves degraded by intermarriages with whites"), the timeframe ("In a few generations the odious distinction of color would pass away"), and the advantages of amalgamation over colonization ("amalgamation may speedily take the place of the detestable one of transportation and banishment").[57] The fullness of this ironic criticism took form as the argument replicated the logical appeals made by colonizationists at their meeting, leaving one to either be suspect of the original logic or be open to racial amalgamation.

The editors' labeling of the Counter Memorial as "well-meant irony" invited a singular, almost humorous reading of the text. Yet, as this discussion shows, the indecipherability of the author allowed readers to interpret the text as either an anticolonization or a procolonization argument. As an anticolonization argument, the Counter Memorial ironically challenged the claims that colonization was expedient and practicable. The words of the "free people of colour" become a literary conceit for use by a white rhetor, compromising the agency of free blacks that was explicitly articulated by the text. Moreover, proclaiming amalgamation as a solution (and that black men would not feel "degraded" by taking up with white women) ironically inverted social roles, mirroring the ridiculous proposition of colonization.

A procolonization perspective surfaced in the Counter Memorial's argument for amalgamation. Despite the concurrent rise of the black rhetor and the occurrence of interracial relationships, the mixing of white and black blood signified a threat to the white-dominated social order. Eddie S. Glaude explains, "The threat of amalgamation then was a not-so coded way of constituting national identities through difference and, if necessary, violence."[58] Reminding the audience that failure to colonize could allow the races to amalgamate would for many whites intensify the need to support the removal of free blacks to western Africa. As an anticolonization argument, the Counter Memorial questioned the stability of the rhetorical foundations of colonization by revealing the lack of strength driving the colonizationists' scheme. As a procolonization argument, the Counter Memorial attempted to enact a playful irony of pretending to be a free person of colour only to provide a stark warning to racist whites that their safety and purity depended upon colonization.

Without understanding if the author was serious or not—or if their purpose was to critique or encourage colonization—a sense of anxiety emerges from the ironic voice. Such anxiety would only expand when coupled with concerns about the insurrection of blacks and the fear of racial mixing that permeated public discourse in many states. The ironic voice, perhaps more than either the serious or the signifying voices, performed between diasporic and deliberative discourses of colonization. Only the ironic voice asked the reader to assume the author as white and pretend (along with the author) that they spoke as the free people of colour. Performing as black, even in defense of free blacks, forwarded a diminished conception of black agency that was central to the deliberative arguments of white colonizationists. The free black was not *speaking* in the ironic voice; rather, the free black was being *spoken for*. The ironic voice did little to establish a clear voice, making judgments about the necessity of colonization harder to discern, or peculiar.

The editors seemingly attempted to diminish the critical impact of the Counter Memorial, but they offered little that stabilized the meaning behind the irony. "We have seen that in political or moral satire," writes Wayne Booth, "the reconstruction of ironies depends both on a proper use of knowledge or inference about the author and his surroundings."[59] With uncertainty about the author and point of view, the instability of the irony manifest. Regarding unstable ironies, Booth states, "Though such ironies have an element of stability—we *know* that something is being undermined—we don't really know where to stop in our underminings."[60] A reader could "stop their underminings" with the editors' subscription. Perhaps many in 1816 did precisely that. Yet, given the peculiarity of race in the text and context, calling the Counter Memorial ironic does little to stabilize either position on colonization.

The Signifying Voice: Free Black Implied Author, Anticolonization, Self-Determination as Motive

Bruce argues that the Counter Memorial sounded like other memorials and remonstrances authored by free blacks against colonization, but that the suggestion of amalgamation means that the Counter Memorial was "an early, ultimately procolonization effort to parody ... what was already shaping up as a significant body of argument in opposition to the society."[61] Yet, Bruce continues, later memorials by free blacks used many of the same arguments against colonization that appeared in the Counter Memorial. The presence of both a serious argument and a subversive force suggests the potential for a third voice, one that emerged from African American rhetorical practices wherein the serious and ironic synthesize within the signifying voice.

Signifying is a strategy of the double-voicedness, subversion, and misdirection that emerged from the African folk tradition and the American experience of slavery.[62] Signifying, in the context of early nineteenth-century American rhetorical practice, was the strategy of invoking the language of the powerful as a means to direct attention away from the subversive and constitutive meanings within the same discourse. The complexity of meaning in signifying leads the hearer to be "constrained to all potential meaning-carrying symbolic systems in speech events."[63] What makes signifying different than irony or satire, Henry Louis Gates Jr. argues, is that "black formal repetition always repeats with a difference, a black difference that manifests itself in specific language choices."⁶⁴ That is to say, signifying is connected to the unique experience of being African American. By signifying on the rhetoric of the colonization meeting, the Counter Memorial not only refuted the published arguments of colonizationists but used the idea of amalgamation to reveal and challenge the implied social order of the colonization project.

Signifying, a rhetorical strategy that depended upon the difficult balancing of the multiple meanings within the immediate and historical contexts, stems from what W. E. B. Du Bois termed the "two-ness" of the African American experience. In his 1907 work *The Souls of Black Folk*, Du Bois notes that for black people in the United States, "one ever feels his two-ness,—an American, a Negro; two souls, two thoughts, two unreconciled strivings; two warring ideals in one dark body."⁶⁵ According to John Arthos Jr., the two-ness of African American experience manifests in the "surface" (the voice to the master) and "depth" (the voice to the slave) of the discourse.⁶⁶ Signifying gains rhetorical force by inching ever so close to exposing the depth of the discourse while maintaining the veneer of the surface. If the surface meaning falls short of passing as the dominant voice and allows the depth to be realized by those in power, then the misdirection element of signifying has failed, and a rhetor is left open to the repercussions of dissent. If the depth of discourse is too subverted, leaving the surface mode of address to control the meaning of the discourse, then the subversive element of signifying has failed, and a rhetor offers little constitutive force to the powerless audience. The ratio between the voices is an important factor in how signifying functions as a rhetorical strategy of the disempowered.

Signifying can occur at varying levels of explicit critique. The earliest instances of signifying emerged when white texts were made to speak with a black voice—what Gates calls the trope of the Talking Book.⁶⁷ In eighteenth- and early-nineteenth-century America, the mere presence of a black rhetor in traditionally white-only endeavors—such as poetry, literature, or public forums—conveyed meaning beyond the explicit content of the work. Because of the peculiarity of a black voice in a traditionally white endeavor, early signifying tended to adhere closely to the dominant modes of address. Significant departure from the norms of address might increase scrutiny to the point that the rhetor could incur censorship or punishment. Thus, the earliest practices of signifying carefully negotiated blacks' participation in and critique of public life without appearing too hostile to the social order.

During the early nineteenth century, signifying in public discourses began to grow. Songs became one locus of signifying, which allowed blacks to "be relatively candid in a society that rarely accorded them that privilege."[68] Petitions for freedom bore the mark of signifying, as Jacqueline Bacon and Glen McClish argue, by "using excessively polite statements that implicitly disparage, reversing roles, and exploiting the master's own ideals and language to undermine the power structure."[69] Sermons also proved an early and frequent locus of the Talking Book trope. Peter Williams Jr., Absalom Jones, William Hamilton, and others gave sermons that delivered their message as a white preacher would, offering a biblical passage, providing an exegesis of that passage, and closing with a lesson for the audience. In a more pointedly political effort, Jones and Richard Allen publicly refuted the wealthy white businessman Matthew Carey's claims that free blacks had acted immorally during an outbreak of yellow fever in Philadelphia. The response of Jones and Allen did not deviate from the norms of public arguments in the pamphlet medium; they isolated troublesome claims made by Carey, made counterclaims, and marshaled statistical data and anecdotes in support of their claims concerning the portrayal of free blacks in Carey's pamphlet. For example, of the claim that blacks extorted whites, Jones and Allen responded that most free blacks were poor and that Carey made more money through the "sale of his 'scraps' [his account of the epidemic] than a dozen of the greatest extortioners among the black nurses."[70] Whether in song, petition, pamphlet, sermon, or any other discursive act, adhering to the dominant form preempted criticism on the basis of appropriateness and allowed for greater consideration of the message.

Signifying that used harsh wit and biting irony was not yet common practice in the public discourse of the 1810s. However, sermons, again, provided a vehicle for comical signifying during the early nineteenth century. Lemuel Haynes, a black pastor in New England during this time, provided an early example in his 1805 sermon "Universal Salvation." In this impromptu oration Haynes refuted the teachings of a guest (white) preacher at his church by offering a lesson about the "preacher"—the devil—who infiltrated Paradise and sought to turn back the prohibitions of the Almighty. One need not read too carefully to understand the double meaning Haynes gave to the term "preacher," representing both the devil and the white preacher, with whom Haynes did not agree.[71] Closing his remarks, Haynes "trusts no one will feel himself personally injured by this sort of sermon . . . for it has ever been a maxim with me, render unto all their dues."[72] Even in his apology, Haynes manages to imply that his interlocutor received his due. Haynes's sermon used the wordplay that would come to define signifying as an oft-used African American rhetorical strategy.[73]

When read within the immediate context of signifying practices and anticolonization sentiment, the Counter Memorial sounded both resonant and discordant notes. The Counter Memorial engaged the subject of colonization with decorum and reason in much the same way that free black rhetors like Jones and Allen had addressed mischaracterizations of the black population in Philadelphia. There were also dimensions of the Counter Memorial that seemed to mock colonization and, more generally, the hypocrisies of racial hierarchy in the United States. In a practical sense, arguing for amalgamation would likely decimate the perceived reasonableness of the free people of colour and make colonization appear even more necessary. However, the rhetorical impact of signifying concerned more than just the practical considerations of the immediate context. Analyzing the Counter Memorial within the developing African American rhetorical practice of signifying demonstrates that despite losing adherence with a white audience, the Counter Memorial succeeded in revealing the rhetorical peculiarities of the colonizationists' scheme.

Much like the ironic voice, the free people of colour used the rhetorical norms of the time—such as the memorial form and appeals to American symbols—to legitimize their claims against colonization. Groups frequently expressed their purpose through memorials.[74] By offering a counter memorial, the free people of colour participated in the appropriate mode of address. Additionally, the free people of colour appealed to notions of rights that were part of two fundamentally American idioms: the Declaration of Independence—with its appreciation of freedom, liberty, and autonomy—and the Constitution—with its inscription of laws and process. As these appeals were familiar to an elite white audience, the free people of colour spoke in the first voice. Such familiarity provided the necessary diversion to make a more subversive argument about the status of free blacks in the United States. Being black and subversive was much more difficult in public discourse than being white and ironic. Securing the trust of the white audience was all the more important for the signifying voice than it was for the ironic voice. Once the surface of the Counter Memorial matched the decorum required of public discourse, the free people of colour were able to capitalize on the colonizationists' peculiar argumentation, highlighting inconsistencies inherent in colonization's peculiar argumentation.

As the free people of colour built their argument, the foolishness of colonization became pronounced through signifying. The memorialists began by responding to colonizationists' claims that free blacks could not be happy living in the United States, a claim that Caldwell had advanced in his peculiar argumentation at the colonization meeting. The free people of colour countered this claim, first, by repositioning the relationship between free blacks and "naturalized" citizenship and, second, through an argument of self-determination. Colonizationists argued that free blacks maintained a "peculiar" standing as neither slaves nor freepersons—as Henry Clay claimed in his opening remarks of the meeting. To assert the normality of free blacks, the Counter Memorial made the language of citizenship speak in favor of blacks. The first line of the Counter Memorial defined the memorialists as "free persons of colour, resident in the district of Columbia, born in the United States, and of parents born there also." The memorialists "know no country but that of their birth" and are of "good morals."[75] Defining the memorialists in this manner mirrored the language of citizenship from late-eighteenth- and early-nineteenth-century legislative acts.[76]

The Counter Memorial stopped short of explicitly claiming that free blacks were citizens; such a claim would be difficult to defend given the prerequisite "whiteness" of citizenship at the time. Instead, the Counter Memorial's tacit argument from similarity—that the memorialists in fact shared many characteristics of a naturalized citizen—shifted the social position of free blacks closer to that of a naturalized citizen (where the term "naturalized" carried the implicit sense of normality, not peculiarity). Even more, the implication of naturalization in the legal sense responded to the scientific arguments concerning the "natural" intellectual inferiority of blacks. Working from the rhetorical foundation that suggested free blacks were similar to naturalized citizens, the free people of colour questioned the legality of colonizing free blacks qua naturalized citizens.

The deeper meaning of the free people of colour's signifying on citizenship shifted agency from white colonizationists to the free blacks. The shift was made evident in the following passage:

> They [free people of colour] are free men and consider themselves in every respect qualified to determine for themselves what is, and what is not, for their own benefit and advantage; that indeed of all the rights and privileges which they hold under the constitution and laws, they consider the right to determine for themselves whether they be happy or not, by far the most natural, the most precious, and most inviolable, and your memorialists are firmly resolved never to part with it but with their lives.[77]

The free people of colour returned to the theme of what was natural, claiming that the right to choose "whether they be happy or not" was "by far the most natural" of rights. Taking the implication of naturalization to its extreme metaphorical meaning, the free people of colour asserted that they were not suspended in social limbo but were instead rooted in the United States.

The free people of colour not only undermined the colonizationists' claims of unavoidable unhappiness for free blacks in the States; they went on to critique the colonizationists' claim that colonization would resolve insecurity. Rather, according to the signifying voice of the Counter Memorial, colonization would create it. At the germinal meeting of the ACS, colonizationists trod lightly when discussing the fear of slave insurrections and the interracial mixing of the bloodlines, suppressing the intense emotion of these fears by using subdued terms and phrases. Free blacks were, according to Clay, "peculiarly situated"; it was the "unconquerable prejudices resulting from their color" that hindered their ability to "amalgamate with the free whites of this country."[78] Caldwell went so far as to apply the Declaration of Independence to free people of color:

> We say, in the Declaration of Independence, "that all men are created equal," and have certain "inalienable rights." Yet, it is considered impossible, consistently with the safety of the state, and certainly is impossible, with the present feelings towards these people, that they cane [sic] ever be placed upon this equality, or admitted to the enjoyment of these "inalienable rights," whilst they remain mixed with us.[79]

Caldwell's featured address created a space for free blacks in the political realm through his reference to the Declaration of Independence—perhaps *the* symbol of American political autonomy. Clay, Caldwell, and the colonizationists' peculiar argumentation attempted to situate their endeavor as the resolution to the dilemma of slavery as they saw it.

From this premise, the free people of colour then noted that the colonizationists had taken it upon themselves to pass judgment upon the happiness of free blacks, a claim already undermined by the signifying of citizenship. The Counter Memorial continued on the theme of self-determination and happiness:

> When therefore your memorialists are informed that arbitrary associations of men assume to themselves the power to decree that your memorialists are miserable . . . when in truth and in fact they are content and happy, they cannot forbear in duty to themselves to call the attention of your honorable body to a species of despotism as

unprecedented in this or any other country, as it is replete with evil to the best interests of your memorialists now and hereafter.[80]

Despotism was a political fear, a concern for those engaged in the body politic. Fear of despotism and tyranny motivated the patriot cause in the American Revolution. Coordinate terms were used to support fears of despotism, as the free people of colour referred to colonization as "voluntary exile."[81] Where the safety concerns of whites went virtually unmentioned and unexplained in the colonization meeting discourse, the free people of colour brought fear to the forefront, explicated fear in the political terminology of despotism, and implicated colonizationists in the perpetuation of despotism.

The free people of colour also mocked colonizationists by exploiting the meanings associated with Africa and its native inhabitants. As discussed in chapter 1, at the ACS meeting Africa was characterized as both a problem and a solution. Africa was the land of the savage, yet it was also supposed to provide the trappings of civilization that free blacks could not attain in the United States. Caldwell argued that Africa provided the necessary climate for blacks (the Pacific Northwest of the United States being deemed too cold); yet, earlier in the deliberations, Clay used climate as a justification for the early failures of the British free black colony at Sierra Leone (although Clay did claim that the climate was "not at all insurmountable").[82] Clay admitted that previous attempts to colonize Africa—made by Great Britain—confronted significant barriers "resulting from the ignorance, barbarity and prejudices of the natives."[83] For example, Clay asked, "Can there be a nobler cause than that which whilst it proposes to rid our own country of a useless and pernicious, if not dangerous portion of its population, contemplates the spreading of the arts of civilized life and possible redemption from ignorance and barbarism of a benighted quarter of the globe?"[84] Colonizationists were stuck trying to make Africa sound like a fruitful location for colonization, while also maintaining the depiction of Africa's inhabitants (and decedents) as intellectually inferior. In their efforts to address two audiences—northern reformers and southern slaveholders—colonizationists created logically and ideologically peculiar arguments.

Where Clay and Caldwell were constrained by their choice to depict Africa as a site of savagery as well as a hospitable location for free blacks to willingly relocate to, the memorialists' adoption of the ironic, anti-Africa position was full-throated in its description of the horrors of Africa. In the Counter Memorial, nearly all of the negative characteristics associated with Africa were boldly asserted as reasons to resist colonization. Africa was described as "a country inhabited only by savages and wild beasts—with a burning sun and torturing insects—poisonous exhalations, corrupted water and unwholesome food." The memorialists "cannot forbear to indulge a suspicion that something more is intended than meets the eye," that the colonizationists "are in truth and in fact resolved ... to deliver them over to be devoured by wild beasts, or destroyed by ferocious savages or a pestilential climate."[85] The free people of colour turned the racist renderings of Africa into an argument that explicitly debunked colonization as a benevolent endeavor. By using the implicit racism of white colonizationists' characterization of Africa against them, the free people also made the colonizationists look foolish. Exploiting this opening in the colonizationists' peculiar argumentation allowed the Counter Memorial not only to provide more clarity on the issue of colonization, but to do so using many of the colonizationists' own arguments.

Unlike most public discourses by blacks during this time, the Counter Memorial audaciously introduced social and sexual mixing into the public discussion of slavery and colonization. Advocating amalgamation as the solution to the problems of free blacks, the Counter Memorial pushed the second voice (the depth) beyond the cover provided by the first voice (the surface). The memorialists' progression toward amalgamation began with the discussion of the concept of color. "It is known to your memorialists," the free people of colour stated, "that they have been represented, by some, nuisances in the society in which they live, and that they will continue to be so, so long as the prejudices exist against the *color* of your memorialists." If color were the only problem concerning free blacks, then the nation already had within its means the ability to address the problem of color. Or, as stated in the Counter Memorial, "[the memorialists] were inclined to cherish the belief, that philosophers and statesmen would see in those prejudices a remedy, at once natural, easy and efficacious—your memorialists mean the remedy of *amalgamation*." The free people of colour continued asserting that colonization was not necessary, as "in a few generations the odious distinction of color would pass away, and the posterity of your memorialists would find themselves blended with the great American family."[86] Using the premise of "color," which colonizationists used to justify their plans, the memorialists confronted the reader with the peculiar arguments set forth at the colonization meeting.

By signifying on colonizationists' peculiar argumentation, the Counter Memorial offered another voice, one marked by blackness and subversion, to the peculiarity of the text. Reading the text as an act of signifying, amalgamation took the place of colonization and, thus, free blacks took the place of the white colonizationists. The societal order was turned upside down. Instead of the white "self-styled benefactors" of the ACS, there were "enlightened benefactors of the African race" who "would not feel themselves degraded by intermarriages with whites." Agency shifted to the "African race," which, within the framework of the amalgamation solution, had the social standing to define what was beneath them. There was a novelty, and some dissonance, in a free black man implying that some might see his marriage to a white woman as beneath him. The free people of colour assured their readers that free black men would not discriminate against white women. Such a reversal was not unusual within the African American rhetorical tradition, which had a history, according to Gates, of "chiastic fantasies of reversal of power relationships."[87]

The signifying voice conveys a serious meaning through the parody of colonizationist discourse. Parody can be quite powerful, for as Robert Hariman describes, "When language is beside itself, limits are exposed. What had seemed to be serious is in fact foolish, and likewise the powerful is shown to be vulnerable, the unchangeable contingent, the enchanting dangerous."[88] The signifying in the Counter Memorial makes the serious efforts of colonizationists seem foolish. Conversely, one result of such foolishness is the constitution of an empowered black identity in the United States. The act of challenging colonization in a public forum aided in the constitution of blacks as "agents and citizens ... assert[ing] their position in the nation and in the public sphere."[89] Importantly, the signifying voice demonstrated that this new citizen, the free people of colour, wielded far more rhetorical power and skill than an initial understanding of the text revealed.

Conclusion

The Counter Memorial evoked multiple voices in early nineteenth-century discourse, making its meaning more complex than one might initially think. The editors claimed that the Counter Memorial should be read in an ironic voice. This might be accurate in terms of the intent of the author; however, discourse concerning colonization in the ensuing decades demonstrated the strength of the serious and signifying voices in colonization discourse. Almost one month after the first meeting of the ACS, a "meeting of the People of Colour" at Bethel Church in Philadelphia produced and published a series of "Resolutions and Remonstrances" against the efforts of colonizationists in the District of Columbia. Like the Counter Memorial, the "Resolutions and

Remonstrances" offered a response in a deliberative form. One resolution stated, "[W]e never will separate ourselves voluntarily from the slave population in this country; they are our brethren by the ties of consanguinity, of suffering, and of wrongs; and we feel that there is more virtue in suffering privations with them, than fancied advantages for a season."[90] A decade after the "Resolutions and Remonstrances," the editors of *Freedom's Journal*—the first black newspaper in the United States—used the writings of procolonizationists to demonstrate the problems with the relocation scheme.[91] Similarly, "Article Four" of David Walker's 1829 *Appeal* began with long excerpts from speeches given by Clay and Caldwell before Walker systematically rebuked colonization. William Lloyd Garrison—once a member of the ACS—distributed many of the anticolonization tracts by blacks in his *Thoughts on African Colonization*.[92] Arguments about the inferiority of blacks, like those offered by Thomas Jefferson in his support of colonization, seemed foolish in light of the very capable rhetorical performances of blacks against colonization.[93]

The signifying voice would also play a more prominent role in future debates on colonization. In much the same way that the Counter Memorial played with ridicule, abolitionist rhetors responded to colonization with humor and derision. Maria W. Miller Stewart mocked the colonization plans, stating that colonizationists' "hearts are so frozen towards us, they had rather their money should be sunk in the ocean than to administer it to our relief."[94] Frederick Douglass viewed the ACS as "one of the most impudent Societies in the world."[95] In an 1849 speech in New York, Douglass opened by stating:

> Mr. Chairman, ladies and gentlemen: The resolution which I have been called upon to second is an appeal to the people of Great Britain from us, not to unite with our enemies against us, but to set their faces against our enemies and thereby help us. I shall return to this resolution after I have said a few things in favour of Colonization and against ourselves.[96]

Douglass went on to discuss the motivations of colonizationists and the good they claimed to be doing. At the conclusion of this description, he said, "Now are we not an ungrateful class of people?" which received laughter from the audience.[97] Many years later, William J. Wilson, under the pseudonym "Ethiop," wrote an essay entitled, "What Shall We Do with the White People?" a revision of the common refrain of the time, "What shall we do with the Negroes?" Wilson writes that removal of the white people from America would simply not solve the problem of slavery because whites are not fit for self-government, a parody of another common argument levied by many whites against blacks.[98] As the Counter Memorial revealed and later rhetors elaborated, colonizationists provided abolitionists not only with a serious movement to rebut but also with a host of peculiar arguments whose weaknesses could be exposed and ridiculed.

In addition to illuminating the complexity of slavery discourse in the early nineteenth century, the Counter Memorial also engages the peculiar argumentation of white colonizationists and exposes the fissures in their advocacy. Colonizationists claimed that relocation would benefit slaveholders and free blacks alike (with little mention of how this scheme helped blacks still in bondage). The problem for colonization was that a rhetorical stance that attempts to occupy the middle ground is often open to criticism from multiple sides. As David Zarefsky notes, attempts at moderation, or what he calls "a rhetoric of compromise," are effective when the issues at stake are "central, but not volatile."[99] Colonizationists seemed to misjudge their context. The momentary decline in the intensity of slavery discourse owed more to an expectation that the promises of the American Revolution would come to fruition than to a lack of volatility concerning slavery. As an immediate response to the ACS, the Counter Memorial exposed the rhetoric of moderation in the colonization discourse in two ways: by functioning as either pro- or anticolonization in meaning and by recalling more emotional appeals related to slavery that overwhelmed the moderate position of the ACS. Without finding a rhetorical strategy to overcome the instability of claiming the center in the debate over slavery, colonization supporters could not overcome the criticisms they would face.

The Counter Memorial's complexity and rejection of a single, stable voice make it a luminous text for analysis, particularly when viewed within the shifting rhetorical context of slavery discourse in the 1810s. Reading the text as serious, ironic, and/or signifying points to the peculiar voices that unsettled the deliberative discourse of the ACS. The Counter Memorial represents one way in which the voice and presence of blackness complicated the supposedly self-evident good of colonization. However, it was not the only way in which black subjectivity was peculiarly constituted in relation to colonization, as chapters 3 and 4 demonstrate.

CHAPTER 3

Peculiar Planning

Louis Sheridan and the Negotiation of Diasporic and Deliberative Discourse

Born into slavery in 1793 and soon thereafter emancipated, Louis Sheridan was unusually successful for a black man in Bladen County, North Carolina.[1] Sheridan's eventual success and status were evident in many ways. He was a wealthy man (worth an estimated $20,000), a skilled writer; a friend to North Carolina's white former governor, and, curiously, a slaveholder.[2] Sheridan's success as a farmer, merchant, and trader was likely aided by his fair skin, a quality that no doubt made his dealings with whites less transgressive to the racialized social hierarchies of the time.[3] Fair-skinned or not, by any standard Sheridan was part of the upper class of North Carolina in the 1820s and 1830s.

Despite his success, Sheridan remained constrained by the pervasive antiblack racism of the early nineteenth century. He desired a level of freedom that could not be experienced in the Black Belt of North Carolina. In February of 1836 Sheridan began corresponding with the ACS to seek support for the immigration of himself, his family, and others to a colony in Liberia. "I would die tomorrow to be free today," Sheridan wrote to Joseph Gales Sr., the editor of the *Raleigh Register*, treasurer of the ACS, and father of the *National Intelligencer* editor Joseph Gales Jr. who was mentioned in chapter 2.[4] Yet the process of Sheridan's emigration from North Carolina to Liberia was far from smooth. Sheridan's first letter to Gales, on February 16, 1836, expressed the desire to set sail on November 15 of that same year. Almost a year to the day later, Sheridan was still dating his letters from his home in Elizabethtown, North Carolina, inquiring when he and his party might expect to begin their journey to Liberia.[5]

As a wealthy black businessman in the antebellum South, Sheridan put his keen negotiating skills to work when the ACS failed to deliver. Sheridan began making inquiries with auxiliary state-run colonization organizations. On December 30, 1837, Sheridan and seventy-one others boarded the bark *Marine*, a ship provided not by the ACS but by New York and Pennsylvania state colonization groups. Over a month later, on February 8, 1838, the ship reached Edina, Bassa Cove, in Liberia.[6] Sheridan's arrival marked the end of the laborious process of emigration and the beginning of another difficult process of building a life as a settler colonist in Liberia. It also marked the limits of the ACS and the ramifications its peculiar argumentation had on the efficacy of colonization in practice.

This chapter examines Sheridan's negotiation of blackness, power, and material conditions as an enactment of *peculiar planning*. Stefano Harney and Fred Moten argue that "planning" connotes the actions of a person who is self-sufficient and seeking a better future, but who has exclusionary forces arrayed against them. Pushing against planners are policy makers, those who seek to destroy any "fugitive initiation" made by members of the "undercommons."[7] Sheridan's peculiar planning was mostly privately conducted, occurring through an exchange of letters with leaders in various colonization organizations. Unlike the Counter Memorial of the previous chapter or the speeches of Hilary Teage in the next, Sheridan's peculiar rhetoric was not public in the traditional sense. His letters were not printed in a newspaper (with a few exceptions) to be consumed by a broader public. Sheridan's peculiar planning not only negotiated for the favorable terms of a planner; the letters also expressed a deeper negotiation between two orientations toward black subjectivity. Specifically, Sheridan's peculiar planning grappled with notions of Afro-Pessimism and black optimism as different, sometimes conflicting, possibilities for black social and political life. Sheridan did not settle on either a pessimistic or an optimistic outlook but vacillated between these positions, even when his circumstances would seem to warrant a more definitively optimistic or pessimistic perspective. Ultimately, Sheridan's peculiar planning provides a unique connection between the deliberative and diasporic discourses of colonization, as he participates in the colonization scheme while also offering pointed criticism of his treatment by the ACS.

To better understand Sheridan's peculiar planning and its contribution to the larger phenomenon of the peculiar rhetorics of colonization, it is necessary to first outline the critical and historical contexts in which I situate his discourse. Once the context of Sheridan's communiqués with the ACS has been established, I undertake an analysis of Sheridan's correspondence with

Gales to assess the ways in which Sheridan's rhetorical strategies articulate variations of black subjectivity. Finally, I conclude by offering insights into how Sheridan's peculiar planning brings attention to the middleness of black subjectivity.

The Contexts for Sheridan's Peculiar Planning

Sheridan's contribution to our understanding of peculiar rhetorics of colonization comes from his expressions of belonging and alienation during his lengthy negotiation with the ACS. An analysis of Sheridan's peculiar planning and the ways in which it engaged the policymakers and figureheads of the colonization movement opens the space to consider Sheridan's struggle between the positions of Afro-Pessimism and black optimism and that struggle's implications on black subjectivity. In order to understand how Sheridan's peculiar planning enacted the struggle between Afro-Pessimism and black optimism, both the theoretical and historical contexts need elaboration. First, I turn to an account of Afro-Pessimism and black optimism as theories of black subjectivity, illuminating the shared assumptions and points of contention between the two perspectives. Second, I explore Sheridan's historical context to reveal the forces that contributed to the uncertainty and challenges that any free black, and Sheridan in particular, faced in their engagement with the colonization movement. Although I split the theoretical and historical contexts, it is critical to recognize that the historical realities of slavery and antiblack racism are generative of the contemporary theorizing about blackness.

A vibrant area of conversation, debate, and theorization in black studies concerns the structured position of blackness (or Blackness) in American society.[8] What has come to be called Afro-Pessimism might tentatively be defined as "a disposition that posits a political ontology dividing the Slave from the world of the Human in a constitutive way."[9] This critical orientation contends that the advent of modern slavery and the violence of the Middle Passage created Blackness and, parasitically, Whiteness. Frank B. Wilderson III, one of the most prominent theorists of Afro-Pessimism, explains, "This violence which turns a body into flesh, ripped apart literally and imaginatively, destroys the possibility of ontology because it positions the Black in an infinite and indeterminately horrifying and open vulnerability, an object made available (which is to say fungible) for any subject."[10] In Wilderson's theorizing, "the imaginary of the state and civil society is parasitic on the Middle Passage," meaning that all modern structures of power have been built upon the foundation of blacks as fungible objects that exist in a "structured position of non-communicability."[11] The structural suffering experienced by blacks, and the lack of any analogous suffering, renders a unique grammar and, ultimately, "the impossibility of a Black ontology."[12] Or, put more simply by Jared Sexton, "black life is lived in social death."[13]

Wilderson and other Afro-Pessimist theorists build upon the work of, among others, Frantz Fanon, Orlando Patterson, Saidiya V. Hartman, and Hortense Spiller to theorize the relationship among notions of ontology, structural violence, and the meaning of race. Fanon argues that a black ontology—the experience of "being" black—that is, free from the powers of whiteness is impossible. In *Black Skin, White Masks*, he writes, "Ontology—once it is finally admitted as leaving existence by the wayside—does not permit us to understand the being of the black man. For not only must the black man be black; he must be black in relation to the white man."[14] Fanon asks if this position creates "a feeling of inferiority," to which he answers, "No, a feeling of non-existence."[15] Patterson's comparative study of many slave cultures elaborates upon the conditions of "non-existence" that Fanon observes. "Institutionalized marginality," which Patterson also refers to as "the liminal state of social death," is composed of physical violence and death, but also of symbolic notions of honor and power.[16] Spillers expounds further on this "liminal state" and the fluidity and tension of blacks' social position: "Negotiating the ground *between* forms of exile and belonging captures precisely the historic vocation of communities of individuals on the periphery of the dominant order, but it is difficult now to focus on and to keep in view a distinct margin and center."[17] Thus, Afro-Pessimism builds upon the scholarship in black studies that implicitly or explicitly recognizes blackness as the result of violence, oppression, and invisibility, and, as a result, the impossibility of defining black "being" or existence apart from that violence, oppression, and invisibility.

Black optimism shares with Afro-Pessimism an "understanding of blackness as exterior to civil society."[18] Where the two critical positions diverge is in the relationship between the social and the political (and arguments about from which arenas blacks have been excluded). Whereas Afro-Pessimism holds that blacks live in social death and cannot change this condition, black optimism, as explained by Fred Moten, differentiates social death from political death. Black optimism holds that blacks are politically dead and that because of this condition, they are pushed to the social. Moten writes, "Social death is not imposed upon blackness by or from the standpoint or positionality of the political; rather, *it is the field of the political*, from which blackness is relegated to the supposedly undifferentiated mass or blob of the social, which is, in any case where and what blackness chooses to stay."[19] Moten's repositioning of black subjectivity into the social "blob" pushes against the Afro-Pessimist impulse to see blackness as nothingness. Wilderson's articulation of his own nothingness inspires Moten "to assert the presence of something between the subjectivity that is refused and which one refuses and nothing, whatever that is." Perhaps more simply stated, Moten begins to consider "*what nothing is*" and views this process as an optimistic one, opening space for the production of a black ontology apart from the violence through which it was originally constituted.[20]

Moten's larger exploration of "what nothing is" and its relationship to black political death manifests in specific lines of inquiry, such as his differentiation between planning and policy. The dyad of planning and policy explains the tension between the actions of the less powerful to experiment with rhetorical processes that might allow for formal activities (planning), and the top-down imposition of "baseless vision" that communicates to those who plan that there is something "deeply—ontologically—wrong with them" (policy).[21] Planning skews toward black optimism, as the planner "hopes against hope ... in order to survive in the deplorable present."[22] Policy, then, is the product of those with enhanced power and agency, and functions to "correct ... the incorrect, the uncorrected, the ones who do not know to seek their own correction."[23] Those with diminished power and agency, those who constitute the "undercommons," can only plan. It is this betweenness, this subjectivity that is nothing but also something, this constitution within and outside the social blob, that Sheridan's negotiations and planning inhabit.

Analysis of Sheridan's peculiar planning calls attention to a segment of US public address that is often concealed in the shadows of traditional binary categories like antislavery and proslavery, free and enslaved, or black and white. Indeed, Sheridan's peculiar planning reinforces Michelle M. Wright's claim that "black identity has been produced in contradiction."[24] The black identity that Wright discusses is not that of black Africans, but of blacks in the diaspora, which included free and enslaved blacks in the United States. Wright makes the following distinction between the two: "Unlike Black Africans, who ultimately define themselves through shared histories, languages, and cultural values, Blacks in the diaspora possess an intimidating array of different historical, cultural, national, ethnic, religious, and ancestral origins and influences."[25] Sheridan's peculiar planning laid bare the complex subjectivities of blackness that are formed between these contradictions, allowing the rhetorical critic to behold that "intimidating array" of influences as he negotiated with colonizationists in ways that intersected with both deliberative and diasporic discourses.

Like so many elements of the relationships between whites and blacks in a slave society, the presence and recognition of free blacks was complicated. The social situation encountered by Sheridan was a result of decades of slow expansions and rapid contractions of free blacks' rights in the South. Ira Berlin opens his foundational book *Slaves without Masters* by noting the difficulty of ascertaining the number of free blacks residing in the South. Berlin states, "Between the arrival of the first blacks and the codification of slavery in the 1660s, colonial lawmakers hardly recognized [free blacks] at all."[26] Prior to the American Revolution, only Maryland attempted to take serious account of the free black population. That state's 1755 census counted a total population of 153,000, with 28 percent of that population being defined as black.[27] Of the black population, just over 1,800 were listed as free blacks and, interestingly, 80 percent of those persons were considered of mixed race. Maryland was a border state, and, as Berlin argues, there is no evidence to suggest a greater presence of free blacks in other southern states.[28] There was little concern over this population, because it was not yet deemed a threat to the slave system in the South. In the century leading up to the American Revolution, however, "whites sporadically chipped away at the freemen's liberty."[29]

The potential for violence against whites was always lingering among the rationales for restricting the free black population. Other concerns, premised on racist assumptions about black people—like the inferior intellects, poor manners, and meager industriousness of blacks—may have created local and state rules to limit the population. Yet the threat of slave insurrections and the concerns over white female safety, whether heightened by actual events or rumors, created the most definitive changes for the free black population.[30] The slave rebellions of Gabriel Prosser, Nat Turner, and Denmark Vesey; the uprising in Stono, South Carolina; and the successful rebellion in Saint-Domingue left many whites in the South fearful of what could happen if the massive black population turned on them. Although free blacks were rarely part of these uprisings, whites overwhelmingly identified this group as the source for agitation within the enslaved population and enacted harsh restrictions to curb future unrest.[31]

The fear of black violence motivated the creation of policy that worked to supplant peculiar planning. The policies of the powerful imposed "mechanical violence" upon the powerless members of society.[32] Process, procedures, and laws served as the mechanisms for exerting power and control over black subjects. One such restriction that impacted the colonization movement was the enactment in many states of laws concerning the legal emancipation of slaves through wills, a practice known as manumission. By the mid-1830s, most southern states required judicial or legislative approval for slaveholders to free their slaves, and if the manumission was allowed, those freed blacks were required to leave the state.[33] These restrictions on the free black population, born out of the fear of violent insurrection, created a paradox for colonizationists. Requiring judicial or legislative approval to free bondspersons reduced the number of free persons of color available to travel to Liberia, as courts and legislatures were very reluctant to allow slaves to be freed. Yet if slaves were allowed to become free persons, the requirement to leave the state and the difficulties one would face in moving to any other southern state made colonization a more attractive proposition for many "benevolent" masters and free people of color. The supposed freedom granted to free blacks in the South was being eroded, forcing an already compromised people further into a liminal social space.

The expressed motives of colonizationists varied, ranging from missionary zeal to a nascent "separate-but-equal" humanitarianism to antiblack racism. In attendance at the first meeting of the ACS were clergy, wealthy landowners, sitting congressmen, and political operatives.[34] What united the geographically and ideologically diverse group was the recognition that free people of color were neither slave nor free. Colonization, then, was a movement premised on resolving this tension through a synthesis that, as its adherents would argue, could be amenable to northerners and southerners, blacks and whites. The unstated assumption was that neither total enslavement of the black population nor immediate emancipation of the race was "practicable" or "expedient" in the United States.[35] Colonizationists resided in the middle of the politics of race and slavery, just as the population they sought to affect resided in the middle of social life.[36]

Although its supporters approached colonization from a variety of motivations, the ACS was a decidedly political movement. Slaveholders in the South and religious leaders in the North who differed in their reasoning for colonization were united in seeking national and governmental support for colonization. The coalescence of motivations into a political movement was an effort to make the movement more viable. Colonization efforts preceded the ACS's creation, but with little impact. In creating the first national organization to advocate colonization, the supporters of the ACS focused their political efforts on securing public funding. White colonizationists could pursue federal financial support in ways that free blacks could not, for the obvious reason that political agency was readily accessible to the former and not to the latter. White men leading the colonization charge had institutional avenues to effect change, whereas free blacks, particularly in the South, lacked access to many of the formal mechanisms of action—the courts, the legislature, or virtually any public forum. Ironically, white men with a variety of motivations and from a vast array of backgrounds could unite together to garner political support for colonization, but the very population they claimed to "aid" lacked the standing to fully participate.

On the surface Sheridan seemed insulated from the tensions associated with freedom, race, colonization, and commerce. A man with property, income, and white allies, Sheridan could have continued living an enviable life in Elizabethtown. In that context, Sheridan had little use for colonization, at one point calling it "the greatest humbug ever palmed off upon the American people."[37] But Sheridan's successes were nonetheless constrained by his race and the increasing restrictions on free blacks in North Carolina. Although Sheridan was free and allowed to reside in the state, in 1831 a state law was passed that restricted manumission to an act of the Superior Court, and even then, any freed slave was required to immediately leave the state.[38] Furthermore, laws were passed in North Carolina that hampered the ability of free blacks to hold property. For example, when the North Carolina state constitution was revised in 1835, it disenfranchised free blacks and stipulated that if a free black remained outside the state for more than ninety days, they would forfeit their entire estate.[39] North Carolina was more permissive than some slave states in its efforts to create a social equilibrium with whites and blacks. But, as John Hope Franklin argues, in North Carolina "there developed the feeling that the free Negro had no place at all in the social and economic life of North Carolina, and the sooner the State was rid of him the better."[40]

Perhaps a sign of the uneasiness of the status of free blacks in North Carolina was the multitude of local colonization auxiliaries. In 1819 one of the early supporters of the ACS, Rev. William Meade, created the Raleigh Auxiliary Society for the Colonization of Free People of Color. By 1829 eleven organizations in support of colonization operated within North Carolina.[41] The strong presence of the ACS in North Carolina coupled with the increased restrictions on free blacks created a situation in which even a well-to-do businessman like Sheridan was inspired to sell his goods and move to Liberia. In a letter excerpted in *Colored American*, Sheridan opined, "Under the existing state of things, we free people of color are denuded all privileges marking the attributes of a man."⁴²

Without these privileges, Sheridan began considering colonization. Sheridan reasoned that it would be better to make plans for oneself than to wait for the moment when free blacks "*would be compelled to leave the country.*"⁴³ Once opposed to colonization, Sheridan responded to the increasing restrictions of free blacks by viewing colonization as not only a chance to experience true freedom but also an enactment of providence and a fulfillment of destiny. "If by our acquiescence [to travel to Liberia] a high destiny awaits us & the Almighty will bring good out of evil," Sheridan wrote, "it would [only] become me to murmur at his providences."⁴⁴ Although Sheridan had once seen himself as of a different "caste" than other free blacks, increasing restrictions on blacks in his home state compelled him to embrace his "destiny" in Liberia.

To colonizationists, free blacks' precarious social, political, and rhetorical position necessitated their scheme. It also necessitated money. So when a wealthy free black man like Sheridan expressed interest in colonization, the ACS reciprocated with express interest in Sheridan. Their mutual affection did not, however, ameliorate the anxieties of the colonization endeavor, or of the free black liminal status. Negotiating these anxieties, Sheridan's rhetorical energies expressed the tension of black subjectivity in his peculiar planning.

Struggling between Afro-Pessimism and Black Optimism: The Rhetorical Enactment of Sheridan's Peculiar Planning

Sheridan's enactment of peculiar planning negotiated the dialectical tensions between Afro-Pessimism and black optimism. However, his dealings with the ACS compelled him ultimately to transition from a mostly optimistic to a mostly pessimistic view of black subjectivity. In the beginning, the relationship between the ACS and Sheridan seemed mutually beneficial. Sheridan initially engaged in the genteel conventions of epistolary correspondence and demonstrated his knowledge and business savvy by asking questions about the journey he would undertake. Alongside his optimism throughout the early months of correspondence, Sheridan remained somewhat uneasy about colonization. When the ACS failed to meet Sheridan's expectations for support, scheduling, and timely correspondence, Sheridan was galvanized to assert a more pessimistic perspective on how he and free blacks were being treated. Sheridan questioned the benevolence of the ACS and attempted to leverage his negotiations with other colonization organizations to achieve his goals. Even in the face of mounting frustrations, Sheridan coupled his pessimism with an optimistic pursuit of colonizationists' support for moving to Liberia.

The ACS became aware of Sheridan—his erudition, his willingness to relocate, and, most importantly, his money—through one of his white associates.[45] In his capacity as an ACS officer, Gales was traveling throughout his home state of North Carolina on a fundraising tour. By this point in the history of the colonization movement, the ACS's internal strife was not only splintering the movement into different groups but also depleting its financial resources. Gales viewed Sheridan as an ideal settler colonist. In a letter to Ralph Randolph Gurley, the secretary of the ACS, dated July 29, 1835, Gales described Sheridan as a "wealthy, talented, and highly respected man of color" who initially "did not give me much encouragement as [he] could not wish to be more comfortably situated than he is at present (except the single circumstance of inferiority of caste)." Gales went on to describe a series of correspondences with Sheridan in which the latter grew more interested in colonization and requested more "light on the subject." Believing that Sheridan could legitimize colonization and, furthermore, elevate the quality of settler colonists, Gales wrote, "If Sheridan concludes to go to Liberia, he will carry with him, or draw after him most of the intelligent and respectable free colored men of North Carolina."[46] The encouraging communication with Sheridan led Gales to request that the ACS board of managers appoint Sheridan as a colonial agent in Liberia.[47]

Sheridan's peculiar planning for his journey was conducted through letters, in which his adherence to the conventions of the letter genre and his expressions of deference conveyed an optimistic tone. Sheridan's expressions of respect and deference, common of the letter-writing genre, exhibited his optimism insofar as they implied his willingness to question the assumption of black social death and to imagine a future life. Sheridan's letter writing conformed to the standards of the time, which included overt expressions of humility. Salutations of "Respected Sir," and valedictions that evoked some version of "I am your most obedient and humble servant," were standard in Sheridan's letters, regardless of the letters' content. Sheridan also called attention to his decorum while also deferring to his interlocutor. For example, Sheridan remarked in his first letter to Gales, "You will perceive from these remarks at least a shadow of propriety in my at present calling your attention to the matter" of setting a date for departure.[48] It would be difficult to interpret Sheridan's letter as a violation of social custom; thus, his wish that his preceding comments be seen as containing "at least a shadow of propriety" functioned as a hyperbole that called attention to the utter normalcy of his letter. Sheridan's participation in generic deference also demonstrated his level of education. Historian Claude A. Clegg III notes that after Sheridan was freed from bondage, "he was able to obtain a liberal education."[49] Sheridan's generic participation also enacted a desire for belonging, for recognition in the community that engaged in polite, educated communiqués.

In the language of black optimism, Sheridan imagined colonization with "futurial presence," or a sense of hope that simultaneously recognized the possibility of the future and the challenges of the present.[50] In the February 16, 1836, letter in which Sheridan actively began negotiating with Gales and the ACS, Sheridan confessed, "Destiny seems to point me to that Country [Liberia] & to that alone."[51] Sheridan was not blindly optimistic in his hopefulness. He expressed a cognizance of the challenges that settler colonists would confront. Sheridan tacitly observed the racist motivations of many colonizationists, who would be pleased with the "mere removal" of free blacks from the United States, regardless of what awaited the settler colonists in Africa. These motivations were the "evil" from which Sheridan hoped good would come. Sheridan resisted the full embrace of skepticism by acknowledging the good that could come from colonization for free blacks. His resistance was biblically justified, as his mention of "murmuring at his providences" suggested.[52] To murmur at God was to question God and his methods. Sheridan affirmatively resolved the tension implicit in his imagining of "futurial presence," but not before expressing his awareness and concern for the motives of white colonizationists.

Sheridan's display of his expertise demonstrated his hope for colonization while also expressing his dependence upon the white organization to achieve his goals. Sheridan requested information about timing, ship size, food, and water. Such requests included demonstrations of expertise and expressions of deference but were heavily weighted toward the former. Sheridan's early correspondence shows his deep engagement with the process of and planning for his relocation to Liberia. In Sheridan's letter of February 16, 1836, he endeavored to "review with [Gales]" the subject of colonization and "recollect" the terms of their "former arrangements."[53] In this letter Sheridan pushed for a firm departure date of November 15, which he made clear by use of underlining. For Sheridan to close his affairs and prepare, he needed information faster than Gales could provide it. Sheridan's March 25 missive reminded his correspondent that "I only now await your word to <u>begin</u> &

even under the determination much time will be necessary to accomplish all that will be incumbent on me to do."⁵⁴ To make the point clear, Sheridan enumerated seven questions, prefaced with, "You will be pleased to notice the particulars of which I need information":

1st Can a vessel be had at the day I have mentioned & if not then at what time
2d   Will there be others beside our number 40 connected with the expedition
3d   Will any provision be made for us by the society & if so what
4th Shall we be permitted to take any lumber with us & if so how much & what kind
5th Should the providence of God arrange provide & direct our start shall we be destined for any particular seat in the colony under direction of the Board of Managers or be permitted to change our location at will
6th For the Establishment or Establishments we may form in the Colony shall we be permitted to preserve our own inclinations as to our mode of employment or shall there be specific occupation assigned us
7th Can one going there have privilege of returning or departing elsewhere should they not prefer to remain.⁵⁵

Just over one month into the process, Sheridan's directness, his enumeration, and his call for Gales "to notice the particulars of which I need information" represented the demands of someone whose peculiar planning was controlled by those who wielded the power of ACS policy.

Sheridan's persistent questioning conveyed his eagerness to move to Liberia—to escape the "deplorable present"—while it also exposed his growing discomfort with being excluded from the decision-making process. Sheridan's questioning of Gales showed that he was not only an expert but also relentless. Sheridan was particularly keen to know the specifications of the vessel being chartered by the ACS. How will the ship owners be paid, he queried; "Is it paid for by the month or tonnage or number of passengers?"⁵⁶ Failing to receive a timely or sufficient reply, Sheridan sought the expertise of a ship captain from Baltimore. "He says that a sharp built brig of 200 tons is such a vessel as we shall need," Sheridan reported to Gales, adding that "the cost will be at least 600$/ month."⁵⁷ The size of the ship and the cost of the voyage would dictate how many supplies Sheridan could purchase and transport to Liberia. He averred, "Should I be able to retain my stock of goods and take them with me to Liberia their amount in bulk would be considerable I suppose 30 tons at least."⁵⁸ In particular, Sheridan wanted to know how much lumber he could ship to his new home.⁵⁹ Other details mentioned by Sheridan throughout his year-long correspondence included what "culinary preparations" and "provisions of water" the ACS would make for his party, whether a recent visitor to Liberia was an "agriculturalist" and could provide insights into the farming of Liberian soil, and if another visitor to Liberia was planning to leave "a surveyor's compass & chain" that Sheridan "should be glad to buy."⁶⁰ Sheridan's level of detail and sense of equity demonstrates his commitment to making the trip. However, his frustration, albeit tempered, drove him to find answers to his unanswered questions on his own, implying a break in his trust of the ACS.

Sheridan's use of benevolence to both praise and criticize the ACS expressed the nuances of his peculiar planning and his mounting sense of nonexistence. In the reform era, many benevolent associations aimed to provide for the less fortunate. One of the underlying assumptions of many people who engaged in this kind of work was that those who acted benevolently possessed something—wealth, morality, knowledge—that the objects of their actions did not.⁶¹ On multiple occasions Sheridan directly appealed to the benevolence of the ACS to show gratitude for their efforts. In his February 16 letter to Gales, Sheridan stated that "by their [the ACS's] benevolence" the settler colonists could place themselves in a "sphere" in which "we can think & act & feel within ourselves that we are men."⁶² This praise of colonizationists' benevolence occurred early in the process of arranging removal to Liberia. Later, however, Sheridan would turn the ACS's benevolence against it, using the concept as a warrant for his pointed requests of the society. After Sheridan sent the letter asking what provisions he would need to acquire, he received no reply. Sheridan wrote again and asked if water would be provided by the ACS. "Such questions may be deemed frivolous," Sheridan stated, but because he did not want to burden "the benevolence of your Society with any extra expenses[,] the kind indulgence you grant of allowing me to make such enquiries is a sufficient warrant for me doing so."⁶³ If Gales would not respond for the good of Sheridan and his party, then perhaps he would respond if it benefited the ACS's finances and was consistent with the benevolence of the movement. Sheridan seemed to acknowledge that his only means of participating in the political—in the policy conversations with the ACS—was in terms of the benefits to whites, not blacks. Blackness still existed in his appeals, but he subordinated to the concerns of whites in an effort to receive answers. Sheridan was still planning, but not in a manner that expressed outward *black* optimism.

Sheridan's correspondence from February 1836 to August 1836 generally operated from a black optimistic perspective. However, without a ship and with inadequate correspondence from the ACS, his letters in the latter months of 1836 operated from a position that equated blackness with social death. The first line of Sheridan's October 5, 1836, letter to Gales stated, "I have this moment made reply to a letter received from Mr. Elliott Cresson of Philadelphia in which he speaks tho in indirect terms of a proposition to take 100 Emigrants to a point called Bassa Cove."[64] Although the ACS was the largest colonization organization in the United States, and the one with a titular national appeal, there were other colonization organizations. Cresson was the founder of one of these other groups, the Young Men's Colonization Society of Pennsylvania. Sheridan's disclosure to Gales that he was in conversation with a different organization was conducted with great savvy. Sheridan wrote, "I have referred him [Cresson] to you as I suppose all the interests of the Colony of Liberia are One & Indivisible. I hope at least there are no conflicting ones."[65] Sheridan made clear that he was not attempting to negotiate behind the backs of his two potential partners. Even more, he made the idealistic claim that surely all persons involved in colonization want the best for Liberia. However, Sheridan also made clear to both partners that there were others with whom he could do business. Thus, Sheridan deftly demonstrated his ability to leverage power and resources for his ends.

Sheridan's new potential partner in his colonization effort, Cresson, was a white man who had experienced a different form of disenchantment with the ACS. Cresson was a philanthropist from Philadelphia who believed in colonization for humanitarian reasons. Like many northern reformers who supported colonization, Cresson held that slavery should be ended and that colonization was a way to transition toward that end. He stated his frustration to Gurley that the society's main publication organ, *African Repository*, allowed the expression of proslavery views.[66] As a response to the ACS's acquiescence to proslavery opinions, in 1835 Cresson helped create the Young Men's Colonization Society of Pennsylvania for the purpose of aiding in colonization from an antislavery perspective. Cresson's group often worked with another ACS-adjacent group, the New York City Colonization Society, which was formed in 1829 when its founder, Arthur Tappan, was also displeased with the work of the ACS.[67]

Despite these attempts to force the ACS's hand by referencing correspondence with other colonization organizations, Sheridan remained in the subordinate position of needing material support from the ACS. Sheridan's anxiety about the ACS's investment in his emigration grew when it seemed like all of his optimistic planning would yield no result. In a letter dated November 1, 1836, two weeks before the departure date he proposed in his first letter, Sheridan alerted Gales that some of the prospective emigrants rescinded their commitment. Sheridan asked if "it will be insisted on by the managers of the Society that the number 40 emigrants be provided by me or will they be satisfied with any number above the one half."[68] As a sign of his personal commitment, Sheridan wrote with emphasis, "I shall go if I live."[69] Such a statement addressed the tenuousness of life and death, both political and biological. For Sheridan, the feeling of political death in the United States was real, leading him to the conclusion that only biological death would stop him from seeking freedom and a sense of belonging in Africa.

After his aspirational deadline passed, Sheridan communicated with Gales in December to express his despair. Sheridan stated that Dr. David Francis Bacon, the appointed principal colonial physician for the ACS colonies, would make inquiries to the Society on the would-be emigrant's behalf. Sheridan lamented:

> Dr. Bacon of whose amiable qualities your letters had previously given assurance has kindly undertaken to make a representation of my case to the managers of the Amer. Col. Society & I am therefore spared the necessity of rehearsing to you the delicate & painfully mortifying subject but I beg leave to make known Sir a fact that he could not have been apprised of which is the my disappointment & consequent stop in this country could be subject of far greater gratulation than my removal from it & that to accomplish this last I have made such sacrifices as I can never contemplate with any degrees of satisfaction if I am to remain this disappointed.[70]

Despite Sheridan's success as a merchant, his educated correspondence with the ACS, and his practical planning, his lack of control over the means to achieve his destiny resulted in the realization of his social death. Britt Rusert notes that disappointment appears in the "archive of freedom"—archives associated with the black struggle against slavery and for rights—more than most scholars have been willing to discuss. The narrative of "resistance and reparation" that dominates scholarship on early nineteenth-century black rhetoric can sublimate the feeling of disappointment expressed by black writers and speakers, unless that feeling is paired with "some hint of resistance, subversion, or irony."[71] This passage of Sheridan's letter can be read as resistance to the delays of the ACS. But even in that telling, a sense of dispirit and exhaustion tempers the assertion of agency the flowed throughout much of Sheridan's correspondence with Gales.

Embracing a pessimistic black subjectivity, Sheridan nonetheless persisted in planning. Sheridan recognized his inability to be recognized, his seeming nonexistence to the ACS, while continuing to work on the plans to move to Liberia. In a December 16 letter to Gales, Sheridan noted the "uncertainty of what are the provisions" of his party while also thanking Gales for "the many kind expressions you make of good will" and for help "toward obtaining for me a deliverance out of my present bondage."[72] Shortly thereafter, Sheridan declared, "So far from the Agency of Mr. Phelps [a member of the ACS board of managers] contributing to our accommodation it has been means of hindering our voyage to the colony."[73] Sheridan's aspirational departure date had passed, and he had neither departed for Liberia nor received word of when that departure might occur. He enlisted the aid of white colonization supporters to, in his words, "make representation of my case to the managers of the Amer. Col. Society"; thus, he (Sheridan) was "spared the necessity of rehearsing to the delicate & painfully mortifying subject" of his "disappointment."[74] "I have made such sacrifices as I can never contemplate," Sheridan continued. Still, he stated, "permit me to reiterate the assertion of my high consideration."[75]

These passages revealed that white colonizationists were simultaneously Sheridan's problem and solution. On a practical level, colonizationists failed to provide Sheridan with the resources or communication needed to undertake his journey to Liberia, yet he could not abandon the relationship, because he needed their resources. On a rhetorical level, the persistent delays and silences were reminders of the black person's ontological nothingness. That Sheridan not only required the resources of white colonizationists but also required an intermediary—another white colonizationist—to represent his interests to the ACS, reified Sheridan's exclusion from the spheres of power and an Afro-Pessimistic vision of black subjectivity.

Other colonizationists found the ACS's treatment of Sheridan quite troubling but maintained a sense of hierarchy that positioned Sheridan as subordinate. In December of 1836, Bacon met with Sheridan and reported back to the ACS leadership. Bacon made clear that the officials in charge of chartering the ship were to blame for compromising Sheridan's relationship with the ACS. Bacon wrote to Gales on December 21, "For this undesirable though necessary result you may thank those to whom you entrusted the business of chartering the vessel." Bacon elaborated further that the "business was most shamefully neglected in New York" by Anson Phelps. Phelps not only failed to procure an adequately sized vessel, but he conducted the business by "proxy," causing one week's delay due to "the necessity of undoing all that he had done in storing the cargo."[76] What Bacon made clear to Gales was that Sheridan, a planful person who "gave the society due notice" of his transportation requirement, was justified in declining passage on this vessel.

Bacon hoped that Sheridan might accept his invitation to explore Liberia and then return to the United States to make his final arrangements for emigration. In a letter to Gurley, dated three days later, Bacon transcribed Sheridan's letter declining the offer for a visit to Liberia. Bacon referred to the "unfortunate circumstances" that "have frustrated the most important object of this expedition." The word choice was telling. Once can read the sentence as if the term "object" was synonymous with "objective," meaning that the ACS had failed to meet an objective of immigrating Sheridan and his party to Liberia. In another sense, the treatment of Sheridan as an object, or an objective, illuminated the commodification of the North Carolinian. The transcribed letter from Sheridan noted his "disappointment," but also that he hoped to "hail the dawn of a brighter day for poor debased Africa."[77] The paradox of this sentiment speaks the uneasy position of Sheridan's peculiar planning, as he seemed "disappointed" and saw Africa as "poor" and "debased" while he also held out hope for a "brighter day."

In a December 1836 letter to Gurley of the ACS, Bacon expressed Sheridan's tenuous position at length and the implications it had for the ACS's credibility:

> The unfortunate affair has done your society much injury I fear in the opinion of all Sheridan's numerous friends in the mercantile community, and he is looked upon in the light of a much abused man, who after having sold his extensive estate at a sacrifice, broken up his establishment, and kept the great bulk of his movable property packed a whole month for a start is now checked in the execution of a noble scheme in consequence of the culpable remissness of the society's chartering agent, in sending him a vessel which cannot possibly hold even the bare necessaries of life for his followers even without considering the baggage of the other emigrants coming on board here; and more over, of course, of holding the articles of merchandise and building materials which he duly notified the society as the indispensable accompaniments of his expedition.[78]

Bacon provided external validation for Sheridan's mounting pessimism about relocating to Liberia. Even Bacon, a white man supporting colonization, could note the inadequacies of his organization's dealings, the abuses suffered by Sheridan, and the "injury" that their mishandling would cause to the society. Yet again, however, Sheridan was discussed in terms of the material benefits that he could bring to the ACS. Bacon's dissatisfaction was the dissatisfaction of a white colonizationist, not of a man seeking a better future for Sheridan.

Slighted by Gales and the ACS, Sheridan's peculiar planning exhibited his full swing toward an Afro-Pessimistic subjectivity even while he negotiated with another colonization society for support. In a lengthy letter to Gales on August 1, 1837, Sheridan declared his "opposition yea & even hostility to the colonization scheme." "I have always held some cardinal objections to the Colonization Scheme," Sheridan wrote, "and the current harmony at present existing amongst its notaries does not by any means tend to eradicate them."[79] The "harmony" to which Sheridan referred concerned the entreaties made by Cresson and his group for removal to Bassa Cove instead of the ACS-led colony in Monrovia. Perhaps divided loyalties among colonizationists meant divided territories. "**IS LIBERIA DIVIDED?**" Sheridan wrote. His demand for clarification was made apparent in the manner in which the question was written. The use of all capital letters, considerable amounts of ink, and underlining made clear the significance of this question. Sheridan continued, in his normal hand, "Now sir as I am considerably attached to the sayings of a certain old Book called the Bible one of which is that a Kingdom divided against itself cannot stand."[80] The demands of this letter were tinged with dismay and distrust. Sheridan remained disappointed in the delays, as he began the letter by making clear that the lease on the houses he was renting "will expire on the 29th day of October next."[81] Sheridan questioned the status of his destination and not just the means by which he would arrive.

Sheridan typographically and rhetorically demanded from his correspondent to know the status of both his removal to Liberia and the situation within the country. The last line of the letter illustrates Sheridan's exhaustion with Gales and the ACS. Sheridan explained that he received a letter from an ACS agent that was supposed to contain money and that instead contained "a very elaborate epistle asking indulgence." About the matter, Sheridan stated, "I have nothing to say on the subject more than—I need my money."[82] No longer able to defer, entreat, or leverage, Sheridan pessimism took hold and enabled him to fully reject the ACS's policy-making power. No longer did Sheridan view his road to colonization as a rhetorical process. Moreover,

Sheridan's demand for compensation was decoupled from his plan to emigrate; his demand for money was not about optimistic planning but about survival in the face of social death.

The Persistence of Peculiar Planning: Sheridan from Liberia and Double Consciousness

The failures of the ACS and Gales incited Sheridan's incredulity, inspiring him to turn to the joint effort of the Philadelphia and New York colonization groups. On December 30, 1837, Sheridan and seventy-one others boarded the ship provided by Cresson and his collaborators, bound for Bassa Cove.[83] They arrived on February 8, 1838. Sheridan's disillusionment continued to grow, as he made clear in a letter to Lewis Tappan on November 24, 1838. Tappan was a wealthy, white abolitionist from New York, to whom Sheridan was formally introduced in 1834, through a letter from Governor John Owen.[84] Tappan and Sheridan exchanged letters in March of 1837, but their correspondence went silent after a letter arrived in New York via London from Liberia. Sheridan's post elaborated the failings of the colonies in Liberia. It is doubtful that he could have found a better audience for such an account. The letter was then republished, first, in *Colored American*, an abolitionist periodical, and then in the *African Repository and Colonial Journal*, the official publication of the ACS.[85] In both cases, editorial commentary framed Sheridan's letter, albeit with different opinions as to the merit of his insights.

The end of Sheridan's letter to Tappan was representative of his peculiar planning that struggled with optimistic and pessimistic visions of his belonging. Sheridan's sentiment toward the colony seemed firmly cast, as he opined that the "millions of millions of ants," "the chattering of monkeys," and the "unearthly sound of Whaw-whaw" were enough "to drive civilization back to its original darkness, and make chaos come again." Yet a few sentences later Sheridan wrote,

> I know not that our experiment will make for or against the Colonization scheme, as I am not yet prepared to say, whether people ought to come here or not; this is one of the objects I have in view, and to arrive legitimately at these conclusions, will require further experiment than I have yet made. When my conclusions are formed either way (all's alike to me,) you shall have it.[86]

About Sheridan's representation of Africa as "a wretched place" and his supposed reservation of judgment, Rev. John J. Matthias, a former governor of the Bassa Cove colony, replied in the *African Repository* with sarcasm, "So consistent is this veracious correspondent of Mr. Tappan."[87] Matthias's criticism was in line with his colonizationist creed to protect the integrity of the scheme. Within Sheridan's letter to Tappan, and across the years of letters described throughout this chapter, it was clear that Sheridan grappled with colonization and could neither unequivocally support nor denounce the venture.

Sheridan's alleged inconsistency addressed more than the activities associated with moving to Liberia. As Harney and Moten claim, "planning ... is not an activity.... It is the ceaseless experiment with the futurial presence of the forms of life that make such activities possible."[88] Put differently, planning for Sheridan was the imagining of recognition. Sheridan had achieved financial success and a level of freedom most blacks in early nineteenth-century America would never experience. But his blackness constrained his recognition as merchant of equal standing to his white peers. This same lack of recognition, the nothingness, pervaded his correspondence with Gales. Years later Sheridan wrote to the ACS to ask for "important articles of trade" so that the settler colonists would not starve. That letter ended: "Gentlemen, **I am an American exiled**, it is true, but no matter."[89] Sheridan's peculiar planning continued, hoping for recognition as an equal, deserving of assistance in the face of exile but cognizant that his plight was of "no matter" to his audience.

Sheridan's peculiar planning suggests that the rhetorical expression of Afro-Pessimism and black optimism constitutes another dyad of double consciousness in the black experience.[90] Elaborating on double consciousness, Paul Gilroy argues that perhaps all blacks in the West "stand between (at least) two great cultural assemblages"—such as being black and English or black and American—"both of which have mutated through the course of the modern world that formed them and assumed new configurations."[91] For Gilroy, rather than consenting to the mutual exclusivity of these identities, occupying the space between black and English can be "viewed as a provocative and even oppositional act of political subordination."[92] Sheridan's peculiar planning illuminates that Afro-Pessimism and black optimism function not as an either/or proposition. Rather, the case study of Sheridan suggests that both critical dispositions can manifest in the process of peculiar planning. That is, planning can be born of pessimism and fueled by optimism, and born of optimism in the face of a failed or failing policy. By considering these two theories in a situated and material context, Sheridan's peculiar planning offers a provocative example of a rhetor engaging in deliberative and diasporic discourses in the midst of the complexity and undecidability of discourses in the middle of public life.

CHAPTER 4

"Peculiar Obligations"

Hilary Teage and the Constitution of Civic Identity in Liberia

Hilary Teage was Liberia's Benjamin Franklin, Thomas Jefferson, and James Madison. Like Franklin, Teage rose to prominence through the printed word. Teage took over the *Liberia Herald*, one of two newspapers in colonial Liberia and the only one operated by a settler colonist, serving as the editor from 1835 to 1849.[1] Like Jefferson, Teage penned his nation's Declaration of Independence, which asserted the need for Liberia to separate from its American governors in 1847. Like Madison, Teage helped to draft and pass the Constitution of the newly independent country. Although born in the United States, Teage was an extraordinary and influential figure in Liberia. In addition to the endeavors listed above, Teage was also an ordained minister in the Baptist church, a merchant, a founder of the Liberia Lyceum, and a colonial agent for the ACS.[2] It is safe to say that no single settler colonist had more impact on public life in colonial Liberia than Teage.

Teage's contribution to the peculiar rhetorics of colonization emerged from the precarious position of a settler colonist *in* Liberia. Part of the paradox of colonization was the belief by its white supporters that free blacks could develop and contribute to a colony in Africa, but could not do the very same in America. For example, the Parsipanny School in New Jersey, which educated free blacks, stated, "We are not instructing them—for our society—not to form our magistrates or legislators—but preparing them to go home."[3] David Kazanjian explains the competing perceptions of free blacks in terms of "the dual, interrelated roles" of colonization, which were the "racial purification of a domestic space and imperial power over foreign spaces."[4] Deemed unfit for full participation in the white public sphere that governed the United States, upon arriving in Africa settler colonists' identity seemed to change in the eyes of white colonizationists. In colonial Liberia, Kazanjian continues, settler colonists became emissaries of "the supposedly universal and exemplary elements of white America: its Christianity, its capitalist economy, and its governmental system of national statehood."[5] The racial hierarchy of colonization allowed for the empowerment of free blacks only if they were separate from the white population. Even then, white colonial agents governed the various English-speaking colonies in Liberia. For each move toward liberation through colonization, the oppression of antiblack racism seemed to be guiding the effort.

Within the context of postcolonization life, *peculiar obligations* describe Teage's rhetorical efforts to constitute a Liberian civic identity between settlers' current identity as colonists and future identity as citizens of a free and independent Liberia. The phrase "peculiar obligations" derives from Teage's Anniversary Speech on December 1, 1846, in which he stated:

> Let us now turn from those who preceded us, and ask, What are the peculiar obligations which rest upon us: what the particular duties to which we are called? Let us not suppose, that because we are not called upon to drive the invading native from our door—that because we can lie down at night without fear because the savage war-whoop does not now ring upon the midnight air,—therefore we have nothing to do. No mistake can be more fatal. Ours is a moral fight. It is a keener warfare, a sharper conflict.[6]

Teage's peculiar obligations represent the active and engaged process of turning, of connecting where settler colonists had been with where they were going. As Teage suggested, the process of creating a civic identity was "a moral fight." The fights of the past were bloody conflicts with indigenous peoples worsened by the hardships of colonial life. Teage's peculiar obligations recognized that violent past but sought to move the audience to consider the "keener warfare" and "sharper conflict" of building a civic identity and nation.

Teage's peculiar obligations highlight the role that rhetoric plays in the constitution of civic identity. Civic identity is not simply granted by an authority; rather, it is a "performance, rhetorically constituted and socially performed."[7] Robert Asen notes how citizenship "as a mode of public engagement" is "fluid, multimodal, and quotidian."[8] Living as free blacks or slaves in the United States before their removal, Liberian settler colonists previously had limited access to the traditional sites of citizenship—legislative bodies, ballot boxes, and public deliberations. In Liberia participating in these arenas entailed more peculiarity than white male property owners engaging in the same activities in the United States. Settler colonists had experienced degrees of freedom and oppression in the land of their birth. They had experienced emigration from that country by various levels of force and choice. The form of civic discourse might have seemed the same, but the context and experience of the audience were significantly different. Thus, Teage's peculiar obligations refashioned deliberative discourses of citizenship with an understanding of the anxieties of settler colonist identity expressed in diasporic discourse.

Teage used his leadership roles in many civic (and rhetorical) organizations to speak about how settler colonists should define their identity. In those roles, as Marie Tyler-McGraw explains, Teage demonstrated "true talents ... for political philosophy and acute observation of the world around him."[9] Specifically, Teage participated in or created the kinds of institutions that encouraged civic identification: the Liberia Lyceum, the Second Baptist Church, the *Liberia Herald*, and various administrative positions for colonial governance. Tyler-McGraw also contends not only that Teage was "a very bright man," but that he was also "an angry one," a sentiment she claims was "fueled by the exclusion of free blacks from citizenship and opportunity viewed through his own experience in Virginia."[10] Having navigated the tension between exclusion and opportunity, Teage engaged colonization in similar ways as the free people of colour of the District of Columbia (chapter 2) and Louis Sheridan (chapter 3). It seems unlikely that Teage and his family would have relocated to Liberia if they were allowed to fully participate in civic life in the United States. And yet Teage offers a different perspective on peculiar rhetorics based on his context, purpose, and audience. The speeches examined in this chapter were created when Teage was a resident of a Liberian colony, unlike the US-based context for the free people of colour of the District of Columbia or most of Louis Sheridan's correspondence with the ACS. Living in Monrovia, Teage's peculiar obligations emphasized the identity and success of settler colonists *in Liberia*. Teage was not persuading (or dissuading) blacks or whites from supporting colonization, as the free people of colour appeared to do in the Counter Memorial. Nor was he negotiating with (or against) the ACS for goods or considerations, like Sheridan. Teage's peculiar obligations recognized that after the process of colonization had begun, a civic identity among settler colonists was vital to the success of the colonies.

Teage's peculiar obligations and his explication of Liberian civic identity manifested in two of his speeches. These speeches play between deliberative and diasporic discourses in varying ways. In one speech, delivered on May 21, 1845, before the Liberia Lyceum in Monrovia, Teage constituted civic identity through the *peculiar obligation to debate*. Examination of this deliberative speech reveals how Teage emphasized the virtues of debate for settler colonists' development, then situates those virtues in the context of settler colonists' relationship to the ACS. In another speech, delivered on December 1, 1846, marking the founding of the ACS colonies at Cape Mesurado, Teage constituted civic identity through the *peculiar obligation to commemorate*. Examination of this ceremonial speech demonstrates how Teage constructed a narrative of the colony's founding that reminded his audience of the terrible hardships, but also the laudable achievements, experienced by settler colonists.

In both speeches, Teage engaged and subverted the deliberative discourse of white colonizationists, albeit in ways different than the free people of colour of the District of Columbia or Sheridan. In the Liberia Lyceum speech, the emphasis throughout most of the speech was proscriptive, emphasizing the virtues of debate as a key practice for future settler colonists. Toward the speech's end, Teage recounted the ways the ACS abused settler colonists, recasting the peculiar obligation to debate as a way to resist future abuses. In the Anniversary Speech, he emphasized the colony's past, motivating the audience to celebrate their history, a history marked by survival and violence. For Teage, the past should inform settler colonist civic life in the future. Together, these two speeches spotlight how Teage's peculiar obligations linked past and future in constituting settler colonist civic identity.

I examine Teage's peculiar obligations by first providing a brief biography of Teage and how he came to live in Liberia. Next I look to Teage's speech at the Liberia Lyceum in order to understand his articulation of debate's role in the development of civic identity. Then I turn to Teage's 1846 Anniversary Speech to understand how Teage constructs a shared past in order to propel a moral vision of the future. The chapter concludes by considering how the examination of Teage's peculiar obligations expands and makes peculiar the relationship between deliberation and diaspora in colonization discourse.

The Journey of Hilary Teage

The early life of Teage was marked by the exceptional drive and strong religious commitments of his family. He was born to enslaved parents on a plantation in Goochland County, Virginia, in 1805.[11] Hilary's father, Colin

Teage, was a skilled craftsman of saddles and harnesses. Colin and his family, which included his wife, Frances, his son, Hilary, and daughter, Colinett, were enslaved in Richmond until he saved enough to purchase the entire family's freedom for $1,300.[12] The Teages attended First Baptist Church in Richmond, an integrated, though predominantly black, congregation. Although none had received formal education, the entire family could read and write. Their literacy played a role in the Teages' emigration and, as was evident in his later years, would be an enduring part of Hilary's character until his death in 1853. An account in the *Maryland Colonization Journal* told of the elder Teage and his friend Lott Carey becoming interested in emigration to Liberia upon reading an account authored by ACS agents Rev. Samuel J. Mills and Ebenezer Burgess.[13] The missionary element of colonization resonated with Colin Teage and Carey, the latter of whom had helped establish the Richmond African Missionary Society in 1815 for the purpose of bringing the gospel to Africans.[14] After acquiring support from the ACS, Teage, Carey, and their families were among the second group of settler colonists who were removed to west Africa in January of 1821.[15]

The Teages, and Hilary in particular, advocated for the rights that they believed were essential for the success of Liberia. The assertion of their liberty as free persons, and thus their equality to whites, came early in the Teages' time in Africa. After a brief stint in Sierra Leone (a Liberian colony was not yet viable), the Teages moved to Liberia, only to face the tyranny of the ACS colonial agent, a white man named Jehudi Ashmun. When the Teage family arrived in Liberia, Ashmun "unilaterally reassigned land on which some repatriates had built homes," "imposed two-days per week of public labor for each adult," and "threatened to cut off supplies to those who did not perform mandatory labor for the government."[16] The elder Teage was part of a group that resisted these policies, which forced Ashmun to abandon his position for nearly four months in 1826, before being formally replaced by the ACS.

Fighting for the rights of the settler colonists to govern themselves did not end with Colin Teage's stand against Ashmun. In 1835 Hilary entered politics, performing as colonial secretary—the person in charge of the colonies, but who worked underneath the ACS agent. That same year Hilary also took over as editor of the *Liberia Herald*.[17] Both positions were previously held by John Brown Russwurm, a black man known for his role coediting the first black newspaper in the United States, *Freedom's Journal*, and, somewhat controversially, his shift from abolitionist to colonizationist. Russwurm seemed to struggle as the intermediary between the ACS and settler colonists, "hitting his lowest point of disillusionment with Liberia" in 1835.[18] Teage, it seemed, was not disillusioned and did not struggle as Russwurm had. Not only did Teage serve as colonial secretary and *Liberia Herald* editor, but he was also the convention secretary for the group that wrote the "Monrovia Draft" of the Commonwealth Constitution in 1838—an effort to reform colonial governance and give more power to the settler colonists. Those efforts failed to gain traction with the ACS, leading Teage and others to draft a Declaration of Independence in 1847. Thus, almost immediately upon arrival in Liberia, the Teages played important roles in advocating for the rights of settler colonists, advocacy that eventual led to the creation of a free Republic of Liberia in 1847.

The Teages, and settler colonists in general, consistently faced situations in which the rights they sought were being challenged by governing forces an ocean away. Hilary Teage and the other settler colonists were promised freedom and liberty in exchange for their willingness to move to Liberia. Their relocation would also serve a missionary purpose, bringing Christianity to the native African populations they would encounter. The ACS failed to deliver on these promises, leaving many settler colonists feeling first gratitude for the opportunity to be free, and then disappointment that such freedom was denied. Unlike their peculiarity in America, where free blacks existed in a liminal social space between free whites and enslaved blacks, settler colonists in Liberia existed in a liminal space between the promise and the lie of freedom.

The Peculiar Obligation to Debate: The Liberia Lyceum Speech of May 21, 1845, the Future, and Liberian Civic Identity

Teage was deeply committed to the power of language. As a minister, publisher, editor, writer, and speaker, rhetorical practice was central to Teage's public life. Teage also believed that language was a necessary feature of the developing character of the Liberian citizen. For Teage, debate played a central role in the civic identity of settler colonists, as it would make the mind nimble, enable one to confront injustice with gladiatorial might, and allow the truth to emerge. On May 21, 1845, Teage made the case that deliberative discourse was important, while also expressing the tension between belonging and alienation that settler colonists explored in diasporic discourses. The connection between the deliberative and diasporic discourses, situated in Liberia but connected to the United States, shows how the diaspora of free blacks' rhetorical practice spread beyond the borders of the United States.

To that end, the following section begins by situating the Liberia Lyceum in and against the American lyceum culture. Then I account for how Teage outlines the virtues of debate in his 1845 address. The section ends with an exploration of how Teage's Liberia Lyceum speech interacted with African American rhetorical practices in the United States.

The term "lyceum" often refers to a movement for popular education that developed through debating and lecturing in the early to mid-nineteenth century. Antebellum US lyceums often included instruction and exercises in speech and debate, activities also common in organizations called literary societies.[19] Such was also the case with the Liberia Lyceum. The blurry definitional lines between a lyceum and a literary society did not negate for settler colonists the purpose of the institution to encourage popular education. In the United States and in Liberia, both of these terms—"popular" and "education"—defined the rhetorical culture of civic lyceums. The relative heterogeneity and lack of education of the audience, particularly when compared to those who attended literary societies in colleges, the long-standing loci of lecture learning, changed what one could expect of the listeners. The broad circulation of messages to a popular audience also affected the educational content. Lectures that addressed issues specific to the locale and provided entertainment at the same time fared the best.[20]

In the United States, African Americans were often excluded from participating in Anglo-American lyceum culture.[21] This did not mean that African Americans were unaware of or resistant to attending lyceums. Rather, as they did with many aspects of public culture, African Americans were forced to adapt to the oppressive realities of racism as they sought entry into Anglo-American lyceums or built their own organizations. Despite the imposed absence of African Americans from Anglo-American lyceum culture, a sketch of Anglo-American lyceum rhetorical norms provides a basis from which to discuss how these norms were transferred to and translated in the Liberia Lyceum.

Beginning in 1826, but borrowing from the British tradition that came before, the American lyceum movement started as a project to promote mutual education.[22] Josiah Holbrook, writing in the *American Journal of Education* of that year, advocated for "associations for mutual instruction in the sciences."[23] Although Holbrook placed an emphasis on science, he listed "lectures or conversation" as the first requirement for ventures into popular education.[24] Holbrook's advocacy captured a broader sentiment that rhetoric was an implicit part of creating and sharing knowledge. Angela G. Ray explains, "Debating and persuasive speaking were firmly fixed in the minds of many nineteenth-century individuals as an inextricable part of 'education.'"[25] Yet the expectation was that the lyceum lecturer "displayed knowledge rather than asserted strong argument."[26] Occasionally, lecturers made communication the subject of their presentation, such as Dr. A. Comstock's presentation on "Elocution, and the Cure of Stammering."[27] In the main, however, rhetorical prowess was practiced more than discussed in the lyceum.

Although not often the overt subject of lectures, rhetoric was vital to the mission of lyceums. Indeed, bringing popular education to the masses put rhetorical skill front and center. The attempts to draw the broadest possible audience, encompassing "children and adults, men and women, lawyers and blacksmiths, farmers and masons," demanded a level of rhetorical proficiency to engage such a diverse audience while mitigating conflict and controversy.[28] According to Holbrook, the lyceum "aims at the diffusion of knowledge among all classes, all ages, and both sexes. Its doors are open as wide to the poor as to the rich."[29] Holbrook conceived of the lyceum as a republican institution, one that was open to the people and not, like colleges and universities, reserved for the elite. Even as the tenor of lyceums shifted "from mutual education to celebrity entertainment" in the 1840s and 1850s, the emphasis on rhetorical proficiency remained.[30]

The republican ideal of inclusion had its limits in the lyceum. In the United States, African American participation varied in Anglo-American lyceums. Ray explains, "The situation of enslaved African Americans was debated, abstractly, in white members' meetings; individual African Americans like Charlotte Forten sometimes attended sponsored public lectures; and other individuals were sometimes denied membership or equal privileges in these lyceums."[31] Not surprisingly, African Americans created separate lyceums and literary societies as places to learn and to participate in civic life. Dorothy Porter notes that most black literary societies were created after 1828 and were located in larger northern cities like New York and Philadelphia.[32] In the South, there were significantly fewer organizations, as one might expect. Still, there were a few private literary, debating, and benevolent societies in larger southern cities with free black populations, such as Charleston, South Carolina.[33] African Americans sought opportunities for rhetorical education and engagement, but racism and the perpetuation of slavery severely limited those opportunities.

Anglo-American lyceums faced their own obstacles, although they differed in kind and degree from those faced by their African American counterparts. Specifically, Anglo-American lyceums were beholden to newspapers for their success. Donald M. Scott argues that the popular lecture culture of antebellum America "was in many ways a creation of the world of print.... The system could no more have operated without print than the railroad could have operated without tracks." This relationship benefited both parties, but printed word held more power. Newspapers served as the "essential instrument for turning a writer, educator, minister, statesman, journalist, scientist, or aspiring itinerant into an accepted 'professional' lecturer." The newspapers thus functioned as the certifying authority for what made someone popular enough to command an audience for a popular lecture. Newspapers received content and advertising revenue from lecture associations, and yet their reputation was not tied to the groups' success. By contrast, Scott claims, "When a town's newspaper withdrew its support and either attacked or simply ignored the institution, the lecture society had a difficult time surviving."[34] In the United States, there was little question that the lecture system was indebted to newspapers.

Settler colonists in Liberia built upon the Anglo-American lyceum tradition. Monrovia—the main city of the ACS-sponsored settler colonists—supported numerous popular education and rhetorical societies, such as the Liberia Lyceum, the Union Mechanic Association, the Masonic Order of Liberia, and the Young Men's Lyceum.[35] Richard L. Hall emphasizes "how closely [the settler colonists'] culture remained identified with that of their mother country."[36] Article 6 of the Liberia Lyceum constitution provided a representative example: "The object of this Association shall be the diffusion of knowledge throughout the colony as the best method to advance not only general but individual improvement."[37] Similar statements could be found in the constitutions and by-laws of lyceums in the United States.[38] The creation of "mutual aid associations, debating, agricultural, and choral societies," Hall argues, offered familiar American cultural institutions in which settler colonists could participate. These associations also provided "criteria by which settlers distinguished their culture from that of Africans around them"—yet another, though less positive, cultural trace from their American heritage.[39] The unfettered access by settler colonists to these associations was an expression of a civic identity that they had not experienced in the United States.

Lyceums in the United States published pamphlets and newspapers, but none of those organs could match the significance of the relationship between the Liberia Lyceum and the *Liberia Herald*.[40] In colonial Liberia, the Liberia Lyceum and the *Liberia Herald* were uniquely connected.[41] The Liberia Lyceum owned the *Liberia Herald*, a reversal of power from what Scott argues was the traditional dynamic between lyceums and newspapers in the United States. On a local level, the connection between the Liberia

Lyceum and the *Liberia Herald* was the only such relationship between a group organized by settler colonists and a newspaper in Liberia during the transition from colonial to republican government (approximately 1845 to 1855).[42] During a period in which settler colonists began asserting their political independence and crafting a new civic identity, institutions of education and deliberation became increasingly important. The paucity of newspapers in Liberia gave tremendous power to the few publications in the colonies.

As an institution, the Liberia Lyceum was built on similar principles and played a similar role as its Anglo-American counterparts. Popular education, available to the masses and circulated in voice and print, was a commitment shared across the Atlantic. Yet the context in which the Liberia Lyceum emerged had many significant differences from the Anglo-American lyceum. The settler colonists who participated in the Liberia Lyceum were a group in a society marked by betweenness. Their connectedness and disconnectedness to the United States took new forms as settler colonists grappled with their identity in Liberia. These processes, distinct from what most Anglo-American lyceums negotiated, suggest the ways in which the Liberia Lyceum participated in a lyceum diaspora that refracted, rather than reflected, its Anglo-American contemporaries.

Given his role as a founder of the Liberia Lyceum, Teage unsurprisingly believed that lyceums were worthwhile organizations for civic engagement. Early in his May 1845 address, Teage stated: "The existence of our Lyceum indicates our conviction of the efficiency of associations." Still, Teage recognized the faults in lyceums, arguing: "It is to be regretted that in the eager strife of debate truth is too often forgotten in the anxiety for triumph." Calling attention to a common criticism of rhetoric—that truth is sometimes lost in an effort to persuade—might seem an odd move in a speech that aims to support lyceum activities. Teage was not alone in these concerns, however, as his lament tapped into a centuries-old debate in the Western tradition about the role of rhetoric in civic discourse. In *Gorgias* Plato equated rhetoric to cookery, arguing that rhetoric was harmful to the soul just as lavish meals were harmful to the body.[43] Plato made rhetoric seem at best extraneous and at worst damaging to individuals and the polis. Concerns about rhetoric revealed far more than simply a distaste for eloquence. Instead, as Brian Vickers argues, the criticism of rhetoric as harmful to truth often coincided with elites' fear of empowering the disempowered.[44] Discussions of rhetoric and truth were not merely philosophical endeavors divorced from context, particularly for Teage. Such discussions were often a reflection of power dynamics and the contestation over the right to speak experienced by blacks throughout the diaspora.

Teage's position on this age-old controversy was to champion the virtues of rhetoric and debate rather than to denounce them. Teage's justification for debate was offered in terms that suggested the virtues needed for settler colonists to assert their rights and constitute their identity. Specifically, Teage argued that lyceums fostered a nimble mind, provided an arena for gladiatorial engagement with issues, and encouraged the unveiling of deception. Consistent with American lyceum culture (both Anglo-American and African American), Teage mostly valorized rhetoric and debate as essential civic skills for settler colonists. Yet Teage combined this support with a wariness of the ends to which rhetoric and debate could be put.

Teage's promotion of a nimble mind through debate expressed the significant adaptations of Anglo-American rhetorical practice that were undertaken by settler colonists. The process of discovering truths through debate demanded rhetorical activity. The purpose of the Liberia Lyceum, Teage argued, was "to educate and discipline" the intellectual capacity of setter colonists through "vigorous exercise." Debating, Teage argued, "is a species of engagement in which the mind acquires dexterity of movement and elasticity of force." Teage's promotion of "dexterity of movement" addressed the novelty of the situation. Settler colonists were in a new environment, often without their extended families and friends. They confronted new farming challenges, new diseases, and new hostilities, in addition to new freedoms and responsibilities. The novelty of the settler colonists' situation led some to respond poorly to the challenge. Teage's framing of debate in terms of "movement" and "force" obliquely addressed a concern by many settler colonists that some of their peers were being lazy.[45]

More generally, Teage's connection of debate with a nimble mind implicitly refuted the long-standing belief by some that blacks were intellectually inferior to whites. Teage stated, "It is the possession of mind and its capacity of indefinite enlargement and improvement which imparts to man his dignity for apart from mind wherein does he differ from the brute?" Teage adapted a common argument used to denigrate blacks—that they were closer to animals than whites—and used it to encourage the kind of educational experience that would disprove the supposed science of racial difference. A nimble mind would aid settler colonists in addressing the challenges of their new life but also provide a sound rebuke to claims often expressed in the United States of black intellectual inferiority. By encouraging the development of a nimble mind, Teage provided a singular response to a variety of forces that challenged settler colonists' efforts to define their new identity as citizens. It was in that context that Teage's evaluation of a nimble mind reads differently than a similar appeal offered in the developed confines of Boston or New York. In Monrovia, far more was unsettled than settled, a situation that created demands on its citizens not felt in the United States.

A second virtue encouraged in Teage's support of the lyceum was a masculine, gladiatorial engagement with issues. Describing the interaction of a debate elsewhere in his speech, Teage offered the following analogy of debate as physical competition: "The enemy is met in the open field and grappled with hand-to-hand." Teage extended the analogy, stating: "The conspicuousness of the theater—the gaze of congregated spectators—the fire of the eager eye in the hope of the approving award all combined wakens in the mind an ardor, and kindles in it an enthusiasm, and imparts to it an energy it can never hope to feel in the seclusion of the cloister." Here, Teage provided a dialectical counterbalance to his earlier virtue of the nimble mind. One could not simply pursue knowledge without testing that knowledge against other ideas. The "dexterity of movement and elasticity of force" must be "whetted and edged" by debating others.[46] In elaborating this virtue, Teage continued to position the Liberia Lyceum as a place of rhetorical activity.

Teage also continued to challenge the denigrated perception of African Americans pervading much Anglo-American discourse. Using the metaphor of debaters as gladiators, Teage associated the positive, martial characteristics of gladiators—ardor, heroism, fearlessness—with settler colonists in the Liberia Lyceum. Perhaps most transgressive, however, was that Teage used a metaphor with violent undertones to talk about African American intellect, at a time when so many whites feared slave rebellions. In Teage's estimation, settler colonists could be assertive, debating gladiators in the Liberia Lyceum without fear of reprisal, because settler colonists were not slaves, and they were not beasts prone to violence; therefore, they should not be subject to the constraints imposed by white anxiety in the United States.

Teage's masculine framing of argumentation and debate aligned with the gendered public discourse that motivated support for colonization. More women than men sought support for their transportation to Africa, but the reasoning for colonization did not reflect this.[47] Bruce Dorsey argues that "colonization reform assumed a masculine character from its inception."[48] Settler colonists' immigration to Liberia was often positioned in the same light as continental migration across the United States, and, as Dorsey notes, "nothing was considered more manly in this era than westward expansion."[49] In his featured speech at the founding meeting of the ACS, Elias B. Caldwell dismissed the possibility that free blacks would be unwilling to move to Liberia.[50] Teage's description of debate as gladiatorial relied upon gender norms that, in Liberia as in the United States, heralded masculinity as an ideal of civic engagement.[51]

Teage's third enumerated virtue of lyceums was that such groups provided a space to unmask deception. Abolitionists had long believed that colonization was a ruse of the slaveholders—an attempt to remove supposed black troublemakers (read: any free black person) and to create a docile slave population.[52] Settler colonists did not express the same level of disdain, yet the disconnections between their expectations and the realities of colonial life left many feeling deceived.[53] Teage used this sentiment as a rationale for settler colonists to participate in debate. Engaging in the social activity of debate, resisting "the seclusion of the cloister," created a space to confront deception collectively. As Teage stated, "It is in these keen conflicts [debates] that the doublings and evasions of Sophistry are unraveled and exposed, and specious and imposing paradoxes laid bare." Teage explicitly invited controversy into the lyceum. The experience of the settler colonists demanded a sensitivity to duplicity, as a citizen could not naively accept the pronouncements of those in power. For, in Teage's estimation, "It is in the shocks that the sparks of truth are struck out."[54] In this way Teage's deliberative rhetoric about debate simultaneously promoted debate in the colony as a means for survival and identity-building; as well as offer a subversive rebuttal to Anglo-American rhetorical practices that oppressed them. In this way, Teage not only offered a deliberative address; he made deliberation a part of the larger diasporic discourse of settler colonists.

Teage's peculiar obligation to debate accumulated another layer of meaning when put into the context of the African American rhetorical practices in the mid-1800s. Although speaking in Liberia and living under different circumstances than free blacks in the United States, Teage engaged intertextually with African American rhetorical traditions, including the trope of the Talking Book. This trope, discussed in more detail in chapter 2, is worth reviewing for the particular elements of signifying implicated in Teage's Liberia Lyceum speech. The trope of the Talking Book manifested in the writings of African Americans in the late eighteenth and early nineteenth centuries and describes the absence of African Americans from public literary activities. When African Americans practiced literary activities typically allowed for only Anglo-Americans, such as when Phillis Wheatley published her poetry in 1773 or when others composed slave narratives, the presence of a black author was a significant transgression of a racial social order.

These early texts did not contain formal or stylistic departures from their white contemporaries, but, as Henry Louis Gates Jr., explains, the simple act of participation in this previously segregated activity was crucial to African Americans' demonstrating their capacity for reason and constituting themselves as "speaking subjects" rather than commodities or objects. In essence, the Talking Book was the tropological manifestation of "making the white written text speak with a black voice."[55]

Furthermore, the Talking Book was part of what Elizabeth McHenry describes as African American "literary character." McHenry argues that an African American rhetor participating in a previously segregated rhetorical space "offered black Americans a way to refute widespread claims of their miserable, degraded position ... with displays of black genius."[56] The key move was to operate within a white public sphere without any rhetorical difference, other than the quite significant difference of the rhetor's being black and making claims from that racial position. The Talking Book was not a move to revolutionize style, diction, tone, subject, or other traits, as such a radical departure from the norms might only serve as further evidence of difference and would, by extension, further marginalize an already subjugated race. A Talking Book text thus employs the rhetorical conventions of the dominant Anglo-American culture in the service of and authored by African Americans.

The intertextuality of the Talking Book trope comes into relief when Teage's speech is compared to texts authored by Anglo-Americans that are supportive of the lyceum movement. Two decades before Teage's Liberia Lyceum address, Holbrook extolled the virtues of the lyceum in America. He asserted that the creation of "associations for mutual instruction" would spread "with great rapidity" and raise "the moral and intellectual taste of our countrymen."[57] Individuals would cultivate their moral and intellectual tastes, thereby making the American nation better. In Liberia in 1845, Teage echoed Holbrook's sentiment, that the lyceum bettered a democratic citizenry. Teage believed that lyceums were concerned with the "indefinite enlargement and improvement" that makes a man "differ from the brute."[58] Holbrook argued, "Every Lyceum is, in fact, a safeguard of liberty."[59] For Teage, the manner in which lyceums developed human faculties helped to temper the deleterious effects of passions on governance. Teage argued:

> That apparently simplest, and certainly the most unstable of all forms of government, I mean a democracy has been ever found among an ignorant people.... The instability of this form of society and the evils

resulting from it are undoubtedly owing to pride in ignorance.... The education of the people then should be an object of primary importance, as upon it depend in a very great degree their own happiness and the ability of their institutions.[60]

In many ways Teage's speech rehearsed Holbrook's justification for the creation of lyceums. Both sought broad audiences and viewed education as a necessary good for public life. The intertextual dialogue between such justifications—across time, space, and race—reinforced the connections of the Liberia Lyceum to American lyceums and of Teage to other proponents of the value of such associations.

Teage's mostly laudatory comments about debate elided discussion of racial difference until the end of the speech. Befitting the Talking Book trope, the primary marker of difference throughout most of the address was the race of the rhetor rather than the content of the message. Teage's conclusion, however, departed from the norms of Anglo-American lyceum practices and brought to the fore his racialized revision by recognizing the difficult position of settler colonists. Teage admitted that the position of settler colonists was "the most difficult to describe."[61] Settler colonists "enjoyed privileges and exercised rights," he said, but only "under the patronage of the American Colonization Society."[62] Teage told his audience that it was "idle" to "enter on the discussion of right abstractedly or speculatively considered." His discouragement of speculation was tempered shortly afterward, when Teage alluded to Acts 8:1 in describing the situation settler colonists faced: "Like wanderers from Samaria we shall find it certain death to remain here or to return to the city. Hope can be indulged only in going forward."[63] Settler colonists could not be complacent with their current conditions, nor could they return from whence they came (i.e., the United States). Settler colonists, like the Samarians, were displaced peoples. The settler colonists were part of a growing diaspora. Debating and deliberating about public matters was far more than just an exercise in governance. "Going forward" was not only a peculiar obligation of their civic identity, but a matter of survival.

The Peculiar Obligation to Commemorate: The Anniversary Speech of December 1, 1846, the Past, and Liberian Civic Identity

Teage's Anniversary Speech suggested another peculiar obligation of settler colonists, the obligation to commemorate their shared history. The Liberia Lyceum speech examined above proclaimed the kinds of deliberative activities in which the audience should participate—specifically, debate—as well as describing the benefits of debate to settler colonists. By contrast, the Anniversary Speech was less deliberative and more diasporic in the way that it grappled with identity, belonging, and struggle. Teage used the occasion to construct a history of settler colonists—men and women from somewhere else who were not certain they belonged in Liberia—and to celebrate that identity. The history Teage developed was not merely an agreed-upon set of names, dates, and events; rather, he constructed a sense of moral inheritance from the colony's founding. For settler colonists, the history of the Cape Mesurado colony—an area that included Monrovia—was not self-evidently praiseworthy. The intransigence of white colonizationists, high mortality rates, broken promises, violence with indigenous populations, separation from families in the United States, and general hardship all pointed to a history more akin to that of a prison colony than a functional society.

Teage saw the colony's history differently. In his Anniversary Speech, Teage confronted the tensions of diasporic discourse by creating a history that helped to prove that settler colonists belonged in Liberia. This constitutive recounting of history expressed the integral relationship between commemoration and settler colonists' civic identity. As such, Teage worked to make the epideictic genre work toward deliberative ends. In this section, I explain the nature of this peculiar obligation to commemorate by first accounting for the generic conventions of the epideictic genre and conversations about critical memory and sentimental nostalgia that undergird the confluence of ceremonial and deliberative address. Second, by analyzing Teage's speech, specifically his discussion of violence, I reveal the ways in which genre and memory are brought to bear on Liberian settler colonists' civic identity. Finally, I show how the interaction of genre and memory in Teage's address crafts a moral vision for the future of settler colonists.

Teage's speech on December 1, 1846, commemorated the founding of the first colonies in Liberia. The commemoration ceremony offered Teague a fitting occasion to situate settler colonist civic identity in terms of a shared past. The use of epideictic speech occasions and the development of a shared history to constitute communities is far from new. As Celeste Michelle Condit argues, epideictic speaking "serves a three-fold set of paired functions for audiences and speakers," which "include understanding and definition, sharing and creation of community, and entertainment and display."[64] Teage opened the speech by recognizing the generic tradition in which he was participating, stating:

> FELLOW CITIZENS:—As far back towards the infancy of our race, as history and tradition are able to conduct us, we have found the casting every where prevailing among mankind, to mark, by some striking exhibition, those events which were important and interesting, either in their immediate bearing or in their remote consequences upon the destiny of those among whom they occurred.[65]

Teage's "striking exhibition" was important to his audience, for his speech drew from the "history and tradition" of settler colonists in order to understand the "remote consequences upon the destiny" of the founders and, by extension, the settler colonists. In function Teage's Anniversary Speech aligned with American epideictic standard-bearers like John Hancock's Boston Massacre oration in 1774 or Daniel Webster's Bunker Hill address in 1825. The grandeur of language and purpose were on display when Teage noted that speeches of the kind he was delivering marked "epochs in the history of man," "the rise and fall of kingdoms and dynasties," and "the movements of the human mind." Teage both embraced the high stakes of the genre and demurred that successful participation in that genre "requires far higher ability and more varied talent than he possesses who this day has the honor to address you."[66] Teage's self-deprecation belied a clear understanding of the rhetorical practices that were expected for a ceremonial occasion.

Despite his adaptation to some facets of American ceremonial speaking, Teage's address necessarily moved away from the white center of the genre by attending to the particular racial implications of the context. Slavery and epideictic orations have a complicated history in American public address. Edwin Black argues that the sentimental style pervading the ceremonial speeches of Webster and his ilk "repressed" the issue of slavery.[67] "Sentimentality," as Paul Gilroy argues, "blocks shame's productivity, its slow, humble path towards virtue."[68] It is perhaps as a consequence of this sentimental erasure that Teage's address did little to "block" the reality of slavery and colonization through overwrought flourish. Teage noted that the "movement of the human mind" detailed in sentimental orations often tracked "the influence of those movements upon the destinies of the race." He recognized the dual purposes that often motivate ceremonial speaking, stating, on the one hand, that such orations "frequently disclose to us the sad and sickening spectacle of innocence bending under the weight of injustice, and of weakness robbed and despoiled by the hand of unscrupulous oppression."[69] On the other hand, the act of commemorating events involved the selection of only those men and events "as virtue and humanity would approve." Teage recognized the value in expressing the "sad and sickening spectacle" as well as in praising virtuous men and acts, observing that those elements of "an opposite character" to virtue and humanity can be discussed "only as beacons, or as a towering Pharos throwing a strong but lurid light to mark the melancholy grave of mad ambition, and to warn inexperienced voyager[s] of the existing danger." For a person in Teage's position—a settler colonist, a former slave, a leader among free blacks from the United States—race was a subject that required a speaker to balance these complex, seemingly contradictory, features.

The challenge for Teage was incorporating the unique experience of settler colonist life into the generic expectations of a celebratory speech, all in service of a cohesive civic identity, one that simultaneously emulated and subverted Anglo-American rhetorical practice. In particular, Teage needed to interpret the colony's history in a manner that constructed a shared, virtuous past but also recognized the tremendous hardships of the early colonial years endured by many who were still alive. Navigating these different visions of history is what Houston A. Baker Jr. discusses as the definitional crisis of creating a past for the black community. According to Baker, the competing frameworks in this crisis are constituted by "twin rhetorics of *nostalgia* and *critical memory*." Nostalgia has a rhetoric that features "purposive construction of a past filled with golden virtues, golden men, and sterling events," while critical memory recognizes that the experience of blacks in America requires attention to the "cumulative, collective maintenance of a record that draws into relationship significant instants of time past and the always uprooted homelessness of now."[70] Despite their contentious relationship, both nostalgia and critical memory have a place in the ongoing process of identity formation in the African diaspora.

Baker's phrase "the always uprooted homelessness of now" bears unique significance when applied to settler colonists. In Baker's formulation, this notion refers to the critical recognition by African Americans that nostalgia should not mask the struggles of the past that persist in the present. Settler colonists had experienced specific enactments of uprooting and homelessness. The short history of the Liberian colonies combined with still-fluid civic identity of settler colonists made the creation of a national narrative, and the use of nostalgic appeals to a golden age, difficult. However, the easy divide between nostalgia as revisionist history and critical history as realist history became all the more complicated in Teage's speech. For Teage, nostalgia and critical history both played a role in establishing settler colonists as a separate civic identity with a bright and moral future. In his commemorative address Teage used nostalgia to help him establish a venerable past through a patriotic, nationalistic narrative (even in the absence of independent nationhood). Teage's speech also engaged the rhetoric of critical memory by recognizing the hardships and violence of the colony's founding. From these rhetorics Teage looked to the future and prescribed for settler colonists what must be done in order to realize the civic identity he constructed in the speech. Teage's future imagined a people who were grounded, who were of a place, and not adrift in the liminal state rendered by colonization.

Teage engaged with both nostalgic remembrance and critical memory in his framing of the violent confrontations that marred the early years of the Liberian colonies. On November 11, 1822, the earliest settler colonists faced an attack from the Dē, Mamba, and Vai tribes. It was a bloody first encounter, with the colonists greatly outnumbered by the native population. The use of firearms proved the difference in this first encounter; "Great execution was done," contends Liberian historian Harry Johnston.[71] After more bloodshed, peace was made with the chiefs on December 4, 1822. Teage addressed this element of Liberian history without providing specific details of people, places, and dates. Teage stated, "Thanks to the improved and humanized spirit" the actions of the settler colonists against natives, "reeking with the gore of murdered thousands . . . is now regarded only as the savage commissioner of an unsparing oppression, or at best the ghostly executioner of an unpitying justice."[72] In a different era "he who would secure for himself a niche in the temple of undying fame" based upon such violence "must seek some other field than that of battle as the theatre of his exploits."[73] This erasure of specific dates, names, and places was distant from the epideictic practices in the United States at this time. There, epideictic oratories often included excessive details, including the names of virtuous leaders. Teage's evasion of any proper nouns in his commemorative address functioned as a form of critical history, a refusal to praise barbarous acts committed by settler colonists in the past. This erasure of names was particularly poignant given that the men who led the settler colonists against the natives were well known in the colonies.[74] Not only did Teage not identity these founders by name, though they were known, he furthered the implications of critical history by noting that their actions in battle were from a bygone era and not to be lauded.

Although Teage began with the need for a critical memory of the past, he still struck the chords of nostalgic sentimentalism. Specifically, Teage offered a critical reading of the colonial violence of the past, while nevertheless engaging in the adulation of the founders who fought because of the opportunities their battles allowed for in the present. "Still, we honor the heroes of the age that has past [sic]," he stated, and, "No slander can tarnish their hard-earned fame."[75] Teage and his audience were assembled "to commemorate the event for which the founders of our infant Republic toiled, and fought, and bled." Remembering those who died and seeing among the audience members some who fought and survived served to "agitate our bosoms, and marking the character of the resolves which the occasion is ripening." "No sculptured marble" would convey the "fame" of the founders, but, Teage argued, "a nobler monument shall be yours—the happy hearts of unborn millions shall be the shrine in which your names will be treasured."[76] The founders of Liberia set a "high example" of "noble disinterestedness" through their "entire subordination of every thought, and act, and scheme, and interest, to the heaven-born purpose of the human regeneration and human elevation." These passages highlight a nostalgic appeal to the triumphs of the past, because of their implications for the future, not because of their violent clashes with others. In this way, Teage was able to use both nostalgia and critical memory in his attempt to foment a shared civic identity.

Teage's twin rhetorics of critical memory and sentimental nostalgia constituted settler colonists in proud and unsettling terms. The didacticism that Black associates with the sentimental style appeared in the form of Teage's very clear articulation of how he intended to situate the past in his conceptualization of civic identity. The question for his audience "on this occasion, so big with subjects of profitable meditation," was "how we may challenge and secure admiration and gratitude of a virtuous and a happy posterity, by transmitting to them the *patrimony received from our fathers*, not only in all its original entireness, but in vastly augmented beauty, order, and strength."[77] The civic identity of settler colonists should not follow the same trajectory as the past, Teage argued. It must do more. Settler colonists would need to develop, grow, and learn, not least because, as Teage reminded the audience, "of the *peculiarity* of our condition."[78] The rest of the address would "for a moment look back, that from the events of the past we may derive hope for the future."[79]

The "moment" Teage looked back to was slavery. His brief discussion of slavery did not take the same tone as his elaboration of the golden virtues of the founders. Instead, Teage addressed slavery through the tropes of paralepsis (calling attention to a subject while claiming to pass it over) and metaphor. Part of Teage's recalcitrance came from his audience's shared understanding of those horrors. Teage stated, "It is not necessary, and therefore I will not disgust you with the hideous picture of that state of things which followed upon the prevalence of this blasphemous opinion [that blacks were incapacitated]. The bare mention that such an opinion prevailed, would be sufficient to call up in the mind, even of those who had never witnessed its operation, images of the most sickening and revolting character."[80] Saidiya V. Hartman notes the "ease with which scenes" of intense violence against blacks are "usually reiterated" and the "casualness with which they are circulated" in nineteenth-century public discourse.[81] Teage resisted such a practice, relying on the experience of his audience to suffice. Teage stated, "I need not detain you with a narrative of their [the founding colonists'] privations and sufferings."[82] Still, the act of not providing that picture calls attention to the existence of the picture, but in less graphic terms.

Teage's use of metaphors, specifically related to the body, also added a layer of embodiment to the description of slavery in the United States. Teage described the plight of blacks "under the reign of this crushing sentiment" in terms that illustrated the fundamental restrictions on black humanity. Settler colonists born in the United States "drew our first breath and sighed away the years of our youth." The oppression of slavery "chilled every noble passion and paralyzed every arm." Teage described slaves as "inglorious slumberers," on account of the "deep degradation" that surrounded them.[83] Teage's use of metaphor rendered his descriptions of slavery visceral without treading into vivid, detailed accounts of slavery. Such a move allowed Teage to remain somewhat faithful to his claim that it was "unnecessary" to "disgust" the audience with the graphic details, while building a common bond with the audience based on their experience. Even more, the use of rhetorical figuration displayed the intellectual capabilities which the purveyors of racist ideology in America assumed Teage and his race must lack. The horrors of slavery were fundamental to the critical memory of settler colonists. How that common bond was communicated demonstrated Teage's commitment to building a new civic identity rather than remaining mired in the pain of a lack of civic identity.

Teage's framing of past violence—in the United States and in the Liberian colonies—made clear that these events impacted who settler colonists were but would not define them. Teage and his audience came to the colonies aware that it was a compromise. When a black person in the United States "would lift his voice and demand those rights which the God of nature hath bestowed in equal gift upon all His rational creatures," the response from the white man was at first denial and then the proclamation that "LIBERTY and EXPATRIATION are inseparable." "Dreadful as the alternative was," Teage stated, settler colonists were "calm, cool, and fixed in their purpose." If indeed the only way to achieve liberty was through colonization, then, quoting Patrick Henry, Teage declared, "Give me Liberty or give me Death."[84] Once in the colonies, fighting was a matter of circumstance, not desire. Teage opined, "Necessity, stern necessity, unsheathed their sword and forced upon them an alternative from which all the feelings of their heart turned with instinctive recoil." In Teage's telling, settler colonists were active participants in making decisions based upon the circumstances of their past; they were not passive objects being acted upon.

The second section of Teage's speech was more direct in its application of the past to the present. Teage called attention to this shift, stating, "Let us now turn from those who proceeded [sic] us, and ask, What are the peculiar obligations which rest upon us: what the particular duties to which we are called?" Whereas Teage was careful not to overindulge the spirit of violence in the previous section, the second section of the speech encouraged settler colonists to feel the urgency of building a colony. Teage implied that the tasks before his audience were every bit as crucial for their livelihood as their past efforts at defense. "Let us not suppose, that because we are not called upon to drive the invading native from our door," Teage warned, "therefore we have nothing to do. No mistake could be more fatal." For Teage, the process of creating a civic identity was "a moral fight," involving "keener warfare" and "a sharper conflict."[85] The past duty to physically secure the colony was replaced by concerns for how settler colonists would "secure and perpetuate our own prosperity, and transmit it an inheritance to our children."[86] Teage made clear that the creation of a civic identity was an urgent concern, one bound up with notions of governance, freedom, and equality. From these principles, he asked, "By what means shall we advance our prosperity?"[87]

Teage offered a prescription that aligned with the way he developed the peculiar obligation of debate in the Liberia Lyceum speech, describing the "means" through which settler colonists could advance prosperity. Teage's means to achieving prosperity were unity among the population, respect for order, and education of the youth. Teage's elaboration of unity focused more specifically on the ills of self-interest that would undermine a civic identity. Teage said, "The idea of prosperity and stability where disunion reigns ... can only serve to mislead." Teage returned to the motivational power of the colony's violent beginnings, this time invoking the unity required of successful military units. "Can that army, in which faction triumphs among the soldiers and disunion and jealousy distract the counsels of the officers, hope to succeed in a campaign?" By comparing the success of the colony with the success of an army regiment, Teage highlights the importance of unity and shared purpose. The analogy comparing the military to the government continued as Teage blamed disunion on the leaders: "I would observe also, that the complexion of the soldiers' mind will be sure to be tinged by that of their officers." If leaders impact the minds of those that follow them, Teage surmised that leaders must be virtuous. If not, the "unworthy abandonment of the public interests" will be occasioned by "intriguing politicians and unprincipled political demagogues."[88] Thus, unity was key to a successful colony, but only when it was led by strong, virtuous leaders.

But unity and shared purpose would come to nothing without a system to ensure order and appropriate submission to appointed leaders. "Order is heaven's first law," Teage began. He continued, without "subordination" to a republican government, "there can be no security for person nor property."[89] This emphasis on order and law did not mean that Teague advocated a blind devotion to power; rather, he supported "a republican form of government" in which "oppression can have no place." Therefore, the conscientious portion of Teage's statement on submission was imperative. He argued that when "minions of office become so intoxicated with a little brief power... the strong indignation of an outraged public, calmly but firmly expressed" can "awaken the dreamer from his vision of greatness." In other words, it is through the power of the people that "minions of office," unvirtuous leaders, dreaming of power can be awakened from their slumber.[90] As such, the people, in their conscientious submission, have power in Teage's vision of order.

Teage departed from the conventional narrative of republicanism by empowering the average person. He asserted that the people should enact the very obedience to order that they expect in leaders. Not everyone can govern, but "in the intercourse of our daily life we set an attractive example of obedience to the laws" and therefore "equally serve our country."[91] Elevating the actions of the common person even higher, Teage proclaimed, "True dignity, and, I may add, true usefulness, depend not so much upon the circumstances of office as upon the faithful discharge of appropriate duties."[92] For Teage's vision of an ordered republican government to materialize, leaders must be virtuous, the people must demand their leaders to be virtuous, and the people must be virtuous.

According to Teage, for a people to be virtuous, they must be educated. As such, Teage's conceptualization of education emphasized the public good rather than individual benefits. Teage contended, "A virtuous, orderly, educated people, have all the elements of national greatness and national perpetuity."[93] The importance of education for Teage was clear: "Education corrects vice,—cures disorders—abates jealousies—adorns virtue—commands the winds—triumphs over the waves—scales the heavens. . . . Education opens sources of pure, refined, and exquisite enjoyment."[94] Teage refuted the position that self-interest ought to be the main concern of settler colonists, specifically the increase of commerce. "Virtue and independence of a people will be inversely as their attention is wholly given to commerce," he argued. The excesses encouraged by the singular focus on commerce would neglect the overall improvement of the country. Teage noted that "large manufacturing towns and cities" worldwide demonstrated "the deteriorating influence" that the "whole attention" to commerce can create. As a result of such a singular focus on commerce, settler colonists would be "looking constantly abroad to the neglect of the improvement of their own country."[95] Commercial pursuit with other nations may indeed bring improvements, but "it imports vices also."[96] Given the extraordinary benefits of education and the potential evils of commerce, Teage made clear that education should be prioritized in a healthy republic.

Teage did not reject all elements of commercial pursuits. In an ideal setting commerce would result from the hard work and industry of settler colonists, values that Teage certainly did not want to discourage. But Teage and his audience did not live in an ideal situation. To carve out a place for commerce in the civic identity of settler colonists, he grappled with notions of self-interest in more complicated ways than he had when discussing order and unity. "Grant it," Teage conceded, "it is not my purpose to pronounce a wholesale anathema to commerce. I appreciate its high importance in improving our race."[97] But Teage preferred "the primitive employment of agriculture and husbandry." These local pursuits cultivated "virtue and independence" in ways that foreign trade did not.

Teage professed the virtues of what James Oakes terms "yeoman republicanism."[98] A Jeffersonian ideal, yeoman republicanism held that "no one owned the farmer who owned his own land." Oakes explains, "It was precisely this independence that in theory made the self-interest of the yeoman farmer indistinguishable from the greater interest of the commonwealth."[99] If yeoman farmers could produce all that they needed for themselves, then they would be, "ideally, untouched by the temptations of corruption."[100] This yeoman farmer version of republicanism "legitimized the pursuit of self-interest by fusing it to the community interest."[101] Or, in the words of Teage, "Fellow-citizens! Our prosperity and independence are to be drawn from the soil. That is the highway to honour, to wealth, to *private and national prosperity*."[102] Teage even added a layer of Christianity to his yeoman republicanism, reminding his audience that "the Lord God planted a garden eastward in Eden."[103] In the main, Teage spoke in classical republican terms, placing the common good above or before individual advancement. Yet, by encouraging commercial independence, Teage introduced a more synthetic relationship between self-interest and community good.

The peroration to Teage's Anniversary Speech cohered the hardships of the past with optimism for the future. Teage recalled the uniqueness of their collective experience, exhorting, "Fellow-Citizens! we stand now on ground never occupied by a people before."[104] He exhorted them, "Rise to a clear and full perception of your responsibilities," which included nothing short of "the future destiny of your race." Teage also grounded their lineage further back in time, declaring them "the descendants of the mighty Pharaohs."[105] These lofty claims led to a simple question: "Shall Liberia live?" Unsurprisingly, Teage answered, "Yes." At that moment, Teage brought Liberia to life in his audience: "in the generous emotions now swelling in your blossoms—in the high and none purpose now fixing itself in your mind, and ripening into the unyieldingness of indomitable principle."[106] The future of Liberia was no longer just about individual survival, it was about the survival of principles that connected all of the settler colonists. Teage skillfully created a righteous past that would warrant the communal bond needed for the colonies to become a nation.

Teage offered a way to navigate histories of violence without falling into nostalgia (which ignores the negative elements of the past, like violence) and critical history (which ignores positive elements, like founding a new community). Teage's peculiar obligations illustrated what the discourse of the middle/compromise might look like in practice. Such discourse did not artificially merge opposing viewpoints, as the peculiar argumentation of colonizationists did. Rather, it found ways to revise the norms of address to negotiate the context and purpose.

Conclusion

Teage's constitution of a civic identity through peculiar obligations stood apart from how settler colonists discussed their status in colonial Liberia. From 1822 to 1847, Liberia was a collection of colonies that were neither independent nor controlled by a sovereign nation-state. What counted as a citizen did not come from the force of law in any meaningful way. It is telling that during this time, as Tyler-McGraw explains, citizenship was earned by "responsible" conduct and the testimony of three disinterested citizens. Responsibility had certain material components, like owning a home. But there were performative elements as well, like consistently attending church services, dressing in Western clothes, and cultivating the land.[107] To these, Teage elaborated his own peculiar obligations for settler colonist civic identity. Debate was a necessary activity for developing a nimble mind, engaging issues as gladiators, and unmasking deception. These virtues could apply to many audiences, but they had special resonance for settler colonists. The purpose of moving to Liberia was to experience freedom and build a life free from the oppression felt in the United States. Deliberating about matters of public importance served both purposes. The peculiar obligation to debate allowed diasporic discourse to engage and subvert whites' deliberative discourses simultaneously, while addressing a black audience of settler colonists.

Celebrating the past also contributed to settler colonists' sense of freedom and identity formation, but through the act of commemoration rather than deliberation. Rather than reject or forget the past hardships, Teage refashioned them into a source of pride and a motivating principle for Liberians to progress as a people. Teage needed to convince Liberians that liberal individualism would not lead to the exclusionary politics of the United States. Instead, he fashioned a republican civic identity to elevate virtue as key to the new nation and subsumed individualism within the parameters of republican life. The peculiar obligations to debate and to commemorate provided the cohesion among disparate persons, connecting them through civic deliberation and remembrance rather than through the simple fact that they were all just trying to survive.

The peculiarity of Teage's "peculiar obligations" changed when Liberia declared independence and drafted its governing document. In 1847 the settler colonists declared their independence from the ACS and adopted a constitution for their nation. Teage helped to realize both.[108] Teage saw these advancements as planting "a nation of colored people on the soil of Africa, adorned and dignified with the attributes of a civilized and Christian community."[109] Teage purposefully modeled the Liberian Declaration of Independence on the American version, offering a preamble and listing grievances.[110] Importantly, the Liberian Declaration revised the clarion call of "life, liberty, and the pursuit of happiness" in Thomas Jefferson's 1776 text. The Liberian iteration proclaimed, "We recognize in all men certain natural and inalienable rights: among these are life, liberty, and the right to acquire, possess, enjoy, and defend property."[111] The clear emphasis on property also manifested in the constitution's citizenship requirements, which restricted the franchise to black men who owned real estate.[112] Natives could not be citizens, for they were construed as a separate nation. Women were not citizens, although they held certain rights with respect to property owning.[113]

The Liberian emphasis on real estate created a far more liberal notion of citizenship than Teage had advocated in the years leading up to the Liberian Constitutional Convention. The common good and virtue of a civic identity were sublimated to the acquisition of property and means. For all of Teage's probing and careful discussion of the relationship of debate and commemoration in the lives of settler colonists, the declaration and constitution seemed to revert to features of American civic life against which Teage had crafted a more nuanced discourse of Liberian civic identity.

It is not clear why the ideals of the Liberian declaration and constitution were so far afield from those of Teage's 1845 and 1846 oratory. Teage's contributions to Liberian history are understandably weighted toward the official documents he helped create and the leadership positions he held. In addition to being constrained to the texts he created, Teage's early death in 1853 at the age of forty-six left many of his thoughts unsaid and unwritten. And yet, between those texts and roles that are available, it is clear that Teage grappled with what civic life for a settler colonist could be. Kazanjian writes that "black settlers who came to live in colonial Liberia . . . lived unsettled *states of being* or *life* that cannot be reduced to the formal, political, and governmental history."[114] The examination of Teage's speeches and the peculiar obligations therein reveals one settler colonist's efforts to settle those unsettled lives.

CHAPTER 5

Peculiar Proposal

Abraham Lincoln and the Public Policy Advocacy for Colonization

Abraham Lincoln's second Annual Message, delivered to Congress on December 1, 1862, was not among his most noteworthy works. As an annual message—what we would now call a State of the Union address—Lincoln fulfilled his duty as set forth in Article II, Section 3 of the Constitution, to "recommend to their [Congress's] Consideration such Measures as he shall judge necessary and expedient."[1] The most important issue treated in the second Annual Message was slavery, a vehemently contested issue that had already occasioned the secession of eleven Southern states and the military hostilities of the Civil War. Lincoln's message adopted a measured tone as it attempted to chart the path of a compromise policy rather than match the intensity of abolitionists or secessionists. Lincoln recommended constitutional amendments to enact the compensated emancipation of slaves and provide support for colonization as a means to end the war, remove the primary cause of hostilities (slavery), and save the Union. A written message that carefully elaborated his plan and its benefits, the second Annual Message, lacked the overt rhetorical appeal of Lincoln's more famous speeches. Rather, the second Annual Message reported facts and figures, then introduced a carefully reasoned case for Lincoln's proposal.

Lincoln's second Annual Message was, however, far more rhetorically significant and interesting than its bureaucratic tone might suggest. First, the second Annual Message contained the most detailed and direct public policy analysis offered by a public figure in favor of compensated emancipation and, by extension, colonization. The second Annual Message showed a skilled rhetorician at work, but not in the ways that most people think of Lincoln. Most rhetorical scholars focus on Lincoln's forensic or ceremonial discourses, such as the Gettysburg Address, the first and second inaugurals, and his Cooper Union speech.[2] The Lincoln–Douglas debates have occasioned some explication of Lincoln's stance on policies related to slavery, but even those studies recognize the novelty of engaging in policy analysis of Lincoln's discourse.[3] The second Annual Message was different. This was President Lincoln, not candidate Lincoln, wielding the power of the office to advance a policy in the midst of a civil war.

Second, the timing of the second Annual Message gave it increased rhetorical significance. Lincoln faced strong opposition from Northerners and Southerners after his first inaugural address.[4] Later in his first year as president, in his first Annual Message, Lincoln spoke harshly of the South. He referred to seceding states as "a disloyal portion of the American people" who have "been engaged in an attempt to divide and destroy the Union."[5] In the interceding year between annual messages, Lincoln worked to end the war through "all indispensable means."[6] One of those means was colonization, which Lincoln supported dating back to his time in Illinois and which remained a part of his thinking during his presidential years.[7] Another of Lincoln's means to end the war was compensated emancipation. In his first year in office, Lincoln drafted, but never made public, a bill supporting compensated emancipation in the border state of Delaware.[8] Then, on March 6, 1862, Lincoln addressed Congress and called for a resolution to more broadly support compensated emancipation and provide federal funds to border states who passed such measures.[9] Lincoln called a delegation of border-state representatives to the White House on July 1, to urge support for compensated emancipation.[10] (Later that summer, Lincoln invited a delegation of free blacks to the White House to urge support for colonization.) A third means to end the war was total emancipation, which manifested in the Emancipation Proclamation. The second Annual Message was delivered between his announcement of the preliminary Emancipation Proclamation (September 22, 1862) and the final Emancipation Proclamation (January 1, 1863). For one month, compensated emancipation, colonization, and total emancipation were all proposals supported by the president to end the war. And these three means to end the war were not entirely complementary of each other.

This essay situates the second Annual Message within the context of colonization policy discourse to argue that Lincoln's *peculiar proposal* for compensated emancipation and colonization was the apotheosis, and with its failure, an end to colonization policy advocacy in antebellum and Civil War era America.[11] Lincoln's proposal was rendered peculiar by his own situation and the content of the second Annual Message. Within the context of previous colonization argumentation, Lincoln's support of compensated emancipation and colonization offered the best public policy advocacy for the transportation of free blacks to Africa. Important to note is that "best" does not imply it was the most moral or just policy advocacy; rather, it implies that Lincoln's advocacy was the most well-reasoned argument for a policy that was ideologically complicated at best and blatantly racist at worst. In developing this argument I focus on Lincoln's "mediation of material and rhetorical forces," which Robert Asen describes as the central concern of public policy discourse.[12] Asen observes that the debate about rhetoric and materiality "proceeds at an unnecessarily abstract ontological level." The analysis of public policy discourse need not engage in such a debate. Instead, the critic may focus on specific material forces, like "institutional arrangements and money."[13] Attending to material forces in this way emphasizes different features than the moral judgments against Lincoln's colonization support offered by some scholars.[14]

Understanding Lincoln's proposal as the climax of colonizationists' efforts might explain why, having already issued the preliminary Emancipation Proclamation, the president still made one last policy push for colonization. It is not enough to assert that the reason Lincoln supported colonization was that he had supported it in the past. This is certainly part of the story but fails to capture the severity of the situation and Lincoln's capacity for change. Despite his proposal's likely obsolescence in one month's time, when the Final Emancipation Proclamation would take effect, a key to understanding Lincoln's efforts is his indication in the first Annual Message that "all indispensable means must be employed." Equally critical was the next sentence in that statement: "We should not be in haste to determine that radical and extreme measures, which may reach the loyal as well as the disloyal, are indispensable."[15] Lincoln wanted to explore any and all means of ending the war but saw no reason to hastily adopt the most "radical and extreme measures." In the spirit of trying all measures before adopting something as extreme as freeing all of the slaves, Lincoln made the best possible arguments for compensated emancipation and colonization that he could muster.

In the following pages, I offer a reading of the second Annual Message that takes seriously Lincoln's position as policy advocate and the implications of colonization's existing peculiar argumentation on that advocacy. As such, the analysis of Lincoln's peculiar proposal develops in three parts. First, I trace the policy argumentation for colonization that preceded Lincoln's second Annual Message, establishing a set of norms with which to compare Lincoln's advocacy. Second, I analyze Lincoln's second Annual Message as a peculiar proposal, one that mediated material and rhetorical elements of both past colonization discourse and Lincoln's immediate context. Last, I conclude by offering a few remarks about the failure of Lincoln's deliberative discourse.

Policy Argumentation for Colonization before the Second Annual Message

As discussed in greater length in chapter 1 of this book, colonization required the political and economic support of the US government in order to make the significant impact that colonizationists wanted. Working from this assumption, colonizationists made arguments that attempted to justify the necessity of government involvement in removal of free blacks. Colonizationists remained hopeful that Congress would invest its resources and public support in their scheme because, behind the scenes, Congress would mete out small amounts at different times in "not-so-private," but not public, ways.[16] From the founding of the ACS until Lincoln's second Annual Message, the public policy discourses for colonization were primarily of two types: speeches and reports. In the context of colonization advocacy, speeches were characterized by an emphasis on self-evidence and lack of detail, while reports wielded excessive detail to little rhetorical or practical impact.

ACS supporters argued for colonization in terms familiar to the deliberative sphere of American politics, emphasizing the propriety, expediency, and practicability of the scheme. Eric Foner explains, "Absurd as the idea of colonization may appear in retrospect, it seemed quite realistic to its advocates."[17] For example, Clay identified "propriety and practicability" of colonization as the "object of the present meeting."[18] Clay addressed practicability first, referencing the founding of Sierra Leone as evidence that a colony could be created in west Africa, while also suggesting that the transportation of free blacks to Africa would "extinguish a great portion of that moral debt which she [the United States] has contracted to that unfortunate continent."[19] It might seem as if Clay was slipping into the kind of reform-minded advocacy adopted by Northern gradual emancipationists. But Clay was clear that the ACS "constituted no part of the object of this meeting to touch or agitate, in the slightest degree, a delicate question connected with another portion of the colored population of our country."[20] The rhetorical distance that Clay created between the free black population and "another portion of the colored population" was indicative of the tenuous balance Clay and others were attempting to strike between slaveholders and abolitionists. This was the balancing (and for some, Janus-faced) position of colonizationists.

Colonization policy arguments also frequently used moral appeals to answer practical questions. For example, Caldwell stated that he would address the practicability and expedience of colonization; yet expedience was given little attention while practicability was divided into three sub-areas: territory, expense, and the probability of attaining the consent of the free black population. Like Clay's, Caldwell's reasoning about practical considerations slipped into moral appeals, as the latter argued that Africa was the best option for a free black colony because "the Christian religion would be introduced into that benighted quarter of the world."[21] Because of the missionary elements of removal to Africa, Caldwell surmised that all good Christians would seize upon the providence of the colonization project. The moral arguments tied to the question of territory acted as an important buffer to the rather thin reasoning on the expense of the scheme. Caldwell makes no particular argument about the expense, instead relying on the assumption that colonization was a moral imperative. As Caldwell claimed, "it is a great national object, & ought to be supported by the national purse."[22] If the government failed to take part in the "honor and glory which cannot fail of attending the accomplishment of a work so great," then "the liberality and the humanity of our citizens will not suffer it to fail for want of pecuniary aid."[23] For Caldwell and other white colonizationists, the moral imperative was so great that if the government would not support their efforts, certainly private citizens would. A decade later Clay would repeat this same reasoning when pushed to provide justification for the US government bearing the cost of colonization.[24] On matters of territory and expense, colonizationists failed to indicate much in the way of specific details. Instead, areas of practical concern received support with assertions of colonization's necessity.

Colonizationists rarely made specific claims about the costs of colonization, particularly the cost if colonization received a national mandate. Clay's speech at an 1827 ACS meeting made a more substantive policy case than previous efforts but still failed to address the practical elements of a national colonization effort. "Our work has so prospered, and grown under our hands," Clay exhorted, "that the appeal to the power and resources of the public should no longer be deferred." His advocacy purported to offer "indisputable statistical details and calculations" to demonstrate that colonization was "within the compass of reasonable human means."[25] Clay's data-driven reasoning focused on the transportation of free people of color at a rate consistent with their rate of population increase according to the census.[26]

The result would be "a vacuum in society" that would keep the free black population constant and "accelerate the duplication of the European race."²⁷ Clay asked, rhetorically, "Is the annual expenditure of a sum no larger than $120,000, and the annual employment of 7500 tons of shipping, too much for reasonable exertion, considering the magnitude of the object in view? Are they not, on the contrary, within the compass of moderate efforts?"²⁸ Like Caldwell's featured remarks in 1816, Clay's use of rhetorical questions suggested that the answers were self-evident. Clay believed that the plans of the ACS were "not visionary, but rational and practicable."²⁹ However, as a practical measure, colonizationists failed to show how the expenditure would be economically advisable.

The resonance of early colonization policy arguments with Lincoln was displayed in his commemoration of Clay. Upon the death of Clay in 1852, Lincoln delivered a eulogy in the Hall of Representatives in Springfield, Illinois about a man he "loved and revered . . . as a teacher and leader," a man he called "my beau ideal of a statesman."³⁰ Lincoln described the parallel development of a nation (born in 1776) and Clay (1777), stating, "The infant nation, and the infant child began the race of life together."³¹ Lincoln traced the Kentuckian's work as an "intelligent and patriotic American" on issues like the War of 1812, the Missouri Compromise, nullification, and the Compromise of 1850.³² In Lincoln's telling, Clay was "a truly national man" who fought for the republican principles on which America was founded.³³ After much elaboration of Clay's service and virtues, Lincoln concluded his eulogy by discussing Clay's role in the colonization movement. Lincoln quoted at length from Clay's 1827 ACS speech, notably sections about colonization as the "humane" and "benevolent" work "in behalf of the unhappy portion of our race doomed to bondage."³⁴ Lincoln added his own support to the colonization efforts, exhorting, "This suggestion of the possible ultimate redemption of the African race and African continent, was made twenty-five years ago. Every succeeding year has added strength to the hope of its realization. May it indeed be realized!"³⁵ In the praise of Clay, Warren A. Beck argues, "Lincoln expressed the belief [in colonization] which he still held during his first years in the White House."³⁶ Lincoln would make his contribution to colonizationists' policy arguments a decade after praising Clay's work in that area.

A eulogy served as the vehicle for Lincoln's first widely publicized support of colonization, but he would go on to support colonization on other occasions. Jason H. Silverman argues that Lincoln's support of colonization was attuned to the context in which he spoke. Silverman writes, "Lincoln, the astute politician, knew that every speech must be written with a cognizance of the occasion. When delivering his eulogy on Clay, a man firmly committed to colonization, Lincoln appropriately concurred with that principle."[37] Silverman points to later speeches—like Lincoln's reply to Stephen Douglas delivered at Peoria on October 6, 1854—in which Lincoln exhibited more cautious support for colonization. Lincoln was an active member in the Illinois State Colonization Society that was founded in 1845, attending meetings before and after his eulogy of Clay.[38] Lincoln continued to support colonization and would deliver speeches in support of the movement in his various political positions.

The other type of colonization public policy discourse was direct appeals to Congress through memorials and the subsequent reports that legislators created in response to those memorials. Colonizationists' memorials frequently relied upon the same appeals as the speeches, but also included supporting documents to bolster the case for congressional support. The task of producing a report often fell to a member of Congress who supported colonization, leading to a document that simply elaborated the same arguments contained in the memorial. Reports began as rather short statements on the issue, but, as the ACS became more active and more information about colonization was produced, reports became large compendiums of documents with no curation of the evidence for a coherent and persuasive argument for a federal colonization policy.

The practice of the ACS sending memorials that asked for support from the government began shortly after the group's creation. A memorial, signed by ACS President Bushrod Washington, was sent to the House of Representatives and was read aloud on the floor January 17, 1817. The appeals made by Clay and Caldwell at the germinal meeting were conveyed in this first communication with Congress. This memorial referred to the existence of free people of color as an "inherent vice in the composition of society."[39] Free blacks, the Memorial claimed, have "anomalous and indefinite relations to the political institutions and social ties of the community." The 1817 memorial clearly denoted that the problem of free blacks and the potential solution of colonization involved moral and political considerations. Like the meeting that created the ACS, the Memorial made claims about the duty, or "patriotism," of Americans to find a place where free blacks could achieve the "higher rewards of excellence." Although the Memorial noted that this was a moral and political issue, it admitted that it would not "mark out, in detail, the measures which it may adopt in furtherance of the object in view" but would instead "implicitly rely[] upon the wisdom of Congress to devise the most effectual measures."[40] The ACS argued that something must be done but left the specifics of public policy to the legislators.

Over the next fifty years, colonization "remained at the heart of national politics," yet with little support by way of policy or financial support.[41] However, the colonization project was able to gain political traction through creative interpretations of loosely related laws and issues. In response to the initial memorial from the ACS, which was read in the House of Representatives on April 18, 1818, Congress commissioned a report on the efficacy of the policy.[42] The report did not garner congressional action; rather, it was some creative legal interpretations of existing laws that, two years later, provided financial support for the colonization movement. William H. Crawford, secretary of the treasury under President James Monroe, argued that the Slave Trade Act of 1819 gave the president broad powers (and $100,000) to return Africans who were illegally trafficked to the United States, which could include supporting colonization.[43] Monroe used the money to create an official government expedition to west Africa in 1820, but this did not constitute formal, congressional support of colonization. Although many of the legislators were supportive of removing free blacks from areas where whites resided, dissent had already been registered for giving public land or money to free blacks when the same was not done for whites.[44]

The ACS continued to memorialize the government for support, the results of which included either deliberation without a decision or the commission of more, and longer, reports on colonization. An 1827 ACS memorial to the House of Representatives was referred to the Select Committee on the Suppression of the Slave Trade. In response, Representative Charles Fenton Mercer from Virginia drafted the Select Committee's report on the Memorial, publishing a 294-page document on April 7, 1830. Mercer detailed the gains of the movement, described the growth of the Liberia colony, provided quotations from eminent figures in support of colonization, and presented official documents from colonization groups, including tables of emigration statistics and a map. A similar memorial was presented in the Senate, where after some debate, that body refused to send the memorial to a committee.[45] In 1843 the Commerce Committee of the US House of Representatives published a report of more than a thousand pages in response to an ACS memorial from the previous year.[46] Much of the report was gleaned from materials printed by the ACS in their newspaper, *African Repository*. In the years following the creation of the ACS, colonizationists were building a vast archive of supportive material and sharing it through newspapers and the appendices to their memorials. If the grounds for passing legislation were based on the quantity, and not the quality, of information provided to Congress, it is likely that Congress would have passed a bill in support of emigration.

But the volume of anecdotes, statistics, and letters of support failed to generate significant traction with Congress. By the later 1850s, the ACS had become "moribund" and "an old fogy affair."[47] During the era of Lincoln's rise to national prominence, the effectiveness of memorials, reports, and speeches decreased even further from an already-low level of impact on national policy. The communicative processes of colonizationists' policy argumentation—where speeches led to memorials, which often led to reports, which led to longer reports—lacked rhetorical force in the public discourse of slavery. Colonizationists were active communicators but had failed to translate advocacy into significant money, policies, or territory.

Lincoln's Second Annual Message: Compensated Emancipation and Colonization as the Solution to Sectional Tension

Lincoln's peculiar proposal operated at the intersection of colonization speeches and reports, offering more specificity and detail than previous colonization speakers while also using less data and with more explanation than colonization reports. The genre of the Annual Message facilitated this interaction of discourse types. As Karlyn Kohrs Campbell and Kathleen Hall Jamieson explain, an Annual Message offers "public mediations on values" while also assessing facts in the service of policy recommendations.[48] The ratios of these functions within a particular Annual Message illuminate the interests and skill of the individual president. In his second Annual Message, Lincoln's proposal developed in three ways. First, Lincoln naturalized the bonds of union rather than emphasizing separation through his discussion of territory. Second, Lincoln observed that sacrifice from all members of society—North and South—would be required to maintain this union. These two moves established a foundation based on mutuality and practicality that authorized the third move, Lincoln's advocacy for colonization as a means to relieve the potential anxieties of whites and blacks coexisting in a free society.

On the question of territory and colonization, Lincoln played the most significant role of any president since Monroe. Most of Lincoln's work as president that concerned where free blacks would be transported occurred in private. Lincoln's cabinet included three strong colonization advocates: Edward Bates (attorney general), Montgomery Blair (postmaster general), and Caleb Smith (secretary of the interior). Additionally, Lincoln's minister to Guatemala, Elisha Crosby, engaged in secret talks with leaders from that country and Honduras about creating a free black colony in their countries. Not surprisingly, those leaders were unreceptive and asked why the colony would not be created in the American West. Crosby's talks occurred in March of 1861, and one month later Lincoln met with Ambrose Thompson, who claimed to have several thousand acres of land in Chiriquí on the Isthmus of Panama (then part of New Granada, now in Columbia).[49] Blair approached Mexico about starting a colony in the Yucatan Peninsula.[50] Behind the scenes Lincoln was pursuing a variety of avenues related to where free blacks could be colonized. At the same time, fighting at Fort Sumter escalated the tensions between North and South. Some took the conflict as an opportunity to pursue options for where to send "contraband" blacks captured during the fighting.[51] For Lincoln, the year 1861 was marked by his private efforts to secure territory for the colonization of free blacks and a very public fight by Southern states to secure territory for the enslavement of blacks.

The Civil War changed the context for Lincoln's colonization advocacy, which was evident in the way that Lincoln used the concept of territory. The subject of territory enabled Lincoln to discuss compensated emancipation and colonization as parts of the solution to the war. Lincoln constructed the United States as a territory that was naturally united and thus not easily divisible by the actions of humans. Lincoln began by asserting that the essential elements of a country are "its territory, its people, and its laws." "The territory is the only part of which is of certain durability," Lincoln stated. The individuals engaged in the war will not outlive the territory, a point that Lincoln punctuated by quoting Ecclesiastes 1:4: "One generation passeth away and another generation cometh, but the earth abideth forever."[52] The nature of this enduring territory did not allow for easy division and separation. Lincoln quoted at length from his first inaugural address to argue for the "total inadequacy of disunion as a remedy for the differences between the people of the two sections." In the first inaugural Lincoln argued, "Physically speaking, we can not separate. We can not remove our respective sections from each other nor build an impassable wall between them." The quoted portion of the First Inaugural included an analogy to further his point about the natural connection between North and South: "A husband and wife may be divorced and go out of the presence and beyond the reach of each other, but the different parts of our country can not do this."[53] In addition to the quoted parts of the first Inaugural, Lincoln offered another reason against disunion. Lincoln engaged in a lengthy description of the practicable problems of dividing a nation, specifically as it relates to terrain, resources, and trade. Even if Americans wanted to dissolve the Union, he reasoned, "There is no line, straight or crooked, suitable for a national boundary upon which to divide."[54] The sum of Lincoln's logic was that the United States as a territory could not be divided; therefore, another remedy to differences must be found.

Lincoln positioned sectionalism as a violation of natural and practical considerations, making union appear to be the only choice. In the United States, land was connected to more land, with no easy way to make a clean break. If the United States was a natural, unbreakable territory, as Lincoln's reasoning would have his audience believe, then other options ought to be pursued to alleviate the problems between the regions. Lincoln himself offered options by way of a transition to his proposed constitutional amendments:

> Our national strife springs not from our permanent part; not from the land we inhabit; not from our national homestead. There is no possible severing of this but would multiply and not mitigate evils among us. In all its adaptations and aptitudes it demands union and abhors separation. In fact, it would ere long force reunion, however much of blood and treasure the separation might have cost. Our strife pertains to ourselves—to the passing generations of men—and it can without convulsion be hushed forever with the passing of one generation.[55]

The impermanent part from which the national strife sprang was slavery. Lincoln refashioned the notion of territory to address the crisis of sectionalism and to establish the foundation for his proposed constitutional amendments. Lincoln's territory arguments made no reference to colonization, but his reasoning responded to colonizationist thinking in important ways. Unlike previous colonizationists, who framed territory as a matter of difference, division, and fear, Lincoln argued that separation would cost too much in "blood and treasure." Lincoln's efforts to make his audience of legislators feel naturally, reasonably, and inextricably linked by the land they inhabited built a foundation of union. If the land could be seen as a source of unity, rather than division, then the compromise measures he would later propose might also seem natural and reasonable.

Colonizationists always billed their endeavor as a compromise, one that would easily fit with the principles of both emancipationists and slaveholders. Pro-colonization arguments often appealed to self-evidence, as if to say, "Who wouldn't want to support this?" Such an approach was possible among some white audiences when the policy concerned only free blacks, as the argument could be made that removing that population advanced both antislavery and proslavery interests. Proceeding from his discussion of the nation as indivisible territory, Lincoln offered his solution to the ills of the Union in the form of three constitutional amendments. Lincoln's first two constitutional amendments proposed 1) ending slavery by 1900 and compensating the states that ended slavery with bonds based on the slave population according to the census, and 2) allowing slaves who fought for the Union to be free immediately and the slaveholder compensated so long as they were not disloyal to the nation. The third amendment was the shortest and least specific, part of which read, "Congress may appropriate money and otherwise provide for colonizing free colored persons with their own consent at any place or places without the United States."[56] Unlike the previous amendments, the third contains more deference to Lincoln's audience. Congress *may* appropriate funds for colonization. Free blacks *"with their own consent"* could seek support for removal to another country. For whites who could not contemplate living equally among blacks, these conditional statements provided potential relief from the anxieties of racial equality. For those who believed in racial equality, Lincoln's third amendment could be dismissed, because it failed to mandate colonization. Both compensated emancipation and colonization challenged slaveholders' views on the necessity of slavery for their economic livelihood, while also challenging abolitionists' views on the necessity of immediately ending slavery to recognize the rights of those in bondage. The amendments could easily offend Northern and Southern white audiences that Lincoln addressed.

Lincoln viewed these constitutional amendments as compromises that required mutual sacrifice. Lincoln stated,

> Some would perpetuate slavery; some would abolish it suddenly and without compensation; some would abolish it gradually and with compensation: some would remove the freed people from us, and some would retain them with us; and yet there are other minor diversities.... By mutual concession we should harmonize and act together. This would be compromise, but it would be compromise among friends and not with the enemies of the Union.[57]

Lincoln's proposals to end slavery and pay slaveholders for their lost property went further than most colonizationists were willing to go. Recall Clay's insistence in his 1827 speech to the ACS: "The Society, composed of free men, concerns itself only with the free."[58] Unlike Clay, Lincoln could not reasonably claim that his plans would not compromise the principles of either abolitionists or slaveholders. Quite the opposite. Lincoln significantly enlarged the population affected by his policy compared to colonization and, in so doing, raised the barrier for widespread support of his plan. Lincoln's shift from compromise-as-mutual-ease to compromise-as-mutual-concession meant that both sides would sacrifice and, by extension, that neither side could claim a total victory over the other. This shift was by no means the obvious or predetermined choice. No solution that either supported emancipation or treated blacks as property would be agreeable to both sides. Lincoln asserted that the nation could not be divided and that compromise would be difficult. Much like his arguments about territory and the natural connection between North and South, Lincoln's claims about mutual concession emphasized unity over division. From this "mutual concession," Lincoln set out to make another extraordinary argument for a colonizationist, that compensated emancipation paired with colonization was a beneficial policy for the whole nation.

Lincoln's arguments about the time frame and cost of his plan illuminate the peculiar balance he attempted to strike between North and South in his proposal. With regard to timing, colonizationists presumed that their plan was needed and available immediately. Lincoln made timing a much more complicated issue with his proposals for compensated emancipation and the end of slavery. In Lincoln's plan, slavery would be illegal by 1900. He argued that this date was "both just and economical," a phrase that could be used to summarize Lincoln's overall effort at compromise in the second Annual Message.[59] The justness of the proposal was not directed to blacks, but to the whites on either side of the slavery issue. For slavery's defenders, Lincoln rhetorically recognized the anxieties of compensated emancipation. "The emancipation will be unsatisfactory to the advocates of perpetual slavery," Lincoln surmised, but he argued that "the length of time should greatly mitigate their dissatisfaction."[60] For abolitionists, Lincoln reminded them that each state could begin compensated emancipation at its own leisure; 1900 was simply the final deadline. Abolitionists "will hail the prospect of emancipation, but will deprecate the length of time," Lincoln acknowledged. However, he noted additional advantages to allowing some flexibility in emancipation. "The time spares both races from the evils of sudden derangement,"[61] by which Lincoln implied that whites and blacks would need to adjust, albeit gradually, to the new social reality of free blacks (and only free blacks) within their state borders. Eventually, future generations would grow up unburdened by the prejudices of the past. From the inception of the colonization movement, arguments about "expediency" framed the movement in immediate terms: colonization must and can happen immediately. When paired with the bold plan of compensated emancipation and colonization, Lincoln's elongated notion of time allowed the immediate necessity of action to remain while also noting that both races would need time to "spare" them from the difficulties of emancipation.

Having tamped down the fears that his plan required either immediate or indefinite emancipation, Lincoln turned to perhaps the most difficult argument for his plan, or any plan related to colonization: the cost. Colonizationists rarely focused their advocacy on cost. To be clear, colonizationists certainly appealed to Congress and private donors for funds. But they rarely made detailed arguments about the financial costs and benefits of colonization. In the few moments in which they did so, as in Clay's 1827 speech, the math was fairly simple. According to Clay, colonization would cost only $20 per person, with an annual expenditure "no larger than $120,000."[62] More typical of colonization discourse were general requests for financial support framed by appeals that described the cost as a "reasonable exertion" or "moderate effort," particularly in light of the "moral fitness" that financiers would feel when free blacks were relocated to their homeland in Africa.[63] Like so much of colonization advocacy, the issue of cost lacked realistic assessment, and more often than not, focused on the morality of supporting colonization.

Lincoln's purpose and context necessitated a peculiar approach to discussing the cost of any solution to the problems of slavery. Compensated emancipation was a much larger proposal than was colonizing free blacks only. But the stakes for Lincoln were also higher than they had been for other colonizationists. A civil war had begun. With this as the context for his remarks, Lincoln compared the cost of compensated emancipation to the cost of war, rather than considering the cost of colonization an isolated matter. Lincoln's cost-benefit analysis began with a wordy aphorism: "Certainly it is not so easy to pay something as it is to pay nothing, but it is easier to pay a large sum than a larger one."[64] This general sentiment was then applied to the current situation in the United States. "The war requires large sums, and requires them at once," Lincoln argued. The amendments he proposed "would require no ready cash, nor the bonds even any faster than the emancipation progresses."[65] The cost could be spread out over time due to the nature of the payment (bonds) and the individual timeframes for implementation adopted by each state. Beyond the money, Lincoln also noted the cost of human life that could be saved under his proposed amendments. His plan "will cost no blood, no precious life. It will be worth saving both."⁶⁶ The war served as Lincoln's backdrop, which allowed costs—both financial and human—to be considered in terms that would more deeply resonate with a white population during the Civil War than with that same population during times of peace.

The cost of Lincoln's proposal did not focus solely on the war. A secondary line of reasoning analyzed seven decades of US population growth, claiming that the nation could reap the benefits bestowed upon large nations and bear the cost of emancipated compensation. Lincoln supplied a table that showed the rate of population increase in the United States from 1790 until 1860. The data, Lincoln observed, showed "an average decennial increase of 34.60 per cent in population."⁶⁷ Given that this rate of growth never wavered more than 2 percent in either direction, Lincoln then provided a table that projected the total population of the country in ten-year intervals up to 1930. Lincoln concluded, "These figures show that our country may be as populous as Europe now is at some point between 1920 and 1930.... if we do not ourselves relinquish the chance by the folly and evils of disunion or by long and exhausting war springing from the only great element of national discord among us."⁶⁸ Lincoln presumed the benefits of growth by comparing the United States to the European continent. He drew a fine point, however, about how the nation pays for its debts—war or otherwise—with an analogy:

> If we had allowed our old national debt to run at 6 per cent annum, simple interest, from the end of our revolutionary struggle until to-day, without paying anything on either principal or interest, each man of us would owe less upon that debt now than each man owed upon it then; and this because our increase of men through the whole period has been greater than 6 per cent—has run faster than the interest on the debt.⁶⁹

"Thus," Lincoln concluded, "time alone relieves a debtor nation, so long as its population increases faster than unpaid interest accumulates on its debt."⁷⁰ Lincoln reasoned that war was imminent and costly; compensated emancipation was temporally flexible and less costly in life and money. The specificity of cost and the elongation of the time frame made Lincoln's peculiar proposal unlike any colonization discourse that preceded it.

After an exhaustive accounting of the benefits of compensated emancipation, Lincoln turned to his "third article"—colonization. He was quick to state that the proposed amendment "does not oblige, but merely authorizes, Congress to aid in colonizing such as may consent."⁷¹ David Zarefsky notes that the peroration of the second Annual Message, which followed Lincoln's discussion of colonization, is multivocal in the ways that it can be read very differently in its original context versus later eras. Lincoln's brief section on colonization was multivocal in another way, providing a range of possible meanings within the original context. The multivocality in the moment could demonstrate Lincoln's skill or failure as a policy advocate, depending upon which path into the speech one follows.

One interpretation of Lincoln's support for colonization is that his discourse was an earnest effort to support colonization. Lincoln had long advocated colonization, and his statements in the second Annual Message could reflect the wisdom of a thoughtful advocate. This interpretation is supported by historians like Philip Shaw Paludan, who sees colonization "not as Lincoln's *plan* but as *one* of Lincoln's *plans*."[72] Lincoln made it clear that the free black population would not be required to resettle in Africa and was welcome to stay in the United States. "And yet," Lincoln opined, "I wish to say there is an objection urged against free colored persons remaining in the country which is largely imaginary, if not sometimes malicious."[73] Lincoln did not need to agree with the racist sentiments toward free blacks to know that it existed and could cause considerable problems if there was not an avenue to relieve that potential anxiety, for whites and blacks alike. This interpretation understands Lincoln as a policy realist, one who skillfully navigated the rough terrain of the early 1860s. As such, colonization was a necessary element of his proposal because it provided some relief for those members of Lincoln's audience for whom the prospect of living among free blacks would disqualify the president's proposal as a viable solution. Compensated emancipation alone could not address these prevailing racists' ideologies, at least not for the current generation. Thus, Lincoln's support of colonization was short on words and long on significance to potential success of his plan.

A second interpretation questions whether Lincoln's support for colonization was merely a ruse to create more support for total emancipation. Given the careful financial breakdown that Lincoln provided for compensated emancipation, his discussion of colonization was markedly void of such analysis. Even more, as David Zarefsky argues, Lincoln made arguments that "subvert" his supposed support for colonization.[74] Lincoln mentioned that he had received applications from free blacks seeking colonization but that "several of the Spanish-American republics have protested against the sending of such colonies to their respective territories."[75] Zarefsky argues that statements like this, when combined with Lincoln's proposed amendment authorizing but not obligating Congress to support colonization, meant that the president "comes close to acknowledging that his scheme will not work." Lincoln's advocacy was a "stalking-horse" for his preference for total emancipation over colonization.[76] In this interpretation Lincoln's support of colonization is seen as an appeasement strategy to quell the concerns of anxious whites who, regardless of their benevolence, were concerned about the large increase in free blacks that the president's plan would create. Or, in a slightly different light, colonization could be seen as a straw target offered by the president to make his main proposal appear stronger. The lack of argumentative development (compared to his breakdown of compensated emancipation earlier in the message) and the fence-sitting about the potential to acquire the necessary territory for settler colonists allowed the president to seemingly, but not seriously, address the concerns by some whites about the rapid increase in the free black population.

Lincoln's support for colonization in the second Annual Message could be a boon for colonizationists, regardless of interpretation. If one received Lincoln's message as legitimate support, then the benefit to colonizationists would come from claiming the public support of the president. Paludan's perspective, which holds that "the president advocated colonization and honestly believed it," supports the pro-colonization interpretation.[77] If one adopts Zarefsky's view that Lincoln undercut his own support for colonization, then it is still arguable that possibly tepid public support for colonization from the president was still *public support from the president*. What was undeniable was that Lincoln argued for three constitutional amendments, one of which sought funds and support for colonization. Such a move had not been made by a US president before and would not be made by any president after.

Conclusion

Before issuing the preliminary Emancipation Proclamation, Lincoln hosted a delegation of black leaders at the White House on August 14, 1862. The subject of the meeting was colonization. As with the second Annual Message that he would pen nearly four months later, Lincoln emphasized the inalterability of certain situations related to race. However, unlike the second Annual Message's focus on unity, this speech defined racial incompatibility as a "fact." From this fact, Lincoln declared, "It is better for us both, therefore, to be separated."[78] Colonization, Lincoln assured them, "would open a wide door for many to be made free."[79] Lincoln spoke for an hour to the assembled committee and left no time for their response. He asked the committee "to let me know whether this can be done or not."⁸⁰ The response from the free black population was overwhelmingly critical. One black man from Philadelphia wrote to the president, "This is our country as much as it is yours, and we will not leave."⁸¹ Frederick Douglass responded that the president spoke like "an itinerant Colonization lecturer, showing all his inconsistencies, his pride of race and blood, his contempt for Negroes and his canting hypocrisy."⁸² Despite the criticism, Lincoln kept colonization in the second Annual Message.

Lincoln's commitment to colonization, even with the knowledge that many free blacks rejected it, reveals how the deliberative discourse of white colonizationists concealed from their view the diasporic discourses of free blacks. For all of Lincoln's efforts to unite the white Northerners and white Southerners in the second Annual Message, and for all of the careful economic analysis he provided regarding the cost of compensated emancipation, the president reverted back to controvertible claims about the self-evident harm of difference and the self-evident virtue of colonization. There was little to no acknowledgment of the complex negotiation of belonging and fleeing that free blacks expressed in diasporic discourses. Lincoln's peculiar proposal was meticulous in its attention to policy details, which mattered little when placed in the larger social and political maelstrom of American life during the Civil War.

Lincoln's peculiar proposal failed. His three proposed constitutional amendments went nowhere, leaving Lincoln to sign the final Emancipation Proclamation on January 1, 1863. For the next two years, Lincoln withheld public comment about colonization but worked behind the scenes to develop colonization plans.⁸³ In 1862, prior to the Annual Message, Lincoln's administration entered into a contract with Bernard Kock, who claimed to own land on the island of Île à Vache (off the coast of "Hayti"). The results were disastrous, with Lincoln canceling the contract on April 16, 1863, and ordering naval vessels to recover 350 settler colonists in February of 1864.⁸⁴

To the committee of free blacks two years prior, Lincoln had promised that emigrants "shall not be wronged."⁸⁵ However, in the case of Île à Vache, free blacks had been wronged, arriving to an island without shelter or food. Of the $600,000 allocated for the colonization venture, only $38,329.93 was spent on settler colonists. The rest of the funds covered expenses and salaries for white administrators involved with the project.⁸⁶ On March 4, 1865, the US Navy's *Marcia C. Day* set sail from the island with the surviving immigrants. John Hay, Lincoln's private secretary, noted in his diary, "I am glad the President has sloughed off that idea of colonization. I have always thought it as a hideous and barbarous humbug."[87] The failure at Île à Vache was the last effort, public or private, that Lincoln made toward colonization. Although Lincoln made the most specific and well-reasoned policy argument for colonization, his peculiar proposal was marred by his effort to hold as coequal the competing ideologies of equality and antiblack racism. Like many colonizationists before him, Lincoln believed that such colonization could forestall disunion and violence. It could not.

Lincoln's second Annual Message ended with the following peroration, a passage Foner deems "the most eloquent ever composed by an American president."[88]

> Is it doubted, then, that the plan I propose, if adopted, would shorten the war, and thus lessen its expenditure of money and of blood? Is it doubted that it would restore the national authority and national prosperity and perpetuate both indefinitely? Is it doubted that we here—Congress and Executive—can secure its adoption? Will not the good people respond to a united and earnest appeal from us? Can we, can they, by any other means so certainly or so speedily assure these vital objects? We can succeed only by concert. It is not "Can any of us imagine better?" but "Can we all do better?" Object whatsoever is possible, still the question recurs, "Can we do better?" The dogmas of the quiet past are inadequate to the stormy present. The occasion is piled high with difficulty, and we must rise with the occasion. As our case is new, so we must think anew and act anew. We must disenthrall ourselves, and then we shall save our country.

These lines are representative of a Lincoln that lives in the American public memory. A Lincoln that is perceived as eloquent, moral, sober, and hopeful. At the time, the *Continental Monthly* suggested that Lincoln's words be "committed to memory and constantly recalled by every man."[89] Perhaps. But more certain is that the overwhelming majority of the second Annual Message was not eloquent or likely to be committed to memory. The vast majority of it reported the mundane details of the government's previous year. It was a failed attempt at compromise and was, by the standards of many people at the time, and certainly many more people today, morally questionable at the least.

Conclusion

Middle Passages, Emigration, and Peculiar Legacies

The peculiar rhetorics examined in the preceding chapters make the case for an expanded view of colonization's particular significance in American public discourse about race in the nineteenth century. Part of colonization's contribution to rhetorical history concerns the powerful white politicians who attempted to persuade other powerful white politicians that colonization was good for the nation. While most scholarly attention has focused on colonization as a political movement led by whites, the rhetorical complexity of the movement is often elided in favor of a narrative of inevitable failure.[1] This book's appreciation of peculiar rhetorics brings into sharper focus the multiple, shifting, and often conflicting concerns accounted for in the deliberative discourses of Henry Clay, Elias B. Caldwell, and Abraham Lincoln. Clay's and Caldwell's peculiar argumentation at the creation of the ACS failed to resolve the central tension between supporters of slavery and supporters of freedom. Lincoln seemed keenly aware of the tension but, through his pragmatically constructed peculiar proposal of compensated emancipation, sought a compromise based on mutual sacrifice. Separated by almost fifty years, the discourses of Clay and Caldwell and Lincoln shared the common political goal of alleviating sectional tensions among the white population through colonization. That ultimate goal was not achieved, but the story of colonization told in this book is not one of predetermined failure. Rather, this book explains how colonization was a story of rhetorical making and unmaking.

Perhaps more importantly, the chapters between the beginning and end of colonization explicate peculiar rhetorics of black experiences with colonization. Whereas Clay and Lincoln are well-known figures in US history and public address, the texts and rhetors explored in chapters 2, 3, and 4 are not. The rhetors and texts examined in these chapters complicate the African American rhetorical canon, particularly the relationship between the discourses of liberation and freedom. In chapter 2, the peculiar voice of the "free people of colour of the District of Columbia" provided a prism through which to explore the instability and variety of interpretations of the colonization scheme. Who were the free people of colour of the District of Columbia? Were they black? Was their message empowering? In chapter 3, Louis Sheridan's peculiar planning explored his vacillations between Afro-Pessimism and black optimism as he negotiated with the ACS for transportation to Liberia. How is Sheridan's rhetorical prowess properly contextualized when he negotiated with the ACS? What should we make of his lack of public advocacy against slavery? In chapter 4, Hilary Teage's peculiar obligations constituted a settler colonist civic identity for an audience that was *apart from* US white culture but also seeking to be *a part of* a nation in which US principles of liberty and equality would finally apply to blacks. How did Teage's vision for settler colonist civic identity interact with notions of freedom and liberation for African Americans in the United States? The peculiar rhetorics examined in these chapters introduce new questions, concerns, and contexts to African American rhetoric. In so doing, that diasporic corpus begins to look and sound more diverse, representing the wide-ranging, complex, and nuanced black experience. In the space remaining, I offer a brief sketch of the peculiar legacy of colonization.

The end of the Civil War and the subsequent passage of the Reconstruction Amendments changed, but did not end, the colonization movement. Terminology shifted. "Colonization," with its ties to the white-led movement of the previous decades, was replaced by the more empowering "emigration," which some African American leaders adopted. What did not shift were some basic principles of colonization's various stakeholders. The antiblack assumptions that motivated some to support colonization did not dissipate with the passage of the Fourteenth Amendment. Many whites still sought separation and segregation from the black population. The disdain for such racism and desire for true liberty that led many blacks to support colonization also remained after the Civil War. The broken promises of freedom in the United States and appeals to black empowerment kept the dream of Liberia in the imagination of many free and newly freed black people. It certainly seemed more *possible* that a black person could attain life, liberty, and property in a post–Civil War United States, but to many it did not seem more *probable*. Thus, other options, such as emigration, remained open.

Two moments of emigration fervor that occurred in the aftermath of the Civil War revealed the ways in which postbellum rhetorics of emigration interacted with and departed from the antebellum peculiar rhetorics of colonization. The post-Reconstruction emigration movement, led by Henry McNeil Turner, included the ACS while it also fostered the creation of black emigration companies chartered by African Americans. In the 1910s and 1920s, the Back-to-Africa movement, led by Marcus Garvey, emphasized the universal improvement of all Africans. A brief accounting of these two movements, with their vocal leaders and their equally vocal (and famous) detractors, provides a glimpse into still more peculiar rhetorics connected to colonization, emigration, and racial identity.

Henry McNeal Turner and Post-Reconstruction Emigration

Turner became a powerful advocate for emigration as Reconstruction began to wane. Turner was born in 1834, in South Carolina, the oldest son of freeborn parents. He converted to Christianity at a camp meeting in the 1840s and made preaching his vocation in 1853. Like many African American leaders, Turner's interest in emigration began with Haiti. Writing to Massachusetts senator Charles Sumner, Turner professed that Haiti seemed like a good "resting place for the Negro's feet."[2] By 1875 Turner turned his attention to Africa. Once federal troops withdrew from South Carolina in 1877, Turner became part of a group that chartered the Liberian Exodus Joint Stock Steamship Company. Owned and operated by African Americans, this company had the same aims as the ACS, without the influence of antiblack actors. Turner's outspokenness encouraged the creation of other such groups in Arkansas and Oklahoma. "Throughout his career as an emigrationist," James Campbell writes, Turner "argued that erecting a powerful, independent nation in Africa was the only way to rehabilitate black manhood, to restore African Americans' self-respect, and secure the respect of other races and nations."[3] Turner made such arguments up until his death in 1915.

Turner's commitment to emigration shared with colonization its abject failures and lack of practicality. Clay, Caldwell, and Lincoln all made arguments related to expediency and practicability of colonization. All colonization societies were in the business of fundraising thus, demonstrating the viability of a scheme was imperative. Unlike free black colonizationists in the antebellum era, Turner argued for the practicability of colonization using an argument for reparations. In an 1893 speech, Turner claimed, "This nation justly, righteously and divinely owes us for work and services rendered, billions of dollars, and if we cannot be treated as American people, we should ask for five hundred million dollars, at least, to begin an emigration somewhere."[4] Like previous colonization supporters, Turner never saw that sum of money materialize.

Rather, the emigration movement confronted the recurring issues of rampant disease, insufficient funding, and poor planning. In 1878 the Liberia Exodus Joint Stock Steamship Company sent its first, and only, ship to Liberia. A group of 206 men, women, and children boarded the *Azor*, a steam-powered bark the group purchased, while ten thousand well-wishers stood on the docks to bid them farewell. Twenty-three passengers died of measles before arriving in Liberia, and dozens more died of malaria shortly after arriving.[5] This kind of tragedy was not limited to Turner's group. The Liberian Exodus Arkansas Colony was composed of a few hundred would-be emigres who sold most of their possessions and traveled from Arkansas to New York City, where they expected to travel to Liberia with the support of the ACS. More than fifty years after Sheridan (chapter 3) negotiated for agreeable terms with the ACS, the willing group from Arkansas similarly struggled with the ACS to emigrate to Liberia. In 1891 the group found themselves without a ship or any accommodations. It took the ACS two more years to raise funds to sponsor the group, but by that time most in the group had either returned home or become part of the local community. The effort was such a failure that the ACS ended its efforts to support emigration of blacks to Liberia. It would help only skilled workers find transportation to Liberia. The absence of slavery allowed for blacks to be more empowered in creating emigration groups or deciding for themselves that they would make the journey to Africa. But it did not greatly change the impracticability of the journey.

In an effort to acquire the necessary resources to make emigration practical, Turner aligned himself with a faction of American legislators who still believed in the inferiority of blacks. In 1890 South Carolina senator Matthew Butler proposed a bill that would provide five million dollars for the removal of blacks to Africa conditional upon their renouncing US citizenship and attaining citizenship in their new country.[6] The white southern support for the bill noted that this kind of effort had been supported by such esteemed characters as Clay, Daniel Webster, and Lincoln, while it also departs from some previous schemes insofar as the removal to Africa would be voluntary. "If the bill meant compulsory expatriation I would fight it to the death," Turner stated, "but as it is voluntary upon the part of the negro let it pass as soon as possible."[7] Curiously, Butler claimed that his bill was meant as "a piece of sarcasm" meant to force northerners to confront the hypocrisy of their support for blacks from a distance. Turner's support was yet another instance of blacks aligning with white men of odious motivations in order to achieve a desirable end. On a deeper level, Butler saw his bill as a subversive act, while others took it seriously, speaking to the peculiar political position of colonization. The Counter Memorial discussed in chapter 2 represented this instability in numerous ways. Butler's bill was simply an instance of the peculiar performance of colonization discourse taking shape within emigration discourse.

Like colonizationists before them, emigrationists like Turner were criticized for the betraying the fight for equality in the United States. A dominant theme in both colonization and emigration discourse was that Africa was the homeland, even for African Americans. This perspective invited criticism from the abolitionists, who had, prior to the Civil War, argued that colonization was simply an effort to keep rights from blacks. Frederick Douglass's vigilant attacks on colonization, even decades after its viability peaked, seemed to suggest that he was concerned about the likelihood that the peculiar scheme would result in a pernicious afterlife. Speaking about the "future of the colored people of this country" in 1883, on the occasion of the twenty-first anniversary of emancipation in the District of Columbia, Douglass argued that three solutions had been adopted: colonization, "extinction through poverty, disease, and death," and, lastly, "assimilation and unification."[8] Among Douglass's trio of solutions, colonization seemed to occupy the middle ground as being neither death nor full integration. As he had done for many decades prior, Douglass remained clear on his position on colonization, stating, "I will say that I do not look for colonization either in or out of the United States. Africa is too far off, even if we desire to go there, which we do not. . . . Removal to any of the territories is out of the question."[9] Instead, Douglass contended, "Assimilation and not isolation is our true policy and our natural destiny."[10]

The tensions of peculiar rhetoric remained a part of the deliberative and diasporic discourses concerning the social location of black people. Turner embraced the African diaspora as a concept, but his rhetoric conveyed the certainty that was characteristic of deliberative discourse. Opponents of Turner remained unsettled by efforts to transports the black population anywhere. Colonization was never peculiar for Douglass and other abolitionists; it was always viewed as a ruse, a trick to avoid granting full and unfettered rights to African Americans. Additionally, emancipation, Douglass declared, was "a stupendous fraud."[11] Even with the end of slavery and the passage of the Reconstruction Amendments, colonization and emigration lingered in the United States with enough seriousness that Douglass and others felt it necessary to continue to denounce it. Douglass's view reflected the anxieties of diasporic discourse, the ever-present struggle to belong and flee.

Marcus Garvey and the Back-to-Africa Movement of the Early Twentieth Century

Garvey picked up the mantle of leading emigrationists when Turner died. In the 1910s and 1920s, Garvey's Back-to-Africa movement aimed to uplift all blacks. Garvey, a Jamaican immigrant to the United States, was the charismatic leader of the Universal Negro Improvement Association and advocated that blacks everywhere work to reclaim Africa from European colonizers. Garveyism, as it was sometimes called, was most prominent in the United States from approximately 1914 to 1927. During that time, Garvey chartered his own company—Black Star Line—to facilitate emigration. Garveyism differed from colonization in its broader orientation; emigration was just one part of the broader mission of African empowerment. The movement was not led by white people telling the blacks where to go; it was led by blacks telling the whites where to go.

Garvey's emigration plans suffered from many of the same critiques levied against Turner and the white colonizationists of the antebellum era. Prominent black intellectual W. E. B. Du Bois feuded openly with Garvey. As Campbell describes, "To Du Bois, Garvey was everything that black America did not need in a race leader—a bombastic ill-educated 'demagog' with no understanding of history or the 'technic of civilization,' 'no business sense, nor flair for *real* organization."[12] Du Bois argued, "Marcus Garvey is, without doubt, the most dangerous enemy of the Negro race in America and in the world. He is either a lunatic or a traitor."[13] The politics of racial purity and sexuality implicated in chapter 2 emerged in Garvey's response to his critic. Du Bois was an "unfortunate mulatto who bewails every day the drop of Negro blood in his veins.... That is why he likes to dance with white people and dine with them and sometimes to sleep with them, because from his way of seeing things all that is black is ugly, and all that is white is beautiful."[14]

Garvey's plans also brought him into temporary alliances with antiblack racists. Garvey's American supporters—under the name of the Peace Movement of Ethiopia—worked with white supremacists to federally fund the "repatriation" of African Americans. This effort, undertaken in 1937, was called the Greater Liberia Act and was introduced by Senator Theodore

Bilbo from Mississippi. The act aimed to federally fund the removal of twelve million African Americans to help solve the nation's unemployment issues of the time. It was largely through Garveyism, and the peculiar policies that emerged in its wake, that from the period between World War I and World War II, colonization remained a part of the American discourse on race relations in the United States.

Garveyism also revealed the peculiar legacy of colonization within Liberia. Garvey's goal was to uplift all Africans through emigration to Liberia. However, within Liberia, a very clear hierarchy had been established in which the descendants of settler colonists from America, known as Americo-Liberians, held political power over the indigenous population. The peculiar obligations articulated by Hilary Teage and discussed in chapter 4 were superseded by a more odious synthesis of deliberative and diasporic discourses, namely, the oppression of the less powerful by those in power. In 1920 the population of Liberia was approximately five hundred thousand persons, about five thousand of whom were part of the settler-colonist caste. Americo-Liberians held nearly all of the major political offices in the nation. The representation of indigenous groups like the Kru, Bassa, or Vai, in high elected positions, was "the exception rather than the rule." This unequal representation of native voices in government was, in part, the product of a system that had been established in the 1870s in which indigenous groups paid the government $100 for up to two, nonvoting delegates to the national legislature. These delegates were often illiterate and required translation when they spoke to the larger assembly. M. K. Akpan states the unfortunate and obvious about indigenous representatives—"their ability to influence government policy towards securing economic and social improvement for their people . . . was slight."[15]

While the 1870 policy instituted social divisions into national politics, social divisions between settler colonists and indigenous populations predated the establishment of a politically independent Liberia. The colonial governor of Liberia reported in 1836 that "the marriage of a colonist with any one of the neighboring tribes was considered exceedingly disreputable and subjected the individual to the contempt of his fellow citizens."[16] At least one colonist openly maintained that the native Africans ought to be slaves to the colonists.[17] Even after Liberian independence was achieved, the fissure remained. However, he also recognized that "it would require on the part of the man of the least culture, strong moral courage to break through the strong prejudice against the intermarriage of the colonists and natives which prevails here among Americo-Liberians."[18]

The attitude persists even today. Helene Cooper, a Liberian by birth, writes in an April 6, 2008, *New York Times Magazine* article, "In Liberia, we are called the Congo People—my family and the rest of the freed American blacks who founded Liberia back in 1821. It is a somewhat derogatory term, used by the native Liberians.... We got the native Liberians back by calling them Country People—far more derogatory, in our eyes."[19] Thus, a political and social hierarchy took shape in Liberia that mirrored that which appeared in the United States, with settler colonists' descendents playing the role of the elite whites from whom their ancestors fled decades before, which could not be easily toppled by the introduction of even more emigrants.

Perhaps as a result of this contentious history, Garvey's efforts for *universal* improvement of Africans were first supported, then denounced, by the political and social elite in Liberia. One of the legacies of colonization was the tremendous economic hardship that settler colonists faced and that many Liberian citizens have not, even in the twenty-first century, overcome. So, when Garvey promised the Liberian government that he would raise funds for them in exchange for land on which to build facilities for new immigrants, the government agreed. But an influx of new immigrants and increased attention to indigenous groups would ultimately weaken the power held by the political elite. Even more, the United States government viewed Garveyism as an "apparently subversive movement" and communicated as much to the Liberian government. The public manifestation of this concern came with the selection of Du Bois as the representative of the United States at the inauguration of Liberian president C. D. B. King in 1924. One newspaper at the time argued that support for Garvey's new colonization scheme might "throttle us if we espouse it."[20] In his inaugural address, President King stated that it had been necessary "to take such concrete and effective steps as would show to our friendly territorial neighbors and the world at large, that Liberia was not in any way associated or in sympathy with any movement, no matter from what sources arising, which tends to intensify racial feelings of hatred and ill will."[21] Through his address the new president of Liberia intimated that Garvey's efforts were racist, a move achieved by reframing the universal improvement of black people as racial separatism rather than uplift. Edmund David Cronon contends that, with the refusal of the Liberian government, Garvey's Back-to-Africa movement was dead.[22]

Garvey's opponents were able to frame his efforts in a similar vein to previous colonization efforts, despite the presence of a charismatic black leader and transcendent appeals to universal improvement. Although Garvey has often been called the "black Moses," his opponents seemed to treat him more like a black Delilah. Garvey wanted to lead his people to the promised land, but many African Americans, white Americans, and Liberians seemed worried that supporting colonization was akin to allowing the Philistines to shave Samson's head. If the Back-to-Africa movement succeeded, the power of each of these groups would be lost. What seems to cut across speakers, contexts, and generations is an underlying tension between power and powerlessness in peculiar rhetorics of colonization, regardless of the race of the rhetor or the universality of the appeals.

It was curious that Du Bois figured so prominently into the demise of Garveyism, as Du Bois himself moved to Africa—to Ghana—in 1961. After decades of advocating Pan-Africanism, denouncing supposed hucksters like Garvey, and moving further to the political Left, Du Bois eventually joined the Communist Party and left the United States. He could not see the possibility of achieving the full guarantees of life, liberty, and the pursuit of happiness in the United States. Du Bois's journey shared less in common with African colonization than Garvey's on account of the former's individualistic approach to removal. No one else could have received the accommodations Du Bois received. Ghanaian president Kwame Nkrumah provided Du Bois with "substantial financial support" to pursue his *Encyclopedia Africana*.[23]

Du Bois's turn toward emigration, if only for himself and not as a general principle, was more like Sheridan than Teage. Sheridan's accomplishments and wealth could not make him an equal to his white peers in North Carolina. However, unlike Sheridan, Du Bois would ultimately receive the resources he needed to justify the move. Like Sheridan, Du Bois's experiences with white policy makers and business leaders left him pessimistic about the prospect for change in the United States. And although Du Bois seemed to engage in a radical critique of America, like Sheridan, his criticism lacked attention to the underclasses of blacks in America. In fact, Cedric Robinson argues that Du Bois was "blinded by the elitism of his class prerogative."[24] Nevertheless, on October 1, 1961, the ninety-three-year-old Du Bois applied for membership in the Communist Party of the United States and immediately departed for Ghana. On that day, he wrote: "Today, I have reached a firm conclusion. Capitalism cannot reform itself; it is doomed to self-destruction."[25] By triangulating race, class, and emigration in Du Bois's decision to emigrate, "the ambiguous conjuncture" in his treatment of emigration and colonization, despite his own participation in the act of removal, becomes clear.[26]

Neither Turner, Garvey, nor Du Bois would stand for the white movement known as colonization. Emigration was a movement for blacks, by blacks. But emigration bore the imprints of colonization, generating another iteration of a peculiar rhetoric. Black leaders who fought for equal rights in the United States saw emigration, even black-led efforts at worldwide racial uplift, as a concession of defeat. Emigrationist discourse was not peculiar in the same ways that Clay, "the free people of colour of the District of Columbia," Sheridan, Teage, or Lincoln were peculiar. Although peculiar rhetorics changed with their contexts, they continued to grapple with contemporaneous and enduring notions of rhetoric, race, agency, place, and rights.

The Peculiarity of Deliberative and Diasporic Discourses

Colonization played a central role in the American public discourse on race for more than fifty years. During that time, this contentious scheme was contested in deliberative and diasporic discourses by white and black colonizationists. Chapter 1 illustrated how peculiar argumentation manifested in the deliberative discourse of Clay and Caldwell. Clay's and Caldwell's peculiarity was evidenced by the odd ways in which they attempted to appeal to northern and southern audiences, while failing to address free blacks. This lack of engagement was part of the diasporic discourses of the black rhetors examined in the next three chapters. In chapter 2 the Counter Memorial of the free people of colour of the District of Columbia complicated the deliberative discourse of colonizationists by speaking in a peculiar voice. The range of possible meanings of the Counter Memorial illustrates the tension between belonging and fleeing that animates diasporic discourse. Chapter 3 examined the diasporic discourse of Louis Sheridan and his negotiation with the ACS. Sheridan's peculiar planning demonstrated the tension between Afro-Pessimist and black optimist theorizations of black subjectivity. The diasporic discourse of Hilary Teage, taken up in chapter 4, more fully embraced the deliberative elements of colonizationists. However, Teage's peculiar obligations revised deliberative discourse to account for the experience and context of settler colonists in Liberia. Returning to the deliberative discourse of white colonizationists, chapter 6 explored Lincoln's peculiar proposal in his second Annual Message. Lincoln operated between long-standing colonizationist arguments and contemporary exigencies to offer a potential solution to the racial and sectional hostilities. Thus, from 1816 until 1862, an array of peculiar rhetorics emerged from various approaches to deliberative and diasporic discourses.

The examination of peculiar rhetorics in this book demonstrates the value of a turn toward the middle. The public discourse of race has been and continues to be a maelstrom of rhetorical action. Attending to peculiarity or other manifestations of betweenness accounts for inflection, granularities, and movements of discourse that may otherwise be flattened out when read as static, a failure, and/or dichotomous. A turn toward the middle allows for reexamination of texts whose meanings have been settled or glossed by history. A turn toward the middle allows for more voices to enter the cacophony of public debate about race. A turn toward the middle allows for those voices to be unsettled, unsure, disappointed, or unclear. The process of understanding the rhetorics of race, while never finished or settled, ought to account for the complexity of racial issues. *Peculiar Rhetoric* intervenes not to begin or end the scholarly examination of the middle but to contribute to an approach that continuously opens racial discourse to rhetorical examination.

Notes

INTRODUCTION

1. "Notice," *National Intelligencer* (Washington), December 18, 1816, n.p. The *National Intelligencer* was a prominent newspaper in Washington, and its editors were ardent supporters of colonization. See chapter 2 for more about the significance of this newspaper in the colonization movement.

2. "The Meeting on the Colonization of Free Blacks," *National Intelligencer* (Washington), December 24, 1816, n.p.

3. P. J. Staudenraus, *The African Colonization Movement, 1816–1865* (New York: Columbia University Press, 1961), 30n14.

4. "Meeting on the Colonization of Free Blacks" (emphasis added).

5. "Meeting on the Colonization of Free Blacks."

6. A note on terminology: Peculiar rhetorics of colonization involve an array of people of different political and social positions. In general, I use the term "black" to describe a people marked as "other" by the logics of racism and the institution of slavery in the United States. Michelle M. Wright notes that defining blackness is difficult, because it is a "collective identity that intersects with many other collective identities" (3). Furthermore, I agree with Wright's claim that blackness is both a construct and a phenomenology. As a construct blackness can be "implicitly or explicitly defined as a shared set of physical and behavioral characteristics." As a phenomenology blackness is "imagined through individual perceptions in various ways depending on the context" (4). This book's examination of peculiar rhetorics shows how blackness was often defined and contested in the space between construct and phenomenology. In that betweenness, more precise articulations of blackness will be used to focus on a particular population and definition of blackness, such as free black, settler colonist, slave, "free people of colour of the District of Columbia," and indigenous African. When referring to areas of scholarly examination, I default to the field norms (e.g., African American rhetoric). Blackness provides the linguistic space to explore the contestation of race and power that is central to the peculiarity of colonization's discourse. Michelle M. Wright, *Physics of Blackness: Beyond the Middle Passage Epistemology* (Minneapolis: University of Minnesota Press, 2015).

7. Paul Gilroy, *The Black Atlantic: Modernity and Double Consciousness* (Cambridge: Harvard University Press, 1993), 1.

8. For example, Indiana created a new state constitution in 1851, which supported colonization, while also voiding all contracts with free blacks and creating fines for any white that hired black immigrants. See Brandon Mills, "'The United States of Africa': Liberian Independence and the Contested Meaning of a Black Republic," *Journal of the Early Republic* 34, no. 1 (2014): 96–97.

9. "Meeting on the Colonization of Free Blacks."

10. Staudenraus, *African Colonization Movement*, Appendix 1: 251.

11. Ferdinando Fairfax, "Plan for Liberating the Negroes within the United States," *American Museum* (Philadelphia), December 1790, 285. Fairfax attended the germinal meeting of the ACS.

12. Henry Noble Sherwood, "Paul Cuffe: The Redemption of Africa," *Journal of Negro History* 8, no. 2 (1923): 169.

13. "Colony of Free Blacks," *National Intelligencer* (Washington), December 14, 1816, n.p. This was also printed in "Chronicle," *Niles' Weekly Register* (Baltimore), December 14, 1816, 259. Gale L. Kenny provides an in-depth look into the northern missionary elements of colonization in "Race, Sympathy, and Missionary Sensibility in the New England Colonization Movement," in *New Directions in the Study of African American Recolonization*, ed. Beverly C. Tomek and Matthew J. Hetrick (Gainesville: University Press of Florida, 2017), 33–49.

14. In 1815 the Union Humane Society of Ohio called for common action and the removal of blacks away from elite whites. Henry Noble Sherwood, "The Formation of the American Colonization Society," *Journal of Negro History* 2, no. 3 (1917): 211.

In 1816 the Kentucky Colonization Society petitioned Congress for land "to be laid off as an asylum for all those Negroes and mulattoes who have been, and those who may hereafter be, emancipated within the United States." This petition reached the Congress on January 18, 1816, and was referred to the Committee on Public Lands. *Annals of Congress*, 14th Cong., 1st sess., 691.

15. Mercer first became aware of the secret journals after a night of drinking with fellow assemblymen, one of whom had participated in the secret session. C[harles] F[enton] Mercer, "Address of the Hon. Charles Fenton Mercer, at the Anniversary of the Am. Col. Society. January 18, 1853," *African Repository* 24, no. 5 (May 1853): 143. See also Douglas R. Egerton, *Charles Fenton Mercer and the Trial of National Conservatism* (Jackson: University Press of Mississippi, 1989), 105–7.

16. "Colony of Free Blacks," n.p. This was also printed in "Chronicle," 259.

17. Eric Burin, *Slavery and the Peculiar Solution: A History of the American Colonization Society* (Gainesville: University Press of Florida, 2005), 16; US Census Bureau, *A Century of Population Growth: From the First Census of the United States to the Twelfth* (Washington, DC: Government Printing Office, 1909), 133.

18. William Lloyd Garrison, *Thoughts on African Colonization* (1832; repr. New York: Arno Press and New York Times, 1968). Garrison's first issue of the *Liberator* included a rebuke of gradualism and moderation, both virtues heralded by colonizationists. "To the Public," *Liberator*, January 1, 1831, 1. Garrison's critique caused well-known activists Elizur Wright Jr., Amos A. Phelps, and Theodore Dwight Weld to quit the ACS. Burin, *Slavery and the Peculiar Solution*, 21.

19. Maria W. Stewart, "An Address Delivered at the African Masonic Hall, Boston, February 27, 1833," in *Pamphlets of Protest: An Anthology of Early African-American Protest Literature, 1790–1860*, ed. Richard Newman, Patrick Rael, and Phillip Lapansky (New York: Routledge, 2001), 126.

20. Frederick Douglass, "Colonizationist Measures: An Address Delivered in New York, New York, on 24 April 1849," in *The Frederick Douglass Papers*, Series One: Speeches, Debates, and Interviews, vol. 2, ed. John W. Blassingame (New Haven: Yale University Press, 1982), 163. Douglass delivered other addresses against colonization; see Douglass, "The Colonizationist Revival: An Address Delivered in Boston, Massachusetts, on 31 May 1849," in *The Frederick Douglass Papers*, Series One: Speeches, Debates, and Interviews, vol. 2, 203–17; and Douglass, "Henry Clay and Colonization Cant, Sophistry, and Falsehood: An Address Delivered in Rochester, New York, on 2 February 1851," in *The Frederick Douglass Papers*, Series One: Speeches, Debates, and Interviews, vol. 2, 311–25.

21. Thomas R. Dew, *Review of the Debate in the Virginia Legislature of 1831 and 1832* (Richmond: T. W. White, 1832), 80.

22. George Fitzhugh, *Sociology for the South; Or the Failure of Free Society* (Richmond: A. Morris, 1854), 288.

23. Philip C. Wander, "Salvation through Separation: The Image of the Negro in the American Colonization Society," *Quarterly Journal of Speech* 57, no. 1 (1971): 57.

24. Jacqueline Bacon, "'Acting as Freemen': Rhetoric, Race, and Reform in the Debate over Colonization in Freedom's Journal, 1827–1828," *Quarterly Journal of Speech* 93, no. 1 (2007): 61.

25. Stephen H. Browne, "Textual Style and Radical Critique in William Lloyd Garrison's Thoughts on African Colonization," *Communication Studies* 47, no. 3 (1996): 177.

26. Alisse Portnoy, *Their Right to Speak: Women's Activism in the Indian and Slave Debates* (Cambridge: Harvard University Press, 2009).

27. Ousmane K. Power-Greene, *Against Wind and Tide: The African American against the Colonization Movement* (New York: New York University Press, 2014).

28. David Zarefsky, "Presidential Rhetoric and the Power of Definition," *Presidential Studies Quarterly* 34, no. 3 (2004): 608.

29. Erik Doxtader, "Characters in the Middle of Public Life," *Philosophy & Rhetoric* 33, no. 4 (2000): 338.

30. Doxtader, "Characters in the Middle of Public Life," 338.

31. Bradford Vivian, *Being Made Strange: Rhetoric beyond Representation* (Albany: State University of New York Press, 2004), 91, 87.

32. *Oxford English Dictionary*, s.v. "peculiar," http://www.oed.com.proxy-remote.galib.uga.edu/view/Entry/139494?redirectedFrom=peculiar#eid.

33. Kenneth M. Stampp, *The Peculiar Institution: Slavery in the Ante-Bellum South* (New York: Knopf, 1963).

34. David Zarefsky, "Four Senses of Rhetorical History," in *Doing Rhetorical History: Concepts and Cases*, ed. Kathleen J. Turner (Tuscaloosa: University of Alabama Press, 1998), 32.

35. Zarefsky, "Four Senses of Rhetorical History," 31.

36. Daniel Walker Howe, *The Political Culture of the American Whigs* (Chicago: University of Chicago Press, 1979), 3.

37. Jenell Johnson, *American Lobotomy: A Rhetorical History* (Ann Arbor: University of Michigan Press, 2014), 17.

38. See Kenneth Burke, *A Rhetoric of Motives* (Berkeley: University of California Press, 1969); Kenneth Burke, *Language as Symbolic Action: Essays on Life, Literature, and Method* (Berkeley: University of California Press, 1969); Edwin Black, "The Second Persona," *Quarterly Journal of Speech* 56, no. 2 (1970); 109–19; Michael C. McGee, "In Search of 'The People': A Rhetorical Alternative," *Quarterly Journal of Speech* 61, no. 3 (1975): 235–49; and Maurice Charland, "Constitutive Rhetoric: The Case of the *Peuple Québécois*," *Quarterly Journal of Speech* 73, no. 2 (1987): 133–50.

39. James Jasinski, "A Constitutive Framework for Rhetorical Historiography: Toward an Understanding of the Discursive (Re)Constitution of 'Constitution' in *The Federalist Papers*," in *Doing Rhetorical History: Cases and Concepts*, ed. Kathleen J. Turner (Tuscaloosa: University of Alabama Press, 1998), 75.

40. Jasinski, "Constitutive Framework for Rhetorical Historiography," 75.

41. Barbara Biesecker, "Coming to Terms with Recent Attempts to Write Women into the History of Rhetoric," *Philosophy & Rhetoric* 25, no. 2 (1992): 141.

42. Biesecker, "Coming to Terms with Recent Attempts," 141.

43. Biesecker, "Coming to Terms with Recent Attempts," 157.

44. Bonnie J. Dow, "Feminism and Public Address Research: Television News and the Constitution of Women's Liberation," in *The Handbook of Rhetoric and Public Address*, ed. Shawn J. Parry-Giles and J. Michael Hogan (West Sussex, UK: Wiley-Blackwell, 2010), 351.

45. Dow, "Feminism and Public Address Research," 352.

46. Eric King Watts, "The Problem of Race in Public Address Research," in *Handbook of Rhetoric and Public Address*, 375.

47. Watts, "Problem of Race in Public Address Research," 375.

48. Stephanie Burkhalter, John Gastil, and Todd Kelshaw, "A Conceptual Definition and Theoretical Model of Public Deliberation in Small Face-to-Face Groups," *Communication Theory* 12, no. 4 (2002): 401.

49. Kenneth Cmiel, *Democratic Eloquence: The Fight over Popular Speech in Nineteenth-Century America* (Berkeley: University of California Press, 1990), 15, 26–27.

50. "Meeting on the Colonization of Free Blacks," n.p.

51. Robert Asen, *Democracy, Deliberation, and Education* (University Park: Pennsylvania State University Press, 2015), 9.

52. Fred Moten and Stefano Harney, "Policy and Planning," *Social Text* 27, no. 3 (2009): 183.

53. Raka Shome, "Postcolonial Interventions in the Rhetorical Canon: An 'Other' View," *Communication Theory* 6, no. 1 (1996): 44.

54. Kim D. Butler, "Defining Diaspora, Refining a Concept," *Diaspora* 10, no. 2 (2001): 192.

55. Stuart Hall, "Cultural Identity and Diaspora," in *Identity: Community, Culture, Difference*, ed. Jonathan Rutherford, 222–37 (London: Lawrence & Wishart, 1990), 235.

56. Nadia Ellis, *Territories of the Soul: Queered Belonging in the Black Diaspora* (Durham, NC: Duke University Press, 2015), 6.

57. Khachig Tölölyan, "Rethinking *Diaspora*(s): Stateless Power in the Transnational Moment," *Diaspora* 5, no. 1 (1996): 8; Ellis, *Territories of the Soul*, 6.

58. David Zarefsky, "Henry Clay and the Election of 1844: The Limits of a Rhetoric of Compromise," *Rhetoric & Public Affairs* 6, no. 1 (2003): 93. On rhetoric and compromise, see also Cindy Koenig Richards, "'To Restore the National Faith': Abraham Lincoln's 1854 Peoria Address and the Paradox of Moral Politics," *Southern Communication Journal* 76, no. 5 (2011): 401–23; James Jasinski, "The Forms and Limits of Prudence in Henry Clay's (1850) Defense of the Compromise Measures," *Quarterly Journal of Speech* 81, no. 4 (1995): 454–78.

59. David A. Frank and Mark Lawrence McPhail, "Barack Obama's Address to the 2004 Democratic National Convention: Trauma, Compromise, Consilience, and the (Im)possibility of Racial Reconciliation," *Rhetoric & Public Affairs* 8, no. 4 (2005): 572.

60. Frank and McPhail, "Barack Obama's Address," 572 (emphasis mine).

61. John B. Hatch, "Reconciliation: Building a Bridge from Complicity to Coherence in the Rhetoric of Race Relations," *Rhetoric & Public Affairs* 6, no. 4 (2003): 744.

62. On Douglass, see Glen McClish, "Frederick Douglass and the Consequences of Rhetoric: The Interpretive Framing and Publication History of the 2 January 1893 Haiti Speeches," *Rhetorica* 30, no. 1 (2012): 37–73; McClish, "The Instrumental and Constitutive Rhetoric of Martin Luther King Jr. and Frederick Douglass," *Rhetorica* 33, no. 1 (2015): 34–70. On Garnet, see James Jasinski, "Constituting Antebellum African American Identity: Resistance, Violence, and Masculinity in Henry Highland Garnet's (1843) 'Address to the Slaves,'" *Quarterly Journal of Speech* 93, no. 1 (2007): 27–57. On Stewart: Monika R. Alston-Miller, "The Influence of the Pauline Epistles on Maria W. Stewart's Rhetoric, A Political Gospel," *Journal of Communication & Religion* 38, no. 2 (2015): 100–117; Valerie C. Cooper, *Word, Like Fire: Maria Stewart, the Bible, and the Rights of African Americans* (Charlottesville: University of Virginia Press, 2011); Willie J. Harrell Jr., "A Call to Political and Social Activism: The Jeremiadic Discourse of Maria Miller Stewart, 1831–1833," *Journal of International Women's Studies* 9, no. 3 (2008): 284–303. On Walker: Chris Apap, "'Let No Man of Us Budge One Step': David Walker and the Rhetoric of African American Emplacement," *Early American Literature* 46, no. 2 (2011): 319–50; and Peter P. Hinks, *To Awaken My Afflicted Brethren: David Walker and the Problem of Antebellum Slave Resistance* (University Park: Pennsylvania State University Press, 2010).

63. See, for example, Jacqueline Bacon, *The Humblest May Stand Forth: Rhetoric, Empowerment, and Abolition* (Columbia: University of South Carolina Press, 2002); Glen McClish, "William G. Allen's 'Orators and Oratory': Inventional Amalgamation, Pathos, and the Characterization of Violence in African-American Abolitionist Rhetoric," *Rhetoric Society Quarterly* 35, no. 1 (2005): 47–72; Jacqueline Bacon and Glen McClish, "Descendents of Africa, Sons of '76: Exploring Early African-American Rhetoric," *Rhetoric Society Quarterly* 36, no. 1 (2006): 1–29; Glen McClish and Jacqueline Bacon, "'I Am Full of Matter': A Rhetorical Analysis of Daniel Coker's *A Dialogue between a Virginian and an African Minister*," *Journal of Communication & Religion* 29, no. 2 (2006): 315–46; and Glen McClish, "A Man of Feeling, a Man of Colour: James Forten and the Rise of African American Deliberative Rhetoric," *Rhetorica* 25, no. 3 (2007): 297–328.

64. Britt Rusert, "Disappointment in the Archives of Black Freedom," *Social Text* 33, no. 4 (2015): 19.

65. Rusert, "Disappointment in the Archives of Black Freedom," 23.

66. For example, see Aristotle, *On Rhetoric: A Theory of Civic Discourse*, trans. George A. Kennedy (New York: Oxford University Press, 1991), 1.5-6.

67. Stefano Harney and Fred Moten, *The Undercommons: Fugitive Planning and Black Study* (Brooklyn, NY: Autonomedia, 2013), 76.

CHAPTER 1—PECULIAR ARGUMENTATION: HENRY CLAY, ELIAS B. CALDWELL, AND THE ESTABLISHMENT OF COLONIZATION'S DELIBERATIVE DISCOURSE

1. "[No title]," *Maryland Gazette and Political Advertiser* (Annapolis), January 2, 1817, n.p.

2. Aristotle, *On Rhetoric: A Theory of Civic Discourse*, trans. George A. Kennedy (New York: Oxford University Press, 1991), 1.5-6.

3. See the introduction to this book for more details on the colonization advocacy that preceded the ACS. Also, the histories of the ACS highlight the groups' efforts to unite different elements of white society. See, for example, Amos J. Beyan, *The American Colonization Society and the Creation of the Liberian State: A Historical Perspective, 1822-1900* (Lanham, MD: University Press of America, 1991); Eric Burin, *Slavery and the Peculiar Solution: A History of the American Colonization Society* (Gainesville: University Press of Florida, 2005); Penelope Campbell, *Maryland in Africa: The Maryland State Colonization Society, 1831-1857* (Urbana: University of Illinois Press, 1971); Early Lee Fox, *The American Colonization Society 1817-1840* (Baltimore: Johns Hopkins Press, 1919); P. J. Staudenraus, *The African Colonization Movement, 1816-1865* (New York: Columbia University Press, 1961); Henry Noble Sherwood, "Early Negro Deportation Projects," *Mississippi Valley Historical Review* 2, no. 4 (1916): 484-508; Henry Noble Sherwood, "The Formation of the American Colonization Society," *Journal of Negro History* 2, no. 3 (1917): 209-28; and Allan Yarema, *American Colonization Society: An Avenue to Freedom?* (Lanham, MD: University Press of America, 2006).

4. Immediately after the meeting, Clay's and Caldwell's speeches are mentioned in such geographically diverse sources as "[No title]," *Poulson's American Daily Advertiser* (Philadelphia), January 2, 1817, n.p.; "Colonization of Free Blacks," *Albany* (NY) *Advertiser*, January 11, 1817, n.p.; "[No title]," *Georgia Journal* (Milledgeville), January 14, 1817, n.p.; "Colonization of Free Blacks," *Shamrock* (New York), January 18, 1817, n.p.; "Colonization of the Blacks," *Eagle* (Maysville, KY), January 24, 1817, n.p.; "Colonization of Free Blacks," *American Advocate and Kennebec Advertiser* (Hallowell, ME), February 15, 1817, n.p. . Decades later, the speeches remained a part of the conversation. See "Early History of the ACS," *African Repository and Colonial Journal* 12, no. 1 (January 1836): 51-55; and Archibald Alexander, *A History of Colonization on the Western Coast of Africa* (Philadelphia: William S. Martien, 1846), 80-89.

5. Fox, *American Colonization Society*, 60.

6. American Colonization Society, *The Tenth Annual Report of the American Society for Colonizing the Free People of Colour of the United States, With an Appendix* (Washington: Way & Gideon, 1827), 13-14; "Colonization Sketches," *African Repository and Colonial Journal* 13, no. 5 (May 1837): 145-47; "Africa[:] The Great Movements," *African Repository and Colonial Journal* 18, no. 7 (May 1842): 129; "American Colonization Society," *African Repository and Colonial*

Journal 1, no. 1 (March 1825): A1–A2; "Colonization Benevolence: Message of the President," *African Repository* 38, no. 4 (April 1862): 103; "General Walter Jones: The Last of the Founders of the American Colonization Society," *African Repository* 37, no. 11 (November 1861): 321; "The United States Government and Liberia," *African Repository* 52, no. 1 (January 1876): 5.

7. "Colonization of Free Blacks," *Boston Recorder*, April 22, 1817, n.p.; "African Colonization," *Vermont Intelligencer and Bellows Falls Advertiser* (Bellows Falls), September 4, 1820, n.p.; "Colonization Society," *Baltimore Patriot & Mercantile Advertiser*, January 24, 1828, n.p.; and "Colonization Society," *Portsmouth Journal of Literature and Politics*, February 9, 1828, n.p.; Erastus Hopkins, *The Objections to African Colonization, Stated and Answered* (Philadelphia: Russell and Martien, 1833), 9; David Christy, *A Lecture on African Colonization, Including a Brief Outline of the Slave Trade, Emancipation, the Relation of the Republic of Liberia to England, &c.* (Cincinnati: J. A. & U. P. James, 1849), 31; Phillip Slaughter, *The Virginian History of African Colonization* (Richmond: Macfarlane and Fergusson, 1855), 15.

8. Dickson D. Bruce Jr., "National Identity and African-American Colonization, 1773–1817," *Historian* 58, no. 1 (1995): 15.

9. Bruce, "National Identity and African-American Colonization," 15.

10. Bruce "National Identity and African-American Colonization," 27.

11. David Walker, *Walker's Appeal, in Four Articles* . . . 3rd and last ed. (Boston: David Walker, 1830), 50–61.

12. "American Colonization Society," *North American Review* 35, no. 76 (July 1832): 126.

13. Isaac V. Brown, *Biography of the Rev. Robert Finley, D. D., of Basking Ridge N.J.: with an Account of His Agency as the Author of the American Colonization Society . . .* (Philadelphia: J. W. Moore, 1857), 92.

14. David P. Geggus, "Preface," in *The Impact of the Haitian Revolution in the Atlantic World*, ed. David P. Geggus (Columbia: University of South Carolina Press, 2001), ix. For a full account of the situation in Saint-Domingue, see C. L. R. James, *The Black Jacobins: Toussaint L'Ouverture and the San Domingo Revolution* (New York: Dial Press, 1938).

15. Simon Newman argues that the Saint-Domingue revolution accounts, in part, for the growing conservatism in American political culture. See Simon P. Newman, "American Political Culture and the French and Haitian Revolutions," in Geggus, ed. *Impact of the Haitian Revolution*, 72–89.

16. Herbert Aptheker, *American Negro Slave Revolts* (New York: International Publishers, 1974), 73–74.

17. W. E. B. Du Bois, *The Suppression of the African Slave Trade to the United States of America, 1638–1870* (Williamstown, MA: Corner House, 1970), 71–72.

18. *Annals of Congress*, 7th Cong., 2nd sess., 385–86, 424.

19. John R. McKivigan and Stanley Harrold, *Antislavery Violence: Sectional, Racial, and Cultural Conflict in Antebellum America* (Knoxville: University of Tennessee Press, 1999), 6.

20. "Evidence against the Negroes Tried September 11th," in *Calendar of Virginia State Papers and Other Manuscripts from January 1, 1799, to December 31, 1807; Preserved in the Capitol, at Richmond*, vol. 9, ed. William P. Palmer and Samuel McRae (New York: Kraus, 1968), 141.

21. David Brion Davis, *The Problem of Slavery in the Age of Revolution, 1770–1823* (Ithaca: Cornell University Press, 1957), 210.

22. Aptheker, *American Negro Slave Revolts*, 244.

23. Davis, *Problem of Slavery*, 60.

24. Mercer first became aware of the secret journals after a night of drinking with fellow assemblymen, one of whom had participated in the secret session. C[harles] F[enton] Mercer, "Address of the Hon. Charles Fenton Mercer, at the Anniversary of the Am. Col. Society. January 18, 1853," *African Repository* 29, no. 5 (May 1853), 143. See also Douglas R. Egerton, *Charles Fenton Mercer and the Trial of National Conservatism* (Jackson: University Press of Mississippi, 1989), 105–7.

25. The Jefferson–Monroe correspondence can be found in Phillip Slaughter, *The Virginian History of African Colonization* (Richmond: Macfarlane and Fergusson, 1855), 2–5.

26. Staudenraus, *African Colonization Movement*, 53–56.

27. "American Colonization Society," *North American Review*, 126.

28. The detailed accounting of Mercer's role in motivating colonization in 1816 is found in Egerton, *Charles Fenton Mercer*, 107–12.

29. Egerton makes a point to correct the record, which had previously positioned Finley as the impetus for the Society's meeting. See Douglas R. Egerton, "'Its Origin Is Not a Little Curious': A New Look at the American Colonization Society," in *Rebels, Reformers, & Revolutionaries: Collected Essays and Second Thoughts* (New York: Routledge, 2002), 107–19.

30. Finley qtd. in Staudenraus, *African Colonization Movement*, 17.

31. Egerton, *Charles Fenton Mercer*, 110.

32. Bjørn F. Stillion Southard, "The Plain Style in Early Anti-Slavery Discourse: Reassessing the Rhetorical Beginnings of Quaker and Puritan Advocacy," *Quarterly Journal of Speech* 102, no. 3 (2016): 286–306.

33. See, for example, John Hepburn, "American Defence of the Christian Golden Rule..." (1714), excerpted in *Am I Not a Man and a Brother: The Antislavery Crusade of Revolutionary America, 1688–1788*, ed. Roger Bruns (New York: Chelsea House, 1977), 19 (hereafter cited as Bruns); and Benjamin Lay, *All Slave-Keepers, That Keep the Innocent in Bondage, Apostates* (Philadelphia: n.p., 1737), 114, 119.

34. James Otis, "Rights of the British Colonies Asserted and Proved" (1764), in Bruns, 103.

35. Quoted in Mary Stoughton Locke, *Anti-Slavery in America: From the Introduction of African Slaves to the Prohibition of the Slave Trade, 1619–1808* (Gloucester, MA: P. Smith, 1965), 41.

36. Donald G. Mathews, *Slavery and Methodism: A Chapter in American Morality, 1780–1845* (Princeton: Princeton University Press, 1965), 8–9.

37. H. Shelton Smith, *In His Image, But . . . : Racism in Southern Religion, 1780–1910* (Durham, NC: Duke University Press, 1972), 47–48.

38. Sydney V. James, *A People among Peoples: Quaker Benevolence in Eighteenth-Century America* (Cambridge: Harvard University Press, 1963), 227.

39. Abolition groups included Pennsylvania Society for Promoting the Abolition of Slavery for the Relief of Free Negroes Held in Bondage and for Improving the Condition of the African Race (1784) and the Society for Promoting the Manumission of Slaves in New York City (1785). The Society for the Relief of Free Negroes Unlawfully Held in Bondage had been created in 1775, yet its efforts were stalled by the Revolutionary War. Davis, *Problem of Slavery*, 216.

40. Jesse Torrey Jr., *A Portraiture of Domestic Slavery, in the United States: With Reflections on the Practicability of Restoring the Moral Rights of the Slave, without Impairing the Legal Privileges of the Possessor; and a Project of a Colonial Asylum for Free Persons of Colour; Including Memoirs of Facts on the Interior Traffic in Slaves and on Kidnapping* (Philadelphia: n.p., 1817), 48–53.

41. "The Presbyterian Church and Colonization," *African Repository* 36, no. 7 (July 1860): 205–8.

42. Robert Finley, *Thoughts on the Colonization of Freed Blacks* (Washington: n.p., 1816).

43. "Margaret Bayard Smith to Mrs. [Jane] Kirkpatrick, Dec. 5, 1816," in *The First Forty Years of Washington Society, Portrayed by the Family Letters of Mrs. Samuel Harrison Smith (Margaret Bayard) from the Collection of Her Grandson, J. Henley Smith*, ed. Gaillard Hunt (New York: Charles Scribner's Sons, 1906), 131.

44. Paul Cuffe qtd. in Henry Noble Sherwood, "Paul Cuffe: Pathfinder in Negro Colonization," *Journal of Negro History* 8, no. 2 (1923): 194.

45. *Annals of Congress*, 13th Cong., 2nd sess., 1195, 1265.

46. Paul Cuffe to T. Brine, January 16, 1817, qtd. in Sherwood, "Paul Cuffe: Pathfinder in Negro Colonization," 202.

47. "The Meeting on the Colonization of Free Blacks," *National Intelligencer* (Washington), December 24, 1816, n.p. All subsequent references to the speeches of Clay and Caldwell refer to this source.

48. "Petition of Prince Hall and Other Blacks, January 13, 1777," in Bruns, 428.

49. "Quaker Petition to the Continental Congress, October 4, 1783," in Bruns, 495.

50. Kenneth Burke, *A Rhetoric of Motives* (New York: Prentice Hall, 1950), 187.

51. Burke, *Rhetoric of Motives*, 187.

52. Burke, *Rhetoric of Motives*, 10.

53. Kenneth Burke, *Attitudes toward History* (Berkeley: University of California Press, 1984), 336.

54. Burke, *Attitudes toward History*, 336.

55. The Memorial was printed in "Notice," *National Intelligencer* (Washington), January 18, 1817; and in *Annals of Congress*, 14th Cong., 2nd sess., 481–83.

56. *Annals of Congress*, 14th Cong., 2nd sess., 940.

57. Staudenraus, *African Colonization Movement*, 51–56.

58. William Warren Sweet, *Religion in the Development of American Culture, 1765–1840* (New York: Charles Scribner's Sons, 1952), 237.

59. "Memorial to Congress," *Annals of Congress*, 14th Cong., 2nd sess., 482.

60. "Colonization in Pennsylvania," *Maryland Colonization Journal* 1, no. 15 (March 1838): 64. The *Maryland Colonization Journal* obliquely credits the *Commercial Herald, and Pennsylvania Herald* for the article. It is likely that the original they are referencing came from *Commercial Herald and Pennsylvania Sentinel* (Philadelphia).

61. *Eleventh Annual Report of the American Colonization Society* (Washington, DC: The Society, 1828), 425.

62. "The New Nationality," *African Repository* 38, no. 11 (October 1862): 300.

63. "The Meeting on the Colonization of Free Blacks," *National Intelligencer* (Washington), December 24, 1816, n.p.

64. Abraham D. Shad, Peter Spencer, W[illia]m S. Thomas, "Address of the Free People of Color of the Borough of Wilmington, Delaware" (1831), repr. in William Lloyd Garrison, *Thoughts on African Colonization*, 2 parts (Boston: Garrison and Knapp, 1832), 2:38.

65. Edmund Ruffin, "African Colonization Unveiled" (1833), in *Address to the Virginia State Agricultural Society* (Richmond: P. D. Bernard, 1853), 8.

66. Garrison, *Thoughts on African Colonization*, 1:2.

67. William Jay, *Slavery in America: Or, An Inquiry into the Character and Tendency of the American Colonization and the American Anti-Slavery Societies* (London: F. Westley and A. H. Davis, 1835), 80–86.

CHAPTER 2—PECULIAR VOICE: THE COUNTER MEMORIAL OF THE FREE PEOPLE OF COLOUR OF THE DISTRICT OF COLUMBIA AND THE UNSETTLING OF COLONIZATION'S DELIBERATIVE DISCOURSE

1. "A Counter Memorial Proposed to Be Submitted to Congress in Behalf of the Free People of Colour of the District of Columbia," *National Intelligencer* (Washington), December 30, 1816, n.p. (hereafter "Counter Memorial").

2. "Counter Memorial."

3. "Counter Memorial."

4. "Counter Memorial."

5. Erik King Watts, "'Voice' and 'Voicelessness' in Rhetorical Studies," *Quarterly Journal of Speech* 87, no. 2 (2001): 180.

6. Nadia Ellis, *Territories of the Soul: Queered Belonging in the Black Diaspora* (Durham, NC: Duke University Press, 2015), 6.

7. I use "African American" when discussing signifying because of the clear influence of west African traditions and American contexts in the development of the notion of signifying. See Henry Louis Gates Jr., *The Signifying Monkey: A Theory of Afro-American Literary Criticism* (New York: Oxford University Press, 1988), 3–43.

8. Michelle M. Wright, *Physics of Blackness: Beyond the Middle Passage Epistemology* (Minneapolis: University of Minnesota Press, 2015), 3.

9. Toni Morrison, *Playing in the Dark: Whiteness and the Literary Imagination* (Cambridge: Harvard University Press, 1992), 6–7.

10. Morrison, *Playing in the Dark*, 7.

11. Leah Ceccarelli, "Polysemy: Multiple Meanings in Rhetorical Criticism," *Quarterly Journal of Speech* 84, no. 4 (1998): 408.

12. Watts, "'Voice' and 'Voicelessness,'" 184.

13. Winthrop D. Jordan, *White over Black: American Attitudes toward the Negro, 1550–1812* (Chapel Hill: University of North Carolina Press, 1968), 331. See also Alice Dana Adams, *The Neglected Period of Anti-Slavery in America, 1808–1831* (Gloucester, MA: P. Smith, 1964), 2.

14. David Brion Davis, "The Emergence of Immediatism in British and American Antislavery Thought," *Mississippi Valley Historical Review* 49, no. 2 (1962): 215.

15. The scholarly works associated with each of these descriptors are, respectively: John W. Burgess, *The Middle Period: 1817–1858* (New York: Charles Scribner, 1901); George Dangerfield,

The Era of Good Feelings (New York: Harcourt, Brace, 1952); Adams, *Neglected Period of Anti-Slavery* (London: Methuen, 1953); and Matthew E. Mason, "The Rain between the Storms: The Politics and Ideology of Slavery in the United States, 1808–1820" (PhD. diss., University of Maryland, 2002).

16. Edwin Black, "The Sentimental Style as Escapism, or the Devil with Dan'l Webster," in *Form and Genre: Shaping Rhetorical Action*, ed. Karlyn Kohrs Campbell and Kathleen Hall Jamieson (Annandale, VA: Speech Communication Association, 1978), 75–86.

17. The earliest efforts were termed "transportation," along with the terms "deportation," "gradual emancipation," "manumission," "reexportation," and "colonization." Henry Noble Sherwood, "Early Negro Deportation Projects," *Mississippi Valley Historical Review* 2, no. 4 (1916): 484–508. See also Henry Noble Sherwood, "The Formation of the American Colonization Society," *Journal of Negro History* 2, no. 3 (1917): 211.

18. The statement by Clay about the moderation of the ACS is in "The Meeting on the Colonization of Free Blacks," *National Intelligencer* (Washington), December 24, 1816, n.p.

19. William E. Ames, "The National Intelligencer: Washington's Leading Political Newspaper," *Records of the Columbia Historical Society, Washington D.C.* 46 (1968): 73.

20. Ames, "National Intelligencer," 81.

21. It is also worth noting that Joseph Gales Sr. served as the treasurer and agent for the ACS in later decades. The elder Gales's role in colonization plays a significant role in chapter 3. See Clement Easton, "Winifred and Joseph Gales, Liberals of the Old South," *Journal of the Old South* 10, no. 4 (1944): 464–65.

22. Larry Tise, *Proslavery: A History of the Defense of Slavery in America, 1701–1840* (Athens: University of Georgia Press, 1987), 42.

23. Celeste Michelle Condit and John Louis Lucaites, *Crafting Equality: America's Anglo-African Word* (Chicago: University of Chicago Press, 1993), 72.

24. Dexter Gordon, *Black Identity: Rhetoric, Ideology, and Nineteenth-Century Black Nationalism* (Carbondale: Southern Illinois University, 2003).

25. When referencing the purported authors of the Counter Memorial, I use "free people of colour." When speaking of the population beyond the text, I use the term "free blacks."

26. Jacqueline Bacon, *Freedom's Journal: The First African-American Newspaper* (Lanham, MD: Lexington Books, 2007), 23.

27. Dickson D. Bruce, *The Origins of African American Literature, 1680–1865* (Charlottesville: University of Virginia Press, 2001), 110.

28. For examples, see Herbert Aptheker, ed., *A Documentary History of the Negro People in the United States*, 3 vols. (New York: Citadel Press, 1951–73), 1:1–4.

29. Peter A. Dorsey, "'To Corroborate Our Own Claims': Public Positioning and the Slavery Metaphor in Revolutionary America," *America Quarterly* 55, no. 3 (2003): 353–86.

30. Susan Zaeske, *Signatures of Citizenship: Petitioning, Antislavery, and Women's Political Identity* (Chapel Hill: University of North Carolina Press, 2003), 13. Paul Bradley Stewart notes that the "persona of humility" exhibited the petitioners' knowledge of the form of petitioning, regardless of race, class, or gender. See Paul Bradley Stewart, "Early American Petitioning (1789–1829), Public Life, and the Public Sphere" (PhD diss., University of Maryland, 2002), 180–82.

31. Glen McClish, "'A Man of Feeling, a Man of Colour': James Forten and the Rise of African American Deliberative Rhetoric," *Rhetorica* 25, no. 3 (2007): 304. See also Jacqueline Bacon and Glen McClish, "Descendents of Africa, Sons of '76: Exploring Early African-American Rhetoric," *Rhetoric Society Quarterly* 36, no. 1 (2006): 2.

32. Bacon and McClish, "Descendents of Africa," 2.

33. "Counter Memorial."

34. "Counter Memorial."

35. "Counter Memorial." Herbert Aptheker has documented the numerous acts of insurrection perpetrated by slaves, which kept the fear of violent resistance in the consciousness of the dominant culture. Two well-publicized slave insurrections in particular fueled white fears of violence: the uprising in the colony of Saint-Domingue in 1790 and Gabriel's Revolt in Richmond, Virginia. The implications of these insurrections on colonizationist rhetoric is discussed in more detail in chapter 1 of this book. See also Aptheker, *American Negro Slave Revolts* (New York: International, 1974); David Brion Davis, "Impact of the French and Haitian Revolutions," in *The Impact of the Haitian Revolution in the Atlantic World*, ed. David P. Geggus (Columbia: University of South Carolina Press, 2001), 4; David Brion Davis, *The Problem of Slavery in the Age of Revolution, 1770–1823* (Ithaca, NY: Cornell University Press, 1957), 210; and John R. McKivigan and Stanley Harrold, eds., *Antislavery Violence: Sectional, Racial, and Cultural Conflict in Antebellum America* (Knoxville: University of Tennessee Press, 1999), 5.

36. For one example, see *Letter to a Member of the General Assembly of Virginia on the Subject of the Late Conspiracy of the Slaves; with a Proposal for Their Colonization* (Baltimore: Bonsal & Niles, 1801).

37. "Counter Memorial."

38. Widespread public discussion about amalgamation of the races occurred in 1802 and concerned Thomas Jefferson's sexual relationship with his slave Sally Hemings. It was not until the mid-to-late 1820s that public discussion of amalgamation would become an acceptable topic in public discourse. See Elise Virginia Lemire, *"Miscegenation": Making Race in America* (Philadelphia: University of Pennsylvania Press, 2002), 1–10. On the amalgamation of lower social classes, see Leslie M. Harris, "From Abolitionist Amalgamators to 'Rulers of the Five Points': The Discourse of Interracial Sex and Reform in Antebellum New York City," in *Sex, Love, Race: Crossing Boundaries in North American History*, ed. Martha Elizabeth Hodes (New York: New York University Press, 1999), 191–212.

39. Kenneth Stampp, *The Peculiar Institution: Slavery in the Ante-bellum South* (New York: Knopf), 350–51.

40. Joshua D. Rothman, *Notorious in the Neighborhood: Sex and Families across the Color Line in Virginia, 1787–1861* (Chapel Hill: University of North Carolina Press, 2003), 31. The social history of miscegenation in Virginia is detailed in James Hugo Johnston, *Race Relations in Virginia and Miscegenation in the South, 1776–1860* (Amherst: University of Massachusetts Press, 1970).

41. Martha Elizabeth Hodes, *White Women, Black Men: Illicit Sex in the Nineteenth Century* (New Haven: Yale University Press, 1997), 3.

42. See Bruce Dorsey, *Reforming Men and Women: Gender in the Antebellum City* (Ithaca, NY: Cornell University Press, 2006), 151–55.

43. "Counter Memorial."

44. As Kenneth Burke notes, "Irony arises when one tries, by the interaction of terms upon one another, to produce a *development* which uses all the terms." The interaction of many terms is important, for, as Burke warns, "if you isolate any one agent in a drama, or any one advocate in a dialogue, and see the whole in terms of his position alone, you have the purely relativistic." Kenneth Burke, *A Grammar of Motives* (Berkeley: University of California Press, 1969), 512.

45. James P. McDaniel, "Liberal Irony: A Program for Rhetoric," *Philosophy & Rhetoric* 35, no. 4 (2002): 306.

46. Benjamin Franklin to the Federal Gazette, March 23, 1790, in *The Papers of Benjamin Franklin*, available at http://franklinpapers.org/franklin/.

47. Brackenridge's *Modern Chivalry* is made more significant when considered within the relatively sparse production and circulation of literature at the time. From 1779 to 1829, around two hundred works of fiction were produced in the United States, with around twenty works circulating widely. See Helen W. Papashvily, *All the Happy Endings* (New York: Harper, 1956), 2.

48. Hugh Henry Brackenridge, *Modern Chivalry*, ed. Lewis Leary (New Haven, CT: College and University Press, 1965), 131.

49. Brackenridge, *Modern Chivalry*, 132.

50. Nicholas Guyatt, *Bind Us Apart: How Enlightened Americans Invented Racial Segregation* (New York: Basic Books, 2016), 162.

51. Hezekiah Niles, "Mitigation of Slavery, No. 6," *Niles' Weekly Register* (Baltimore), July 17, 1819, 342.

52. Niles, "Mitigation of Slavery, No. 6."

53. "Counter Memorial."

54. "Counter Memorial."

55. "Meeting on the Colonization of Free Blacks."

56. "Counter Memorial."

57. "Counter Memorial."

58. Eddie S. Glaude Jr., *Exodus! Religion, Race, and Nation in Early Nineteenth-Century Black America* (Chicago: University of Chicago Press, 2000), 108.

59. Wayne Booth, *A Rhetoric of Irony* (Chicago: University of Chicago Press, 1975), 120.

60. Booth, *Rhetoric of Irony*, 246.

61. Bruce, *Origins of African American Literature*, 138–39.

62. Gates, *Signifying Monkey*, 51. Gates's work is perhaps the definitive explication of signifying with an eye and ear toward its rhetorical functions. Other works that have approached the concept from other methodological perspectives include: Roger D. Abrahams, *Deep Down in the Jungle: Negro Narrative Folklore from the Streets of Philadelphia* (Chicago: Aldine, 1970); John Miller Chernoff, *African Rhythm and African Sensibility: Aesthetics and Social Action in African Musical Idioms* (Chicago: University of Chicago Press, 1979); Dena J. Epstein, *Sinful Tunes and Spirituals: Black Folk Music to the Civil War* (Urbana: University of Illinois Press, 1977); Henry Louis Gates Jr., *Figures in Black: Words, Signs, and the "Racial" Self* (New York: Oxford University Press, 1987); Paul Gilroy, *The Black Atlantic: Modernity and Double Consciousness* (New York: Verso,

1993); Claudia Mitchell-Kernan, "Signifying," in *Mother Wit from the Laughing Barrel: Readings in the Interpretation of Afro-American Folklore*, ed. Alan Dundes (New York: Garland, 1981); Thomas Kochman, ed., *Rappin' and Stylin' Out: Communication in Urban America* (Urbana: University of Illinois Press, 1972); and Shane White and Graham White, *Stylin': African American Expressive Culture from Its Beginnings to the Zoot Suit* (Ithaca: Cornell University Press, 1998).

63. Mitchell-Kernan, "Signifying," 314.

64. Gates, *Signifying Monkey*, xxii–xxiii.

65. W. E. B. Du Bois, *The Souls of Black Folk* (Millwood, NY: Kraus-Thomson, 1973), 3.

66. John Arthos Jr., "The Shaman-Trickster's Art of Misdirection: The Rhetoric of Farrakhan and the Million Men," *Quarterly Journal of Speech* 87, no. 1 (2001): 43.

67. Gates, *Signifying Monkey*, 131. Here I use "white" to denote the dominant mode of address and interpretation (that is, from those in power to an audience of a similar standing) and "black" to denote the mode of address and interpretation of the less powerful black population. This wording is consistent with the phrasing used by Gates.

68. Lawrence W. Levine, *Black Culture and Black Consciousness: Afro-American Folk Thought from Slavery to Freedom* (New York: Oxford University Press, 1977), 240.

69. Bacon and McClish, "Descendents of Africa," 7.

70. Absalom Jones and Richard Allen, *A Narrative of the Proceedings of the Black People, during the Late Awful Calamity in Philadelphia, in the Year 1793* (Philadelphia: William Woodward, 1794), 87. See also Julie Winch, *Philadelphia's Black Elite: Activism, Accommodation, and the Struggle for Autonomy, 1787–1848* (Philadelphia: Temple University Press, 1988), 35.

71. Lemuel Haynes, "Universal Salvation," in *Lift Every Voice: African American Oratory, 1787–1900*, ed. Philip S. Foner and Robert J. Branham (Tuscaloosa: University of Alabama Press, 1998), 60–65. On the interpretation of Haynes's sermon as satire, see Helen Maclam, "Introduction," in *Black Preacher to White America: The Collected Writings of Lemuel Haynes, 1774–1833*, ed. Richard Newman (Brooklyn, NY: Carlson, 1990), xxix.

72. Haynes, "Universal Salvation," 64.

73. Richard D. Brown notes that Haynes was known for his wit. Although one could argue that this wit was not signifying, Haynes was keenly aware of the role his race played. He tried to eschew it on most occasions. However, upon being asked to leave his church in West Rutland, Vermont, Haynes reportedly said that after his thirty years at West Rutland, the congregation had just figured out that he was black. See Richard D. Brown, "'Not Only Extreme Poverty, but the Worst Kind of Orphanage': Lemuel Haynes and the Boundaries of Racial Tolerance on the Yankee Frontier, 1770–1820," *New England Quarterly* 61, no. 4 (1988): 515–18. On Haynes's later use of signifying, see Rosemary Fithian Guruswamy, "Jupiter Hammon's 'Regards' to Phillis Wheatley," in *Genius in Bondage: Literature of the Early Black Atlantic*, ed. Vincent Caretta and Philip Gould (Lexington: University Press of Kentucky, 2001), 193.

74. On January 17, 1817, the Colonization Society submitted its own memorial to Congress. The memorial outlined the goals of the group and hinted that support from the federal government in the way of resources would aid in their plans.

75. "Counter Memorial."

76. The first Naturalization Act in the United States, passed in 1790, established the conditions of naturalization as free, white, and resident in the United States for two years, resident in a State for one year, of good moral character, and willing to swear an oath to the Constitution. See "Naturalization Act of 1790," Stat. 1–103, March 26, 1790.

By 1816 the naturalization standards for citizenship had changed very little. In 1795 Congress amended naturalization standards. The act amended the residency requirement from two years to five. A new provision was added, requiring that a person seeking citizenship declare their intention at least three years prior to becoming a citizen. In 1802 Congress directed the clerk of court to record the entry of all aliens into the United States.

77. "Counter Memorial."
78. "Meeting on the Colonization of Free Blacks."
79. "Meeting on the Colonization of Free Blacks."
80. "Counter Memorial" (emphasis added).
81. "Counter Memorial."
82. "Meeting on the Colonization of Free Blacks."
83. "Meeting on the Colonization of Free Blacks."
84. "Meeting on the Colonization of Free Blacks."
85. "Counter Memorial."
86. "Counter Memorial."
87. Gates, *Signifying Monkey*, 59.
88. Robert Hariman, "Political Parody and Public Culture," *Quarterly Journal of Speech* 94, no. 3 (2008): 251.
89. Jacqueline Bacon, "'Acting as Freemen': Rhetoric, Race, and Reform in the Debate over Colonization in *Freedom's Journal*, 1827–1828," *Quarterly Journal of Speech* 93, no. 1 (2007): 60.
90. *Resolutions and Remonstrances of the People of Colour against Colonization on the Coast of Africa* (Philadelphia: n.p., 1818), [3].
91. See Bacon, "'Acting as Freemen,'" 58–83.
92. Garrison's critique caused well-known activists Elizur Wright Jr., Amos A. Phelps, and Theodore Dwight Weld to quit the ACS. See Eric Burin, *Slavery and the Peculiar Solution: A History of the American Colonization Society* (Gainesville: University Press of Florida, 2005): 21.
93. See Thomas Jefferson, *Notes on the State of Virginia* (London: Burlington House, 1788), 239–43.
94. Maria W. Stewart, "An Address Delivered at the African Masonic Hall, Boston, February 27, 1833," in *Pamphlets of Protest: An Anthology of Early African-American Protest Literature, 1790–1860*, ed. Richard Newman, Patrick Rael, and Phillip Lapansky (New York: Routledge, 2001), 126.
95. Frederick Douglass, "Colonizationist Measures: An Address Delivered in New York, New York, on 24 April 1849," in *The Frederick Douglass Papers, Series One: Speeches, Debates, and Interviews*, vol. 2, ed. John W. Blassingame (New Haven: Yale University Press, 1982), 163. Douglass delivered other addresses against colonization, see Douglass, "The Colonizationist Revival: An Address Delivered in Boston, Massachusetts, on 31 May 1849"; and Douglass,

"Henry Clay and Colonization Cant, Sophistry, and Falsehood: An Address Delivered in Rochester, New York, on 2 February 1851," in *Frederick Douglass Papers*, ed. Blassingame, 2:203–17, and 2:311–25.

96. Douglass, "Colonizationist Measures," 159.

97. Douglass, "Colonizationist Measures," 159.

98. Ethiop [William J. Wilson], "What Shall We Do with the White People?" *Anglo-African Magazine*, February 1860, 41–45. See also Mia Bay, *The White Image in the Black Mind: African-American Ideas about White People, 1830–1925* (London: Oxford University Press, 2000), 75–76.

99. David Zarefsky, "Henry Clay and the Election of 1844: The Limits of a Rhetoric of Compromise," *Rhetoric & Public Affairs* 6, no. 1 (2003): 93–94.

CHAPTER 3—PECULIAR PLANNING: LOUIS SHERIDAN AND THE NEGOTIATION OF DIASPORIC AND DELIBERATIVE DISCOURSE

1. The exact date and terms of Sheridan's emancipation are unclear. It is believed that Louis Sheridan is the person referred to in the 1800 will of Joseph R. Gautier. Furthermore, in the 1810 Bladen County census, Sheridan was listed as white, a sign of his fair complexion and his likely freedom at the time. See William Stevens Powell, *Dictionary of North Carolina Biography*, vol. 5: P–S (Chapel Hill: University of North Carolina Press, 1994), 332.

2. Loren Schweninger, *Black Property Owners in the South, 1790–1915* (Urbana: University of Illinois Press, 1990), 92. Sheridan's net worth translates to roughly $500,000 in early twenty-first-century dollars.

3. Sheridan's skin color was such that he was recorded in the 1810–1820 North Carolina census as a white man rather than "mulatto." See Claude A. Clegg III, *The Price of Liberty: African Americans and the Making of Liberia* (Chapel Hill: University of North Carolina Press, 2004), 153.

4. Louis Sheridan to Joseph Gales, 20 February 1836. American Colonization Society (ACS) papers, Library of Congress, reel 26 (hereafter cited as ACS Papers).

5. Sheridan to Gales, 22 February 1837, ACS Papers, reel 27.

6. Clegg, *Price of Liberty*, 155.

7. This terminology of "planning" comes from Stefano Harney and Fred Moten, *The Undercommons: Fugitive Planning and Black Study* (Brooklyn, NY: Autonomedia, 2013), 76.

8. Wilderson capitalizes "White," "Black," "Red," "Slave," "Savage," and "Human," "in order to assert their importance as ontological positions and to stress the value of theorizing power politically rather than culturally." Frank B. Wilderson III, *Red, White, and Black: Cinema and the Structure of U.S. Antagonisms* (Durham, N.C.: Duke University Press, 2010), 23.

9. Jared Sexton, "The Social Life of Social Death: On Afro-Pessimism and Black Optimism," *InTensions* 5 (2011): 23.

10. Wilderson, *Red, White, and Black*, 38.

11. Wilderson, *Red, White, and Black*, 38, 58.

12. Wilderson, *Red, White, and Black*, 37.

13. Sexton, "Social Life of Social Death," 29.

14. Frantz Fanon, *Black Skin, White Masks,* trans. Charles Lam Markmann (New York: Grove Press, 1967), 139. The translation of Fanon uses the masculine pronoun, which I have kept. It resonates with much of the colonization discourse that was deeply gendered and used masculine appeals in various contexts. See Bruce Dorsey, "A Gendered History of African Colonization in the Antebellum United States," *Journal of Social History* 34, no. 1 (2000): 77–105.

15. Fanon, *Black Skin, White Masks,* 139.

16. Orlando Patterson, *Slavery and Social Death: A Comparative Study* (Cambridge: Harvard University Press, 1982), 46.

17. Hortense J. Spiller, *Black, White, and in Color: Essays on American Literature and Culture* (Chicago: University of Chicago Press, 2003), 382 (emphasis mine).

18. Fred Moten, "Blackness and Nothingness (Mysticism in the Flesh)," *South Atlantic Quarterly* 112, no. 4 (2013): 740.

19. Moten, "Blackness and Nothingness," 740.

20. Moten, "Blackness and Nothingness," 741 (emphasis in original).

21. Harney and Moten, *Undercommons,* 76.

22. Cornel West, "Reconstructing the American Left: The Challenge of Jesse Jackson," *Social Text* 11, no. 11 (1984–1985): 10–11. Quoted in Harney and Moten, *Undercommons,* 73.

23. Harney and Moten, *Undercommons,* 78.

24. Michelle M. Wright, *Becoming Black: Creating Identity in the African Diaspora* (Durham, NC: Duke University Press, 2004), 1.

25. Wright, *Becoming Black,* 2.

26. Ira Berlin, *Slaves without Masters: The Free Negro in the Antebellum South* (New York: Oxford University Press, 1981), 4.

27. Suzanne Ellery Chappelle, *Maryland: A History of Its People* (Baltimore: Johns Hopkins University Press, 1986), 40.

28. Berlin, *Slaves without Masters,* 4.

29. Berlin, *Slaves without Masters,* 7.

30. See chapter 1 for more about how the fear of slave insurrections impacted the creation of the ACS.

31. Berlin, *Slaves without Masters,* 188.

32. Harney and Moten, *Undercommons,* 78.

33. Benjamin Joseph Klebaner, "American Manumission Laws and the Responsibility for Supporting Slaves, *Virginia Magazine of History and Biography* 63, no. 4 (1955): 443–53.

34. Attendees at the first meeting included: Francis Scott Key (Maryland lawyer), Representative John Randolph of Roanoke (Virginia), Representative Robert Wright (Maryland), Senator Robert H. Goldsborough (Maryland), Ferdinando Fairfax (wealthy Virginia landowner), Reverend Samuel J. Mills (Rhode Island), Reverend William Meade (Virginia), Elias B. Caldwell (clerk of the US Supreme Court), Representative Daniel Webster (New Hampshire), Thomas Dougherty (clerk of the US House of Representatives), General Walter Jones (famous military officer and lawyer in the District of Columbia), and Representative Henry Clay (Kentucky). See P. J. Staudenraus, *The African Colonization Movement, 1816–1865* (New York: Columbia University Press, 1961), 27.

35. "The Meeting on the Colonization of Free Blacks," *National Intelligencer* (Washington, DC), December 24, 1816, n.p.

36. The rhetorical contours of this middle discourse are the subject of chapter 1 of this book.

37. Louis Sheridan, letter qtd. in "From the Pennsylvania Freeman," *Colored American* (New York), August 4, 1838.

38. Berlin, *Slaves without Masters*, 139.

39. Willard B. Gatewood Jr., "'To Be Truly Free': Louis Sheridan and the Colonization of Liberia," *Civil War History* 29, no. 4 (1983): 332–48.

40. John Hope Franklin, *The Free Negro in North Carolina, 1790–1860*, rev. ed. (Chapel Hill: University of North Carolina Press, 1995), 197.

41. Franklin, *Free Negro in North Carolina*, 199.

42. Sheridan, letter qtd. in "From the Pennsylvania Freeman."

43. Sheridan, letter qtd. in "From the Pennsylvania Freeman" (emphasis in original).

44. Sheridan to Gales, 16 February 1836, ACS Papers, reel 25.

45. It is worth noting that after Owen's term as governor ended, he served at the state constitutional convention and voted in favor of the tightening restrictions on free blacks. See Gatewood, "'To Be Truly Free,'" 335.

46. Joseph Gales to Ralph R. Gurley, 29 July 1835, Joseph Gales Letters, New York Historical Society Manuscript Collection (underlining in original).

47. Gales made such a suggestion not only on the strength of Sheridan's character but also because "no white man can live in the African climate." It seemed as if Sheridan would receive the material support he needed, conditionally granted based on the racist assumption that the only way a black person could participate in political life was in a climate inhospitable for whites. Minutes of the Board of Managers, August 13, 1835, qtd. in Gatewood, "'To Be Truly Free,'" 337.

48. Sheridan to Gales, 16 February 1836, ACS Papers, reel 25.

49. Clegg, *Price of Liberty*, 153.

50. Harney and Moten, *Undercommons*, 75.

51. Sheridan to Gales, 16 February 1836, ACS Papers, reel 25.

52. Sheridan to Gales, 16 February 1836, ACS Papers, reel 25.

53. Sheridan to Gales, 16 February 1836, ACS Papers, reel 25.

54. Sheridan to Gales, 25 March 1836, ACS Papers, reel 25 (underlining in original).

55. Sheridan to Gales, 25 March 1836, ACS Papers, reel 25.

56. Sheridan to Gales, 27 May 1836, ACS Papers, reel 26.

57. Sheridan to Gales, 22 July 1836, ACS Papers, reel 26.

58. Sheridan to Gales, 20 May 1836, ACS Papers, reel 26.

59. In a May 20, 1836, letter, Sheridan proposed taking "20 to 50 feet of Boards according to the capacity of the vessel with Shingles for stowage." In an August letter, he proposed "30 to 50" board feet of lumber. Sheridan to Gales, 20 May 1836, ACS Papers, reel 26; and Sheridan to Gales, August 1836, ACS Papers, reel 26.

60. Sheridan to Gales, 16 December 1836, ACS Papers, reel 26; Sheridan to Gales, 20 May 1836, ACS Papers, reel 26; and Sheridan to Gales, 27 May 1836, ACS Papers, reel 26.

61. Bjørn F. Stillion Southard, "Arguing Benevolence in the Colonization Debate, 1816," in *Engaging Argument*, ed. Patricia Riley (Washington, DC: National Communication Association, 2006), 148–54.

62. Sheridan to Gales, 16 February 1836, ACS Papers, reel 25.

63. Sheridan to Gales, 20 May 1836, ACS Papers, reel 26.

64. Sheridan to Gales, 5 October 1836, ACS Papers, reel 26.

65. Sheridan to Gales, 5 October 1836, ACS Papers, reel 26.

66. Beverly C. Tomek, *Colonization and Its Discontents: Emancipation, Emigration, and Antislavery in Antebellum Pennsylvania* (New York: NYU Press, 2011), 120.

67. Tomek, *Colonization and Its Discontents*.

68. Sheridan to Gales, 1 November 1836, ACS papers, reel 26.

69. Sheridan to Gales, 1 November 1836, ACS papers, reel 26 (underlining in original).

70. Sheridan to Gales, 23 December 1836, ACS papers, reel 26.

71. Britt Rusert, "Disappointment in the Archives of Black Freedom," *Social Text* 33, no. 4 (2015): 28, 21.

72. Sheridan to Gales, 16 December 1836, ACS papers reel 26.

73. Sheridan to Gales, 23 December 1836, ACS papers, reel 26.

74. Sheridan to Gales, 23 December 1836, ACS papers, reel 26.

75. Sheridan to Gales, 23 December 1836, ACS papers, reel 26.

76. D. Francis Bacon to Joseph Gales, 21 December 1836, reel 26 (underlining in original).

77. D. Francis Bacon to Ralph R. Gurley, 24 December 1836, reel 26.

78. D. Francis Bacon to Ralph R. Gurley, 24 December 1836, reel 26.

79. Sheridan to Gales, 1 August 1837, ACS papers, reel 26.

80. Sheridan to Gales, 1 August 1837, ACS papers, reel 26 (emphasis in original).

81. Sheridan to Gales, 1 August 1837, ACS papers, reel 26 (double underlining in original).

82. Sheridan to Gales, 1 August 1837, ACS papers, reel 26.

83. Clegg, *Price of Liberty*, 155.

84. Lewis Tappan, "Important Intelligence from Liberia," *Colored American* (New York), December 8, 1838, 165.

85. Cornish was coeditor of *Freedom's Journal* with John B. Russwurm. The two editors parted ways, with Cornish continuing to fight for the abolition of slavery and the equality of rights for black people. Russwurm became disillusioned with the prospects of freedom in the United States and immigrated to Liberia in 1829. See Winston James, *The Struggles of John Brown Russwurm: The Life and Writings of a Pan-Africanist Pioneer, 1799–1851* (New York: NYU Press, 2010), 44–57.

86. "Louis Sheridan's Letter," *African Repository and Colonial Journal* 15, no. 2 (February 1839): 37.

87. John J. Matthias, "Remarks on Louis Sheridan's Letter," *African Repository and Colonial Journal* 15, no. 2 (February 1839): 40.

88. Harney and Moten, *Undercommons*, 74–75.

89. Sheridan to Executive Committee of the ACS, 24 January 1842, ACS Papers (emphasis in original).

90. The implications of double consciousness on the rhetorical choices of anticolonizationists are discussed at greater length in chapter 2 of this book.

91. Paul Gilroy, *The Black Atlantic: Modernity and Double Consciousness* (Cambridge, MA: Harvard University Press, 1993), 1.

92. Gilroy, *Black Atlantic*.

CHAPTER 4—"PECULIAR OBLIGATIONS": HILARY TEAGE AND THE CONSTITUTION OF CIVIC IDENTITY IN LIBERIA

1. I refer to the black emigrants from the United States to the Liberian colonies as settler colonists in order to connote what Lorenzo Veracini calls, "the fundamental ambiguity" implied by the compound title. Veracini writes, "*Settler Colonialism* focuses on ... autonomous collectives that claim both a special sovereign charge and a regenerative capacity." Put simply, settler colonists were both creating something new (as settlers) and re-creating elements of the society that sent them (as colonists). Lorenzo Veracini, *Settler Colonialism: A Theoretical Overview* (New York: Palgrave Macmillan, 2010), 3.

2. Marie Tyler-McGraw, "Hilary Teage: Discord and Nostalgia," *Virginia Emigrants to Liberia*, September 27, 2008, http://www.vcdh.virginia.edu/liberia/index.php?page=Stories&section=Hilary%20Teage.

3. Quoted in Hilary J. Moss, *Schooling Citizens: The Struggle for African American Education in Antebellum America* (Chicago: University of Chicago Press, 2009), 39.

4. David Kazanjian, *The Colonizing Trick: National Culture and Imperial Citizenship in Early America* (Minneapolis: University of Minnesota Press, 2003), 95.

5. Kazanjian, *Colonizing Trick*.

6. Hilary Teage, "Anniversary Speech, Delivered at Monrovia, in Liberia, December 1, 1846," in [Wilson Armistead], *Calumny Refuted, by Facts from Liberia* (London: Charles Gilpin, 1848), 25.

7. Michelle Hall Kells, *Héctor P. García: Everyday Rhetoric and Mexican American Civil Rights* (Carbondale: Southern Illinois University Press, 2006), 215.

8. Robert Asen, "A Discourse Theory of Citizenship," *Quarterly Journal of Speech* 90, no. 2 (2004): 191.

9. Tyler-McGraw, "Hilary Teage."

10. Tyler-McGraw, "Hilary Teage."

11. Carl Patrick Burrowes, "'In Common with Colored Men, I Have Certain Sentiments,'" *American Journalism* 16, no. 3 (1999): 20.

12. Alan Neely, "Teague, Colin," in *Biographical Dictionary of Christian Missions*, ed. Gerald H. Anderson (New York: Macmillan Reference USA, 1998), 660; and Tom W. Shick, *Emigrants to Liberia, 1820 to 1843: An Alphabetical Listing* (Newark, DE: Liberian Studies Association in America, 1971), 96.

13. "Lott Carey—the First American Colored Missionary to Africa," *Maryland Colonization Journal* 4, no. 10 (April 1848): 167.

14. Also referred to as the Richmond Baptist Missionary Society or Richmond African Baptist Missionary Society.

15. "Lott Carey," 167. Some reports erroneously date Teage's arrival in west Africa as occurring in 1819. For example, see *African Repository* 29, no. 10 (October 1853): 302.

16. Carl Patrick Burrowes, *Power and Press Freedom in Liberia, 1830–1970: The Impact of Globalization and Civil Society on Media-Government Relations* (Trenton, NJ: Africa World Press, 2004), 39.

17. D. Elwood Dunn and Svend E. Holsoe, *Historical Dictionary of Liberia* (Metuchen, NJ: Scarecrow, 1985), 166.

18. Winston James, *The Struggles of John Brown Russwurm: The Life and Writings of a Pan-Africanist Pioneer, 1799–1851* (New York: New York University Press, 2010), 76.

19. Angela G. Ray, "How Cosmopolitan Was the Lyceum, Anyway?" in *The Cosmopolitan Lyceum: Lecture Culture and the Globe in Nineteenth-Century America*, ed. Tom F. Wright (Amherst: University of Massachusetts Press, 2013), 26–28.

20. Angela G. Ray, *The Lyceum and Public Culture in the Nineteenth-Century United States* (East Lansing: Michigan State University Press, 2005), 20, 41.

21. In this section, I use the term "African American," rather than black, to describe slaves and free people of color who were excluded from the mainstream lyceums. I adopt this terminology because it provides a clear contrast to the phrase "Anglo-American" and highlights black exclusion from the "Anglo-American lyceum," which is used to describe the lyceum movement in the nineteenth century on account of its linkages with Great Britain.

22. Usage of the phrase "American lyceum movement" and its cognates references the Anglo-American lyceum and its practices.

23. [Josiah Holbrook], "Associations of Adults for Mutual Education," *American Journal of Education* 1, no. 10 (October 1826): 594.

24. Josiah Holbrook, "American Lyceum," *American Journal of Education* 4, no. 1 (January/February 1829): 50.

25. Ray, *Lyceum and Public Culture*, 27.

26. Angela G. Ray, "What Hath She Wrought?: Woman's Rights and the Nineteenth-Century Lyceum," *Rhetoric & Public Affairs* 9, no. 2 (2006): 183–213, 197.

27. Waldo W. Braden, "The Beginnings of the Lyceum, 1826–1840," *Southern Speech Journal* 20, no. 2 (1954): 133.

28. Ray, *Lyceum and Public Culture*, 19.

29. "Republicanism of Lyceums," *Family Lyceum* 1, no. 22 (January 12, 1833): 86.

30. Ray, *Lyceum and Public Culture*, 13–47.

31. Ray, *Lyceum and Public Culture*, 113.

32. Dorothy B. Porter, "The Organized Educational Activities of Negro Literary Societies, 1828–1846," *Journal of Negro Education* 5, no. 4 (1936): 557–58.

33. See Robert L. Harris Jr., "Charleston's Free Afro-American Elite: The Brown Fellowship Society and the Humane Brotherhood," *South Carolina Historical Magazine* 82, no. 4 (1981): 289–310; Michael P. Johnson and James L. Roark, "'A Middle Ground': Free Mulattoes and the Friendly Moralist Society in Antebellum Charleston," *Southern Studies* 21, no. 3 (1982): 246–65; and Angela G. Ray, *"A Green Oasis in the History of My Life": Race and the Culture of Debating in Antebellum Charleston, South Carolina* (Salt Lake City: Department of Communication, University of Utah, 2014).

34. Donald M. Scott, "Print and the Public Lecture System, 1840–60," in *Printing and Society in Early America*, ed. William L. Joyce, David D. Hall, Richard D. Brown, and John B. Hench (Worcester, MA: American Antiquarian Society, 1983), 284, 285; see also Ray, *Lyceum and Public Culture*, 102.

35. Burrowes, *Power and Press Freedom in Liberia*, 66. The Maryland State Colonization Society Cape Palmas colony had the Cape Palmas Lyceum, the Hall Palmas Reading Club, the Cape Palmas Reading Room and Library Association, the Female Benevolent Society, and the Russwurm Literary Association. See James, *Struggles of John Brown Russwurm*, 95; and Charles A. Earp, "The Role of Education in the Maryland Colonization Movement," *Journal of Negro History* 26, no. 3 (1941): 386.

36. Richard L. Hall, *On Afric's Shore: A History of Maryland in Liberia, 1834–1857* (Baltimore: Maryland Historical Society, 2003), 348.

37. Qtd. in *Liberia Herald* (Monrovia), May 31, 1845, 1.

38. See, for example, *Charter, Constitution and By-Laws of the Troy Lyceum of Natural History* (Troy, NY: John F. Prescott, 1850), 3; and Daniel Appleton White, *An Address Delivered at Ipswich, before the Essex County Lyceum, at Their First Annual Meeting* (Salem, MA: Foote and Brown, 1830), 52.

39. Hall, *On Afric's Shore*, 348.

40. In the United States, lyceums and black newspapers provided spaces for African Americans to assert their rhetorical agency and participate in public discourse. See Shirley Wilson Logan, *Liberating Language: Sites of Rhetorical Education in Nineteenth-Century Black America* (Carbondale: Southern Illinois University Press, 2008), chaps. 3 and 4.

41. Other Liberian mutual education and rhetorical societies are listed above, see n. 33. Another newspaper—*Africa's Luminary*—was based out of Bassa Cove and was run by white missionaries.

42. See Burrowes, *Power and Press Freedom in Liberia*, 27–86.

43. *Liberia Herald* (Monrovia), May 31, 1845, 1; Plato, *Gorgias*, trans. W. D. Woodhead, in *The Collected Dialogues of Plato*, ed. Edith Hamilton and Huntington Cairns (New York: Pantheon Books, 1961), 462d–65e.

44. Brian Vickers, *In Defence of Rhetoric* (Oxford, UK: Oxford University Press, 1988), 88–90.

45. *Liberia Herald* (Monrovia), May 31, 1845, 1. See Russell's "Liberia No. 1," *Liberia Herald* (Monrovia), November 6, 1846, 6, subsequently reprinted in *African Repository and Colonial Journal* 23, no. 2 (February 1847): 48–53.

46. *Liberia Herald*, May 31, 1845, 1.

47. Debra Newman Ham, "'Teaching Them to Observe All Things': African American Women, the Great Commission, and Liberia in the Nineteenth Century," in *New Directions in the Study of African American Recolonization*, ed. Beverly C. Tomek and Matthew J. Hetrick (Gainesville: University Press of Florida, 2017), 90.

48. Bruce Dorsey, "A Gendered History of African Colonization in the Antebellum United States," *Journal of Social History* 34, no. 1 (2000): 78.

49. Dorsey, "Gendered History of African Colonization," 84.

50. "The Meeting on the Colonization of Free Blacks," *National Intelligencer* (Washington), December 24, 1816, n.p.

51. According to Burrowes, women settler colonists in Liberia had slightly more rhetorical agency than most women in the United States, as they "engaged unhindered in public speaking and political activism especially if they were related by blood or marriage to politically active men." See Burrowes, *Power and Press Freedom in Liberia*, 139.

However, even with greater ability to speak publicly, women were still denied voting rights and often discussed as what Linda K. Kerber calls "Republican Mothers" rather than rhetorical gladiators. As Kerber describes, Republican Motherhood emerged in the United States after the American Revolution. During that time and well into the nineteenth century, the role for (white) women in politics was discussed as being dedicated to "the nurture of public-spirited male citizens" and to "[guarantee] the steady infusion of virtue into the Republic." Linda K. Kerber, *Women of the Republic: Intellect and Ideology in Revolutionary America* (Chapel Hill: University of North Carolina Press, 2000), 11.

An example of the rhetoric of Republican Motherhood in Liberian discourse can be found in another speech delivered at the Liberia Lyceum and reprinted in the *Liberia Herald*. In an address by E. J. Roye on February 9, 1848, he states, "You Ladies of this new Republic cannot know too well the great influence you exert either for weal or wo upon every citizen.... It is your province, ladies, to put your signal veto and condemnation on any immodest thing, to discountenance independently of a sacrifice of any temperal [sic] good, all counterfeit characters either among your own or our sex." *Liberia Herald* (Monrovia), June 30, 1848, 35.

52. For example, see William Lloyd Garrison, *Thoughts on African Colonization* ... (Boston: Garrison and Knapp, 1832); and David Walker, *Walker's Appeal, in Four Articles* ... (Boston: David Walker, 1830).

53. James, *Struggles of John Brown Russwurm*, 72–74.

54. "Address delivered by H. Teage before the members of the Liberia Lyceum ..." *Liberia Herald* (Monrovia), May 31, 1845, 1.

55. Henry Louis Gates Jr., *The Signifying Monkey: A Theory of African-American Literary Criticism* (New York: Oxford University Press, 1988), 130, 131.

56. Elizabeth McHenry, *Forgotten Readers: Recovering the Lost History of African American Literary Societies* (Durham, NC: Duke University Press, 2002), 85.

57. [Holbrook], "Associations," 594.

58. "Address delivered by H. Teage," 1.

59. Holbrook, "American Lyceum," 47.

60. "Address delivered by H. Teage," 1.

61. "Address delivered by H. Teage," 1.

62. "Address delivered by H. Teage," 10.

63. "Address delivered by H. Teage," 10.

64. Celeste Michelle Condit, "The Functions of Epideictic: The Boston Massacre Orations as Exemplar," *Communication Quarterly* 33, no. 4 (1985): 284.

65. Teage, "Anniversary Speech," 15.

66. Teage, "Anniversary Speech," 16.

67. Edwin Black, "The Sentimental Style as Escapism, or the Devil with Dan'l Webster," in *Form and Genre: Shaping Rhetorical Action*, ed. Karyn Kohrs Campbell and Kathleen Hall Jamieson (Falls Church, VA: Speech Communication Association), 80.

68. Paul Gilroy, *Darker than Blue: On the Moral Economies of Black Atlantic Culture* (Cambridge, MA: Belknap Press of Harvard University, 2010), 75.

69. Teage, "Anniversary Speech," 16.

70. Houston A. Baker Jr., "The Black Public Sphere: Critical Memory and the Black Public Sphere," in *The Black Public Sphere*, ed. Black Public Sphere Collective (Chicago: University of Chicago Press, 1994), 7.

71. Harry Johnston, *Liberia*, 2 vols. (New York: Dodd, Mead, 1906), 1:138. For a full account see Johnston, *Liberia*, 1: 137–40.

72. Teage, "Anniversary Speech," 17.

73. Teage, "Anniversary Speech," 17.

74. Among those whom Johnston features in his historical account are Jehudi Ashmun (the first governor of the ACS colonies in Liberia, a white man), and Elijah Johnson and Lott Carey (among the first settler colonists, black men). See Johnston, *Liberia*, 1: 125–60.

75. Teage, "Anniversary Speech," 17.

76. Teage, "Anniversary Speech," 17–18.

77. Teage, "Anniversary Speech," 18 (emphasis added).

78. Teage, "Anniversary Speech," 18 (emphasis added).

79. Teage, "Anniversary Speech," 18 (emphasis added).

80. Teage, "Anniversary Speech," 19.

81. Saidiya V. Hartman, *Scenes of Subjugation: Terror, Slavery, and Self-Making in Nineteenth-Century America* (New York: Oxford University Press, 1997), 3.

82. Teage, "Anniversary Speech," 20.

83. Teage, "Anniversary Speech," 19.

84. Teage, "Anniversary Speech," 19.

85. Teage, "Anniversary Speech," 25.

86. Teage, "Anniversary Speech," 25.

87. Teage, "Anniversary Speech," 26.

88. Teage, "Anniversary Speech," 28.

89. Teage, "Anniversary Speech," 27.

90. Teage, "Anniversary Speech," 27.

91. Teage, "Anniversary Speech," 29.

92. Teage, "Anniversary Speech," 30.

93. Teage, "Anniversary Speech," 31.

94. Teage, "Anniversary Speech," 31.

95. Teage, "Anniversary Speech," 32.

96. Teage, "Anniversary Speech," 32.

97. Teage, "Anniversary Speech," 32.

98. James Oakes, "From Republicanism to Liberalism: Ideological Change and the Crisis of the Old South," *American Quarterly* 37, no. 4 (1985): 553.

99. Oakes, "From Republicanism to Liberalism, 553.

100. Oakes, "From Republicanism to Liberalism, 553.

101. Oakes, "From Republicanism to Liberalism, 553.

102. Teage, "Anniversary Speech," 35 (emphasis added).

103. Teage, "Anniversary Speech," 36.

104. Teage, "Anniversary Speech," 37.

105. Teage, "Anniversary Speech," 37.

106. Teage, "Anniversary Speech," 38.

107. Marie Tyler-McGraw, *An African Republic: Black and White Virginians in the Making of Liberia* (Chapel Hill: University of North Carolina Press, 2007), 165.

108. Regarding the Liberian Constitution, Robert T. Brown debunks the myth that it was written by Simon Greenleaf, a white law professor at Harvard University. See Robert T. Brown, "Simon Greenleaf and the Liberian Constitution of 1847," *Liberian Studies Journal* 9, no. 2 (1980–81): 51–60.

109. *Thirtieth Annual Report of the American Colonization Society* (Washington: C. Alexander, 1847), 21.

110. Tyler-McGraw, *African Republic*, 164.

111. *The Independent Republic of Liberia: Its Constitution and Declaration of Independence; Address of the Colonists to the Free People of Color in the United States* . . . (Philadelphia: William F. Geddes, 1848), 8.

112. *Independent Republic of Liberia*, 4.

113. *Independent Republic of Liberia*, 7.

114. David Kazanjian, *The Brink of Freedom: Improvising Life in the Nineteenth-Century Atlantic World* (Durham, NC: Duke University Press, 2016), 54.

CHAPTER 5—PECULIAR PROPOSAL: ABRAHAM LINCOLN AND THE PUBLIC POLICY ADVOCACY FOR COLONIZATION

1. US Const. art. 2, § 3.

2. David Zarefsky, "The Continuing Fascination with Lincoln," *Rhetoric & Public Affairs* 6, no. 2 (2003): 368. Essays on Lincoln's ceremonial addresses include: James R. Andrews, "Oaths Registered in Heaven: Rhetorical and Historical Legitimacy in the Inaugural Addresses of Jefferson Davis and Abraham Lincoln," in *Doing Rhetorical History: Concepts and Cases*, ed. Kathleen J. Turner (Tuscaloosa: University of Alabama Press, 1998), 95–117; Edwin Black, "Gettysburg and Silence," *Quarterly Journal of Speech* 80, no. 1 (1994): 21–36; Ronald H. Carpenter, "In Not-So-Trivial Pursuit of Rhetorical Wedgies: An Historical Approach to Lincoln's Second Inaugural Address," *Communication Reports* 1, no. 1 (1988): 20–25; Corrine K. Flemmings, "Gettysburg Revisited," *Communication Quarterly* 14, no. 2 (1966): 26–30; Michael C. Leff, "Dimensions of Temporality in Lincoln's Second Inaugural," *Communication Reports* 1, no. 1 (1988): 26–31; Marie Hochmuth Nichols, "Lincoln's First Inaugural," in *American Speeches*, ed. Wayland Maxfield Parrish and Marie Hochmuth Nichols (New York: David McKay, 1954), 60–100; Ronald F. Reid, "Newspaper Response to the Gettysburg Addresses," *Quarterly Journal of Speech* 54, no. 1 (1967): 50–60; Amy R. Slagell, "Anatomy of a Masterpiece: A Close Textual Analysis of Abraham Lincoln's Second Inaugural Address," *Communication Studies* 42, no. 2 (1991): 155–71; Linda Selzer, "Historicizing Lincoln: Garry Wills and the Canonization of the 'Gettysburg Address,'" *Rhetoric Review* 16, no. 1 (1997): 120–37; Martha Solomon, "'With Firmness in the Right': The Creation of Moral Hegemony in Lincoln's Second Inaugural," *Communication Reports* 1, no. 1 (1988): 32–37; David Zarefsky, "Approaching Lincoln's Second

Inaugural Address," *Communication Reports* 1, no. 1 (1988): 9–13. Essays concerning Lincoln's forensic speaking include: Michael C. Leff and Gerald P. Mohrmann, "Lincoln at Cooper Union: A Rhetorical Analysis of the Text," *Quarterly Journal of Speech* 60, no. 3 (1974): 346–58; Gerald P. Mohrmann and Michael C. Leff, "Lincoln at Cooper Union: A Rationale for Neo-Classical Criticism," *Quarterly Journal of Speech* 60, no. 4 (1974): 459–67; Michael W. Pfau, "Evaluating Conspiracy: Narrative, Argument, and Ideology in Lincoln's 'House Divided' Speech," *Argumentation & Advocacy* 42, no. 2 (2005): 57–73; Michael W. Pfau, *Political Style of Conspiracy: Chase, Sumner and Lincoln* (East Lansing: Michigan State University Press, 2005); David Zarefsky, "Lincoln and the House Divided: Launching a National Political Career," *Rhetoric & Public Affairs* 13, no. 3 (2010): 421–54.

Stillion Southard and Stillion Southard discuss the forensic and ceremonial genres as they relate to the two featured speeches at Gettysburg. Campbell and Jamieson use Lincoln as an example of where forensic and ceremonial elements are brought into the otherwise deliberative genre of the State of the Union Address. Bjørn F. Stillion Southard and Belinda A. Stillion Southard, "Edward Everett, 'Gettysburg Address' (19 November 1863)"; Abraham Lincoln, 'Gettysburg Address' (19 November 1863)," *Voices of Democracy* 1 (2006): 130–47; Karlyn Kohrs Campbell and Kathleen Hall Jamieson, *Deeds Done in Words: Presidential Rhetoric and Genres of Governance* (Chicago: University of Chicago Press, 1990), 71–72.

3. Little has changed since Zarefsky observed, "Few scholars have focused on the debates as 'rhetorical action,' addressing the rhetorical choices displayed in the text functioned in the context of the situation." David Zarefsky, "The Lincoln–Douglas Debate Revisited: The Evolution of Public Argument," *Quarterly Journal of Speech* 72, no. 2 (1986): 163. Zarefsky expands upon his analysis of public argument in the Lincoln–Douglas debates in *Lincoln, Douglas, and Slavery: In the Crucible of Public Debate* (Chicago: University of Chicago Press, 1993).

4. Larry Tagg, *Unpopular Mr. Lincoln: The Story of America's Most Reviled President* (New York: Savas Beatie, 2009), 144.

For example, a South Carolina schoolteacher called it "stupid, ambiguous, vulgar and insolent," while Frederick Douglass called the speech "a double-tongued document [that] conceals rather than declares a definite policy." Page Smith, *Trial by Fire: A People's History of the Civil War and Reconstruction* (New York: McGraw-Hill, 1982), 30; and Frederick Douglass, "The Inaugural Address," in *Life and Writings of Frederick Douglass*, ed. Philip S. Foner, 5 vols. (New York: International, 1950), 3:72.

5. Abraham Lincoln, "First Annual Message," in *The Collected Works of Abraham Lincoln*, ed. Roy P. Basler. 8 vols. (New Brunswick: Rutgers University Press, 1953), 5:36 (hereafter, *CW*).

6. Lincoln, "First Annual Message," *CW*, 5:49.

7. Michael Vorenberg, "Abraham Lincoln and the Politics of Black Colonization," *Journal of the Abraham Lincoln Association* 14, no. 2 (1993): 25–28.

8. Lincoln, "Draft of a Bill for Compensated Emancipation in Delaware," in *CW*, 5:29–31.

9. Lincoln, "Message to Congress," in *CW*, 5:144–46.

10. Lincoln, "Appeal to Border State Representatives to Favor Compensated Emancipation," in *CW*, 5:317–19.

11. It should be noted that although the president gives more attention to compensated emancipation than colonization, the former shared more in common with the latter than with the immediatism of abolitionists' claims for emancipation.

12. Robert Asen, "Reflections on the Role of Rhetoric in Public Policy," *Rhetoric & Public Affairs* 13, no. 1 (2010): 126.

13. Asen, "Reflections on the Role of Rhetoric," 125.

14. For example, in a book that claims to "reintroduce authenticity" into the discussion of Lincoln and the Emancipation Proclamation, Harold Holzer refers to the president's support for colonization and compensated emancipation as a "ludicrous and heartless" position that was conveyed in the "painfully inconsistent 1862 annual message." Harold Holzer, *Emancipating Lincoln: The Proclamation in Text, Context, and History* (Cambridge, MA: Harvard University Press, 2012), 3, 124–25.

15. Lincoln, "First Annual Message," in *CW*, 5:49.

16. See David F. Ericson, "The American Colonization Society's Not-So-Private Colonization Project," in *New Directions in the Study of African American Recolonization* (Gainesville: University Press of Florida, 2017), 111–28.

17. Eric Foner, *The Fiery Trial: Abraham Lincoln and American Slavery* (New York: W. W. Norton, 2010), 17.

18. "The Meeting on the Colonization of Free Blacks," *National Intelligencer* (Washington), December 24, 1816, n.p.

19. "Meeting on the Colonization of Free Blacks."

20. "Meeting on the Colonization of Free Blacks."

21. "Meeting on the Colonization of Free Blacks."

22. "Meeting on the Colonization of Free Blacks."

23. "Meeting on the Colonization of Free Blacks."

24. See Henry Clay, *Speech of the Hon. Henry Clay before the American Colonization Society . . . January 20, 1827* (Washington: Colombian Office, 1827), 10, 7.

25. Clay, *Speech of the Hon. Henry*, 7.

26. One example of Clay's statistics reasoning was as follows. The annual rate of increase of the free black population was six thousand per year; the tonnage requisite for such transportation was two persons per five tons ("which is the provision of existing law"), equating to fifteen thousand tons. He notes that "mercantile and military marine might be occasionally employed on this collateral service." The cost would be twenty dollars per person, meaning that $120,000 per year would be needed to execute this plan.

27. Clay, *Speech of the Hon. Henry Clay*, 7.

28. Clay, *Speech of the Hon. Henry Clay*, 9.

29. Clay, *Speech of the Hon. Henry Clay*, 11.

30. Quoted in Daniel Walker Howe, *The Political Culture of the American Whigs* (Chicago: University of Chicago Press, 1979), 272. See also John Stauffer, *Giants: The Parallel Lives of Frederick Douglass and Abraham Lincoln* (New York: Twelve, 2009), 87.

31. Abraham Lincoln, "Honors to Henry Clay," in *CW*, 2:121.

32. Lincoln, "Honors to Henry Clay," 2: 127, 127–30.

33. Lincoln, "Honors to Henry Clay," 2: 131.

34. Lincoln, "Honors to Henry Clay," 2: 131.

35. Lincoln, "Honors to Henry Clay," 2: 132.

36. Warren A. Beck, "Lincoln and Negro Colonization in Central America," *Abraham Lincoln Quarterly* 6 (1950): 165.

37. Jason H. Silverman, "'In Isles beyond the Main': Abraham Lincoln's Philosophy on Black Colonization," *Lincoln Herald* 80, no. 3 (1978): 113.

38. Gary R. Planck, "Abraham Lincoln and Black Colonization: Theory and Practice," *Lincoln Herald* 72 (1970): 61.

39. "Memorial of the President and Board of Managers of the American Society for Colonizing the Free People of Colour of the United States," *Maryland Gazette and Political Intelligencer* (Annapolis), January 30, 1817, n.p.

40. "Memorial of the President."

41. Nicholas Guyatt, *Bind Us Apart: How Enlightened Americans Invented Racial Segregation* (New York: Basic Books, 2016), 267.

42. *Report of the Committee, to Whom Was Referred the Memorial of the President and Board of Managers of the American Society for Colonizing the Free People of Color of the United States* (Washington, DC: E. De Kraft, 1818).

43. Staudenraus, *African Colonization Movement*, 53–56.

44. The Kentucky Abolition Society requested land in the United States for free blacks. One member of the Committee on Public Lands argued, "The Government is not in the habit of granting such advantages to white citizens, nor can they well perceive why they should be expected in favor of those of any other color." *American State Papers*, 14th Congress, 1st Sess., Miscellaneous 2:279.

45. 19th Cong., 2nd Sess., Senate, 289–96; 318–34.

46. *Report of Mr. Kennedy, of Maryland, from the Committee on Commerce of the House of Representatives of the United States, on the Memorial of the Friends of African Colonization . . .* (Washington, DC: Gales and Seaton, 1843).

47. Foner, *Fiery Trial*, 123; and *New York Herald* (New York), January 12, 1860, qtd. in Foner, *Fiery Trial*, 123.

48. Karlyn Kohrs Campbell and Kathleen Hall Jamieson, *Presidents Creating the Presidency: Deeds Done in Words* (Chicago: University of Chicago Press, 2008), 139.

49. Foner, *Fiery Trial*, 184–85.

50. Foner, *Fiery Trial*, 185.

51. Blair suggested that blacks captured in the war be sent to "Hayti." See Foner, *Fiery Trial*, 184.

52. Lincoln, "Second Annual Message," in *CW*, 5:527.

53. Lincoln, "Second Annual Message," 5:527–28.

54. Lincoln, "Second Annual Message," 5:528.

55. Lincoln, "Second Annual Message," 5:529.

56. Lincoln, "Second Annual Message," 5:530.

57. Lincoln, "Second Annual Message," 5:531.

58. Clay, *Speech of the Hon. Henry Clay*, 13.

59. Lincoln, "Second Annual Message," in *CW*, 5:531.

60. Lincoln, "Second Annual Message," in *CW*, 5:531.

61. Lincoln, "Second Annual Message," in *CW*, 5:531.

62. Clay, *Speech of the Hon. Henry Clay*, 9.

63. Clay, *Speech of the Hon. Henry Clay*, 9, 11.

64. Lincoln, "Second Annual Message," in *CW*, 5:532.

65. Lincoln, "Second Annual Message," in *CW*, 5:532.
66. Lincoln, "Second Annual Message," in *CW*, 5:534.
67. Lincoln, "Second Annual Message," in *CW*, 5:533.
68. Lincoln, "Second Annual Message," in *CW*, 5:533.
69. Lincoln, "Second Annual Message," in *CW*, 5:534.
70. Lincoln, "Second Annual Message," in *CW*, 5:534.
71. Lincoln, "Second Annual Message," in *CW*, 5:534.
72. Phillip Shaw Paludan, "Lincoln and Colonization: Policy or Propaganda?" *Journal of the Abraham Lincoln Association* 25, no. 1 (2004): 29.
73. Lincoln, "Second Annual Message," in *CW*, 5:534.
74. David Zarefsky, "Lincoln's Annual Message: A Paradigm of Rhetorical Leadership," *Rhetoric & Public Affairs* 3, no. 1 (2000): 10.
75. Lincoln, "Second Annual Message," in *CW*, 5:520.
76. Zarefsky, "Lincoln's Annual Message," 11.
77. Paludan, "Lincoln and Colonization," 25.
78. Lincoln, "Address on Colonization to a Deputation of Negroes," *CW*, 5:372.
79. Lincoln, "Address on Colonization to a Deputation of Negroes," *CW*, 5:372.
80. Lincoln, "Address on Colonization to a Deputation of Negroes," *CW*, 5:375.
81. James M. McPherson, *Battle Cry of Freedom: The Civil War Era* (New York: Oxford University Press, 1988), 509.
82. Frederick Douglass, "The President and His Speeches," in *Life and Writings*, 3:267.
83. Foner, *Fiery Trial*, 244–58; Paludan, "Lincoln and Colonization," 35–36.
84. Foner, *Fiery Trial*, 258; Lincoln, "Proclamation Canceling Contract with Bernard Kock," *CW*, 6:178–79; Graham D. Welch, "Île à Vache and Colonization: The Tragic End of Lincoln's "Suicidal Folly,'" *Gettysburg College Journal of the Civil War Era* 4 (2014): 45.
85. Lincoln, "Address on Colonization to a Deputation of Negroes," in *CW*, 5:374.
86. Welch, "Île à Vache and Colonization," 61.
87. *Inside Lincoln's White House: The Complete Civil War Diary of John Hay*, ed. Michael Burlingame and John R. Turner (Carbondale: Southern Illinois University Press, 1997), 217.
88. Foner, *Fiery Trial*, 236.
89. "Editor's Table," *Continental Monthly* 3 (January 1863), 126.

CONCLUSION—MIDDLE PASSAGES, EMIGRATION, AND PECULIAR LEGACIES

1. See David Kazanjian, *The Brink of Freedom: Improvising Life in the Nineteenth-Century Atlantic World* (Durham, NC: Duke University Press, 2016), 11.
2. Stephen Ward Angell, *Bishop Henry McNeal Turner and African-American Religion in the South* (Knoxville: University of Tennessee Press, 1992), 119.
3. James Campbell, *Middle Passages: African American Journeys to Africa, 1787–2005* (New York: Penguin Press, 2006), 108.
4. Henry McNeal Turner, "Justice or Emigration Should Be Our Watchword," in *Lift Every Voice: African American Oratory, 1787–1900*, ed. Philip Sheldon Foner and Robert J. Branham (Tuscaloosa: University of Alabama Press, 1998), 788.

5. Campbell, *Middle Passages*, 110.

6. Thomas Adams Upchurch, *Legislating Racism: The Billion Dollar Congress and the Birth of Jim Crow* (Lexington: University Press of Kentucky, 2004): 23–45.

7. Quoted in "Bishop Turner Favors Butler's Bill," *Chicago Tribune*, January 15, 1890, 2.

8. Frederick Douglass, "The United States Cannot Remain Half-Slave and Half-Free," in *Frederick Douglass: Selected Speeches and Writings*, ed. Philip S. Foner and Yuval Taylor (Chicago: Lawrence Hill Books, 2000), 668.

9. Douglass, "United States Cannot Remain Half-Slave and Half-Free," 668.

10. Douglass, "United States Cannot Remain Half-Slave and Half-Free," 668.

11. Frederick Douglass, "I Denounce the So-Called Emancipation as a Stupendous Fraud," in *Frederick Douglass: Selected Speeches and Writings*, 715–19.

12. Campbell, *Middle Passages*, 236.

13. W. E. B. Du Bois, "A Lunatic or a Traitor," *Crisis*, May 1924, 8–9, repr. in *The Emerging Thought of W. E. B. Du Bois: Essays and Editorials from the* Crisis *with an Introduction, Commentaries, and a Personal Memoir*, ed. Henry Lee Moon (New York: Simon and Schuster, 1972), 325.

14. *Negro World* (New York), February 17, 1920.

15. M. B. Akpan, "Liberia and the Universal Negro Improvement Association: The Background to the Abortion of Garvey's Scheme for African Colonization," *Journal of African History* 14, no. 1 (1973): 109.

16. Joseph J. Roberts, "Annual Message," *African Repository* 21, no. 4 (April 1851): 117.

17. Archibald Alexander, *A History of Colonization on the Western Coast of Africa* (New York: Negro Universities Press, 1969), 511.

18. Daniel B. Warner to William Coppinger, May 24, 1879, qtd. in M. B. Akpan, "Black Imperialism: Americo-Liberian Rule over the African Peoples of Liberia," *Canadian Journal of African Studies* 7, no. 2 (1973): 225.

19. Helene Cooper, "In Search of a Lost Africa," *New York Times Magazine*, April 6, 2008, http://www.nytimes.com.

20. *Liberia News*, August, 1924, 3–4, qtd. in Edmund David Cronon, *Black Moses: The Story of Marcus Garvey and the Universal Negro Improvement Association* (Madison: University of Wisconsin Press, 1962), 130.

21. Qtd. in Cronon, *Black Moses*, 130.

22. Qtd. in Cronon, *Black Moses*, 130.

23. Kwame Nkrumah to W. E. B. Du Bois, cablegram, February 15, 1961, W. E. B. Du Bois Papers, University of Massachusetts-Amherst, identifier: mums312-b153-i156 (hereafter, "Du Bois Papers").

24. Cedric Robinson, "DuBois and Black Sovereignty: The Case of Liberia," *Race & Class* 32, no. 2 (1990): 39.

25. Du Bois to Gus Hall, 1 October 1961, Du Bois Papers, identifier: mums312-b153-i071.

26. Robinson, "DuBois and Black Sovereignty," 39.

Index

Africa: "Back to Africa," 16, 134, 137–40; benevolence toward, 38; character of, 20, 60, 94; Christianity in, 5, 27, 30, 34–35, 87, 91, 110; descriptions of, 84, 111; repatriation, 6; Sierra Leone in, 5, 25–29, 34–36, 60, 90; slaveholders from, 50; slave trade, 21; uplift for, 138; western coast of, 3, 29, 53, 116, 120
African Institution, 25
African Repository, 19, 38, 78, 83–84, 120
African Repository and Colonial Journal, 83
Afro-Pessimism, 15, 66–68, 73, 84, 133
Allen, Richard, 56–57
amalgamation, 41, 48–49, 52–55, 57, 61–62
American Colonization Society (ACS), 13–17; auxiliaries, 19; as benevolent society, 38, 77; character of, 20; colonial agents for, 86, 90; Counter Memorial against, 40–64; founding, 6–7, 20–22; funding for, 36; negotiations with Sheridan, 65–85; petitions, 36–37; post-Reconstruction, 134; speeches at founding, 26–36; treasurer, 65
American Society for Colonizing the Free People of Colour of the United States, 3
"American Africanism," 43

"Back-to-Africa," 16, 134, 137–40
Bacon, David Francis, 79–82
Bates, Edward, 121
benevolence, 35, 37–39, 74, 77, 93, 129

blackness: performance, 43; social death and, 78; structured position, 67–70, 77; voice, 61
black optimism, 12, 15, 66–69, 73–75, 78, 84, 110
Blair, Montgomery, 121–22
Brackenridge, Hugh Henry, 50
Butler, Matthew, 125

Caldwell, Elias B., 13–14, 18–39
Carey, Lott, 90
Carey, Matthew, 56
Carroll, Charles, 24
citizenship, 4, 111; attaining, 135; defining, 87; language of, 58–59; petitioning as, 47; requirements, 112
Clay, Henry: 1827 speech to ACS, 117–19, 126; Counter Memorial response to, 46, 52, 58, 60; criticism of, 6; importance of, 13; speech at founding of ACS, 3–4, 10, 13, 18–39; Walker response to, 63
Colored American, 72–73, 83
compromise, 11, 21, 26, 34, 64; Lincoln and, 113, 118, 123–25, 131; H. Teage and, 107, 110
Congress: as audience for the ACS, 13, 21, 23, 25–26, 31; as audience for Lincoln, 113–20, 124–28
Constitution: of the ACS, 40; of black identity, 62, 67, 69; of civic identity, 86–112; Commonwealth, 91; discursive, 8–9; of the Liberia Lyceum, 94; of the US, 57–58, 113, 123–24, 129–30

Index

cost: of Clay's plan, 169n26; of colonization, 10, 13, 32, 35, 117; of colonization for Sheridan, 76; of Lincoln's plan, 125–27; of separating the Union, 123
Counter Memorial, 14, 40–64
Crawford, William H., 37, 120
Cresson, Elliott, 78, 82, 83
Crosby, Elisha, 122
Cuffe, Paul, 5, 25–26

Dê, 104
debate: Lincoln-Douglas, 114; peculiar obligation to, 89, 91–112; about rhetoric and materiality, 115; about slavery, 7, 44, 64
Declaration of Independence: American, 29, 31–32, 52, 57, 59; Liberian, 86, 91, 112
deliberative discourse, 11–16, 18–39; challenging, 40–64; and diaspora, 10; public sphere, 9
Dew, Thomas R., 5–6
diaspora, 15–16, 65–85, 89, 96, 100, 103, 136; and deliberation, 10–12
Douglass, Frederick, 6, 12, 16, 63, 130, 136–37
Du Bois, W. E. B. (William Edward Burghardt), 9, 16, 55, 137, 139, 140
education: of colonization goals, 41, 46; lyceum as, 93–96, 100, 108–9; of Sheridan, 75; of H. Teage, 90–92
emancipation: and benevolence, 38; compensated, 113–15, 121–22, 125–30; in the District of Columbia, 136; Douglass's opinion, 136; gradual, 5, 116; laws governing, 71; Proclamation, 13, 16; religious support for, 24, 38; in Saint-Domingue, 21
emigration: African Institution support for, 25; Back-to-Africa movement, 16; Civil War and, 133–34; compared to colonization, 20, 133; Du Bois and, 140; Garvey and, 16, 137–38; post-Reconstruction, 133–41; Sheridan and, 14, 65–66, 79, 81; H. Teage and, 88–90, 120–21; H. M. Turner and, 134–36
equality, 15, 21, 30–34, 47, 52, 59, 90, 107, 124, 131, 133, 136

Fairfax, Ferdinando, 3, 5
Fanon, Frantz, 68
Finley, Robert, 5, 20, 23–25
First Baptist Church (Richmond, VA), 90
Fitzhugh, George, 6
Franklin, Benjamin, 50, 86
freedom: appeals to, 20, 52, 57, 132; archive of, 79; black, 4, 12, 24, 38, 39; petitions for, 24, 32, 46, 56; settler-colonists, 88; Sheridan and, 14, 65, 71–73, 79, 84; H. Teage and, 90–91, 96, 107, 11; violence and, 22; white, 50

Gales, Joseph, 65, 67, 74–84
Gales, Joseph, Jr., 41, 45, 46, 65
Garnet, Henry Highland, 12
Garrison, William Lloyd, 5–6, 38–39, 63
Garvey, Marcus, 16, 134, 137–40
Gurley, Ralph Randolph, 74, 78, 81

Haiti, 134
Hall, Prince, 32
Hamilton, William, 56
Haynes, Lemuel, 56
Holbrook, Josiah, 92–93, 99–100

irony, 41, 46, 49–56, 80, 155n44

Jay, William, 39
Jefferson, Thomas, 22, 63, 86, 109, 112
Jones, Absalom, 56–57
Jones, Walter, 36

Key, Francis Scott, 3, 20, 23, 36
King, C. D. B., 139
Kock, Bernard, 130

Liberia Exodus Joint Stock Steamship Company, 134–35
Liberia Herald, 86, 88, 90–91, 94
Liberia Lyceum, 86–100, 107, 165n51
Lincoln, Abraham: admiration of Clay, 16, 118; Illinois State Colonization Society membership, 119; Lincoln-Douglas debate, 114; peculiar proposal, 15, 121–29;

second Annual Message to Congress, 15, 113, 121–29

Madison, James, 6, 25, 86
Mamba, 104
Marcia C. Day, 130
Maryland Colonization Journal, 90
Maryland Gazette, 18
Matthias, John J., 83
Meade, William, 3, 72
Mercer, Charles Fenton, 5, 20, 22–24, 120–21
Middle Passage, 67–68, 132
middle rhetoric, 7
Mills, Samuel J., 5, 25, 90
Monroe, James, 6, 22, 25, 37, 120

National Intelligencer, 14, 40–46, 49–50, 65
negotiation, 15, 36–37, 65–85
Niles, Hezekiah, 50–51
Nkrumah, Kwame, 140

order: dialectical, 33–35; ultimate, 33–34

Phelps, Anson, 80–81
Pickering, Timothy, 36
Plato, 95
practicability, 3, 19, 27–36, 116–17, 134–35
Prosser, Gabriel, 21–22, 70

Raleigh Auxiliary Society for the Colonization of Free People of Color, 72
Randolph, John, 3, 40
Russwurm, John Brown, 90–91

Saint-Domingue, 21–22, 70
Seaton, William, 41, 45–46
Second Baptist Church (Bassa Cove, Liberia), 88
Sheridan, Louis: background, 65–67; peculiar planning, 73–85
Sierra Leone, 5, 25–29, 34–36, 60, 90
signifying, 42, 44, 53–64, 98
Slave Trade Act of 1808, 44
Slave Trade Act of 1819, 36, 120

Smith, Caleb, 122
Smith, Margaret Bayard, 25
Smith, Samuel Harrison, 25
social death, 64, 68, 74, 78, 83
Stewart, Maria. W. Miller, 5–6, 63

Tappan, Arthur, 78
Tappan, Lewis, 83–84
Teage, Colin, 89–90, 91
Teage, Hilary: background, 86–91; peculiar obligations to debate, 91–100; peculiar obligation to commemorate, 101–11
territory, 30, 33, 117, 121–25, 129
Turner, Henry McNeal, 16, 134–37, 140
Turner, Nat, 70

Vai, 104
Vesey, Denmark, 70
voice: diasporic, 14; ironic, 42, 49–54; middle, 7; peculiar, 40–64; serious, 42, 46–49; signifying, 42, 54–62

Walker, David, 5–6, 12, 20, 63
Washington, Bushrod, 27, 36, 119
Webster, Daniel, 3, 6, 102, 135
Wheatley, Phillis, 98
Williams, Peter, Jr., 56
Wilson, William J., 63
Wright, Robert, 40

Young Men's Colonization Society of Pennsylvania, 78

www.ingramcontent.com/pod-product-compliance
Lightning Source LLC
Chambersburg PA
CBHW032135250426
43661CB00077B/2143